The Challenge for the Development of European Integration:
Behind the Multiple Crises
多重危机下对欧洲一体化发展的挑战

课题编号：No.574575-EPP-1-2016-1-CN-EPPJMO-CoE

机遇与挑战：

多变世界里中国与欧盟关系的可持续发展

Opportunities and Challenges

Sustainability of China-EU Relations in a Changing World

主编 石坚 [德]海杜克
Edited by Jian SHI, Guenter Heiduk

中国社会科学出版社
CHINA SOCIAL SCIENCES PRESS

图书在版编目(CIP)数据

机遇与挑战：多变世界里中国与欧盟关系的可持续发展 = Opportunities
and Challenges: Sustainability of China-EU Relations in a Changing
World：英文 / 石坚，（德）海杜克（Guenter Heiduk）主编. —北京：
中国社会科学出版社，2019.5
　　ISBN 978-7-5203-4464-7

　　Ⅰ. ①机⋯　Ⅱ. ①石⋯ ②海⋯　Ⅲ. ①中外关系-研究-欧洲联盟-
英文　Ⅳ. ①D822.35

中国版本图书馆CIP数据核字（2019）第095091号

出 版 人　赵剑英
责任编辑　赵　丽
责任校对　王秀珍
责任印制　王　超

出　　　版　中国社会科学出版社
社　　　址　北京鼓楼西大街甲 158 号
邮　　　编　100720
网　　　址　http://www.csspw.cn
发 行 部　010-84083685
门 市 部　010-84029450
经　　　销　新华书店及其他书店

印　　　刷　北京君升印刷有限公司
装　　　订　廊坊市广阳区广增装订厂
版　　　次　2019 年 5 月第 1 版
印　　　次　2019 年 5 月第 1 次印刷

开　　　本　710×1000　1/16
印　　　张　18.5
字　　　数　353 千字
定　　　价　95.00 元

Contents

Introduction 001

Part I Challenges to EU-China Relations

"The Belt and Road" Initiative: A Modern China-Europe Silk Road? 007

The Implications of Brexit for China-EU Economic Relations 061

China's investments and infrastructural expansion in Central and Eastern
 Europe...084

BRI and EU-China connectivity: European perceptions, aims and concerns........104

A Study of Sino-Turkey Relationship under the Framework of the Belt and
 Road Initiative 121

Preparing for the Challenges: To Promote the Dialogue between the Youth of
 China and EU 138

Part II Sustainability and Opportunities for EU-China Relations

EU-China Cluster Collaboration Initiative-The Role of Clusters in
 Economic Development 159

The perspectives on interregional cluster cooperation under BRI Frame..............189

Competitiveness of Poland's exports to China: Comparison with other
 Visegrad countries 210

Sino-European research and academic cooperation under BRI Framework:
 Social Sciences as a tool to improve Europe-China relations 234

EU-China Experimental Research-Cooperation between Sichuan
 University and Bonn University for nearly Two Decades...............................247

A Brief Academic CV of the Contributing Authors of this collection 283

Introduction

Jian Shi and Guenter Heiduk

Since the establishment of diplomatic relations between the EU and China in 1975, more than sixty institutionalized dialogue formats provide a solid and sustainable framework for cooperation in areas such as trade and investment, environmental protection, energy, research and innovation, education, people-to-people exchanges. European companies invested considerably in China's manufacturing industries, thus contributing to the export-oriented growth model in the three decades after China's gradual opening-up started in the early 1980s. China is now the EU's number two ranked trading partner behind the United States, and the EU is China's number one ranked trading partner. In the wake of China's accession to the WTO in 2001, its "Going Global" policy predominantly resulted in foreign direct investments (FDI) in the tertiary sector, the main sub-sectors being leasing and commercial services, followed by in the primary sector. The sectoral concentration is reflected in the geographical distribution of China's FDI in the first decade of the 21st millennium. In 2010, only five percent of China's global FDI stock was invested in Europe. Since then, two major changes in China's "Going Global policy have connected Europe more closely with China". First, the moving up in the value chain from low-tech to high-tech manufacturing has resulted in a significant increase of Chinese M&As in Europe. It is estimated that by the end of 2017 China has taken over approximately 360 European companies which contributes to exceed China's European FDI compared to FDI in the United States by

45%.[①] In this context, the EU-China High Level Innovation Cooperation Dialogue which was set up in 2012 and started in 2013 is-according to the European Commission-aiming to improve mutual understanding of EU's and China's innovation systems and policies, promote effective innovation policies and support measures, and tackle the framework conditions for innovation. The ongoing negotiations on a comprehensive EU-China investment agreement which was launched in 2013 are further evidence for the deepening of EU-China relations. Second, in the five years since President Xi Jinping proposed the "Belt and Road Initiative" (BRI), the "Silk Road Economic Belt" and the "21st Century Maritime Silk Road" have considerably intensified China's economic relations with European countries. In addition to the aforementioned Chinese M&As and greenfield investments in Europe, the BRI is improving the transport connectivity between China and Europe through investment in infrastructure. The cooperation is institutionalized in more than 50 bilateral MoUs with a focus on countries in Central Eastern and Southeastern European countries. The scope of the MoUs is ranging from setting up the general framework for cooperation under the BRI to specific infrastructure project related agreements.The fast growth of China-Europe freight train routes attracted the greatest attention. Approximately 70 Chinese and European cities are now conncected by regular direct freight services. In 2017, more than 3670[②] cargo trains, mainly transporting clothes, automobile parts and components, smart phones and computers, travelled from China to Europe. Despite the impressive increase in the number of freight trains since the China-Europe land route was launched in 2013, the share on total China-Europe trade value reached just 4% in 2016[③]. The two flagship projects-the Chinese investment in the port of Piraeus and the modernization of the Belgrade-Budapest rail link-

---

① Corre, P. (2018). On Chinese Investment and Influence in Europe, Carnegie Endowment for International Peace, May 23, 2018, Washington, DC.

② https://finance.ifeng.com/a/20180826/16470325_0.shtml Accessed December 21, 2018.

③ Jakub Jakóbowski, Konrad Popławski, Marcin Kaczmarski, "The Silk RailroadThe EU-China rail connect ions: background, act ors, interests", p.5. OSW STUDIES, No. 72, 2018.

show that it is necessary to intensify the EU-China cooperation under the BRI framework. The plan to establish a new "China-Europe Land-Sea Express Route" is far from being implemented to the extent that its advantages can be fully exploited.

Despite the fact that EU-China relations are based on the solid framework of the "EU-China 2020 Strategic Agenda for Cooperation", signed by the EU and China in 2013, the BRI projects which are part of the agenda of the "EU-China Connectivity Platform" clearly show that the main beneficiaries are cities/regions in the eastern part of Europe. From an economic point of view there is evidence that the EU and China have not succeeded in integrating the BRI and the European Commission's Investment Plan for Europe ("Juncker Plan") into an overarching key pillar of EU-China relations. This especially refers to synergies between the Trans-European Transport Network Policy and the BRI. In this context it should be noted that the Brexit which is scheduled for March 29, 2019 will most probably pose new challenges for EU-China relations as well as for UK-China relations.

Taking into account the rather negative economic consequences of the pervasive forces of "nation-first" attitudes in certain countries, the EU and China should send a clear signal that cooperation creates benefits for all. The EU and some of its western member states have the challenging task to find answers to the concerns which seem to be a barrier for pro-actively promoting the BRI. China's challenge is to demonstrate how BRI creates benefits for a wider Europe.

The present collection of papers from Chinese and European scholars aims to highlight opportunities and challenges for EU-China relations with focus on BRI projects in Europe, and its sustainability. The collection of papers also approaches to the diversified issues in the areas related closely to the EU-China relations and offers some insightful ideas and suggestions.

The contributors of this collection of papers are from different countries such as Poland, Hungary, Germany and China, and from different disciplines. They provide multi-faceted perspectives on different topics that are valuable for our readers, and hopefully the discussions will inspire and provoke the readers to carry out more thoughtful researches in these fields.

We would like to take this opportunity to give our thanks to Prof. Zhuyu Li and Prof. Dan Yi of Sichuan University for their consistent support and assistance in organizing the roundtable, dialogue and communication among the contributors of this collection of papers, which make this publication possible. And we would also like to give our gratitude to Ms. Li Zhao in China Social Sciences Press at Beijing for her patience and careful editing work to help us ensure the quality of this publication.

PART I

CHALLENGES TO EU-CHINA RELATIONS

"The Belt and Road" Initiative: A Modern China-Europe Silk Road?

Guenter Heiduk

> *"If you want to develop, build a road"*
> Chinese phrase

Abstract

China's "the Belt and Road" Initiative (BRI) is regarded as the most ambitious program of a single country after WWII, namely in terms of geographic reach, financial engagement and diversity of actions. It is neither embedded into an institutional framework nor fixed in time, space and content. Cooperation should guarantee win-win results, whereas connectivity should link the different fields of activities. The official BRI document, published in 2015, reads like a mix of principles of free trade, development aid and social integration. The rapidly growing number of statements and reports predominantly deal with the realized, ongoing and planned projects. Another strand of publications discusses China's real motives behind BRI. Critical voices are outnumbered until now. Analytical studies with economic focus are rare. The paper does not claim to deliver an original study on expected effects of the BRI Initiative, nor does it deliver a comprehensive overview on all initiated and planned projects. But it rather aims to provide an overview on the official Chinese view of the BRI Initiative, including its reflections in media, academics, politics in China, Europe and the USA. It is a snapshot five years after the BRI initiative had been announced. The focus is on its implications for China's relations with the European Union.

Abbreviations

ADB	Asian Development Bank
AIIB	Asian Infrastructure Investment Bank
ASEAN	Association of Southeast Asian Nations
BRICS	Brazil, Russia, India, China, South Africa
CEE	Central and Eastern Europe
CETA	EU-Canada Comprehensive Economic and Trade Agreement
HKTDC	Hong Kong Trade and Development Council
IMF	International Monetary Fund
MoU	Memorandum of Understanding
NDB	New Development Bank
OEM	Original equipment manufacturer
BRI	the Belt and Road Initiative
SOEs	State-owned companies
TTIP	Transatlantic Trade and Investment Partnership

1. Introduction

Since China's opening up to the outside world at the beginning of the 1980s, the country emerged from a closed, backward, predominantly agricultural country to a global manufacturer, until recently labelled as the "workbench of the world". Deng Xiaoping's "invite-in" policy motivated foreign companies to establish production plants, especially for manufacturing parts and components in core industries such as automobiles and electronics. As a result of China's export-led strategy the country is now the world's largest economy (on a purchasing power parity basis), manufacturer, merchandise trader, and holder of foreign exchange reserves (HKTDC, 2018). Since 2010 exports and fixed investment as main drivers of China's growth in real GDP have slowed down. The pre-2008 global financial and economic crisis real GDP growth rate of around 14% has halved and is expected to weaken gradually to about 5.5% by 2023 (IMF, 2018: 3). President Xi Jinping's "Thought on Socialism with Chinese Characteristics for a New Era"— presented at the 19th National Congress of the Communist Party in November 2017—could be interpreted from an economic point of view as a turning point from quantitative to qualitative economic growth and from external to internal driving forces. In contrast to DENG Xiaoping's export-led growth model, the new model aims to achieve the goal of a "moderately prosperous society" by 2020 and to accomplish the "great rejuvenation of the Chinese nation" (Daekwon, 2017). Xi Jinping will promote more balanced economic growth with a special focus on long-marginalized regions in western and central China. In 2016, the IMF already recommended to replace the export- and investment-driven growth model by a more sophisticated model which allows an external, internal, environmental and distributional rebalancing (IMF, 2016a). Recent fiscal and monetary policies and sudden financial market reactions as well as the difficult-to-assess debt burden generate rather uncertainties than stabilities at home and abroad. Countries in Southeast Asia fear negative spillovers from China's decline in economic growth due to their dependence on China-dominated Asian production networks. Duval et al (2015) estimate that the median Asian economy will lose 0.3% GDP growth if China's GDP growth rate declines by 1%. Some developed countries have concerns about Chinese companies' fast growing outward FDI. There are fears that the fast growing number of acquisitions of high-tech companies leads to technological transfers at the expense of the acquired companies. Taking China's global geo-political ambitions into account, it is explainable that China's political leaders are interested in offering new types of benefits to its broader neighborhood. Of course, these benefits have to serve as one of the pillars in building a China-centered world. Wu (2016: 7) argues that "old" power-creating factors-inward FDI flows, low-tech manufacturing and trade within regional and global production networks-will be rather complemented than substituted by new instruments, especially technology acquiring outward FDI, internationalization of the Chinese currency Renminbi, promotion of new financial institutions and initiating infrastructure alliances. Global, mostly positive attention has been paid to the decision of the IMF (2016b) to add the Renminbi to the official currency basket with a weight of 10.92%. The decision came into effect on October 1, 2016. In contrast, the China-initiated establishment of the Asian Infrastructure Investment Bank (AIIB) and the BRICS New Development Bank (NDB) was accompanied by critical voices. The U.S. government expressed worries over lax procurement and environmental standards (Economy, 2016). Alliances under the umbrella of the Chinese BRI initiative should give new incentives for trade and investment with focus on the broader Eurasian region. Despite the rapid developments in BRI-EAEU dialogue (Svetlicinii, 2018) so far, the AIIB financed only three projects in Eurasian countries, namely in Azerbaiyan, Georgia and Tajikistan. The majority of these projects are located in Southeast Asia. It is worth noting that until now BRI-projects in Europe are not financed by AIIB or NDB. China's dominance in the AIIB and the NDB should guarantee that BRI-labeled infrastructure projects will be financed from these banks. After President Xi Jinping launched the initiative in 2013, Western politicians, academics and media tended to categorize it rather as a vision than a concrete plan or even simply ignored it. From Eastern perspective, Wo-lap (2016) noted that "they [members of the National People's Congress and the Chinese People's Political Consultative Conference] have started to notice that this strategy is a sloppy and poorly conceived idea that Xi came up with on his own to serve his ego without implementing any careful studies and plans beforehand, and there are more and more signs in recent months indicating that this plan is simply financially unsound and unsustainable." Meanwhile many critics changed their minds, partly because of intensive Chinese "marketing activities", partly because of verifiable activities. But the latter offer new ground for criticism. Khanna (2016: 15) noted that "the timing of the Belt and Road Initiative is propitious. Just as the crumbling post-colonial and former Soviet republics on its periphery desperately need new infrastructure, China is converting its piles of cash into credit for distressed neighbours to rebuild themselves-by buying China's overproduction of steel and cement and with the assistance of Chinese labour." As described in detail later, there is an obvious divide in the perception of BRI within Europe, namely between the Eastern European 16+1 countries and the Western European countries including the EU.

The paper proceeds as follows: Chapter II introduces into the-from a Chinese point of view important-historical background of BRI, followed by highlighting the emergence and vision of this initiative (Chapter III). Then, chapter IV provides an overview on the realization, real motives and critics of BRI. Finally, the special relevance of BRI for Europe is highlighted in chapter V. The conclusion (VI) summarizes the current stage of the theory, politics and reality of the BRI Initiative.

2. The historical Silk Road

Since ancient times trade routes connect civilizations. They contribute to cultural and technological diffusion and often pave the way for migration. Most prominent are trade routes under the headline of "Ancient Silk Road" which connected China with the Roman Empire via a network of trade routes through Central Asia, Persia, Mesopotamia. "The Silk Road and its maritime Spice Route lie at the origins of globalization not only in the transmission of goods, but in the transmission of ideas, knowledge, culture, religions, science and technology. The Silk Road lasted and flourished from the first century BCE until the mid-15th century, challenged and ultimately superseded by the rise of the Portuguese seaborne empire" (Lehmann, 2015). From an economic point of view one of the most important features of Silk Road trade was the two-directional exchange of goods. Chinese silk was a major product traded from East to West, whereas manufactured products from the Mediterranean region were traded from West to East.

A number of Silk Road studies (Cheung and Lee, 2015; Beckwirth, 2009; Elisseeff, 2000; Frachetti et al, 2017; Frankopan, 2016; Lehmann, 2015; Mark,

2014; Neewitz, 2017) highlight the role of cities at the starting (Chang'an-today known as Xi'an) and ending point (Venice, Rome) of the routes as well as along the routes. The flourishing trade oasis such as Kashgar in China and Palmyra in Syria became rich and developed into commercial hubs where several trade routes crossed. In addition to its function of exchanging goods, the Silk Road also served as a route of communication with the result of cultural and technological learning. At the same time, maritime trade routes emerged between Guangzhou in China and ports on the Red Sea with subsequent overland transport to the Nile, Alexandria and finally to Rome. Documents from the Tang Dynasty (Sixth Century) provide evidence that Chinese migrants moved along the Silk Road to the West. It is a debate going on to which degree trade and westward migration contributed to the development of stop over locations such as the Turfan Oasis[1]. Hansen (2005: 304) describes its high standard of rules, regulations and institutions such as travel passes, taxes, border controls, even partnerships between Silk Road merchants from far-distance cities[2] and concluded that "Silk Road trade in the century of Tang rule had clearly visible spill-over effects on the Turfan economy, which was highly monetized and in which all transactions were subject to high interest rates. Most likely, Silk Road trade was initiated and promoted by the one-sided opening up of the political leaders of the Han Dynasty located in the former capital Chang'an. According to present knowledge, mutual cooperation agreements with trading posts along and at the Western end of the Silk Road did not exist. Uncodified partnerships might have been emerged, firstly build on power but later replaced by mutual trust (Heiduk and McCaleb, 2015).This suggests that the educational level of the elites were developing with their commercial success. Frankopan (2016) noted that besides

---

[1]　Turfan lies about 180 kilometers southeast of the city of Ürümqi on the main northern route of the Silk Road.

[2]　"The geographic range of these merchants 'operations is impressive. Based in Chang' an, Li Shaojin and Cao Yanyan formed a partnership in Gongyuecheng (modern-day Almaligh), which lies some 2500 kilometers to the west in the Yili River basin close to modern China's border to Kazakhstan." Hansen, 2005: 292.

competence in trade, financial expertise also played an important role for the development of trading hubs: Those who were able to build credit networks did particularly well. Minority groups bound over long distances by family connections, religious practices and common identities developed systems to lend, borrow and pay for goods that were sometimes thousands of miles away. Last but not least, evidence suggests that political and military control on the trade route were crucial in establishing and securing empires, but also could contribute to their fall. Frankopan (2016) notes that in medieval times the Mongols "copied some of the economic ideas of ancient Silk Road by carefully investing into major urban centres. "They employed what we would today call progressive tax policies, which encouraged trade within and between cities to stimulate greater revenues for the state."

Lehmann (2015) can be supported in his summarizing characterization that "the Silk Road and the Spice Route of the past were very much about money. There was a pecuniary goal. But the cultural wealth that was generated was immense. Global civilization would be much the poorer without it. The historical Silk Road is a major source of inspiration, wonder and dreams."

The following chapters will show whether the new Silk Road idea-mostly headlined as "The Belt and Road" Initiative-will deserve to be compared with the reality of the ancient Silk Road as far as we know it. Entering into the 21st Century, the question arises whether BRI might contribute to intensify the economic and cultural relations between China and Europe.

3. The BRI Initiative

What the official document tells about the BRI vision

In September 2013 President Xi Jinping for the first time presented the idea of a China-Central Asia cooperation belt during his visit in Kazakhstan.

In the following years China "invited" countries in Southeast Asia, Central Asia, Middle East, Africa and Europe to join this initiative. After authorization by the State Council the official document on the "Vision and Actions on Jointly Building Silk Road Economic Belt and 21st-Century Maritime Silk Road" (NDRC, 2015) was jointly issued by the National Development and Reform Commission and the involved ministries. The document directly refers to the ancient Silk Road as a model for the BRI idea. In the preface of this document it is stated that "more than two millennia ago the diligent and courageous people of Eurasia explored and opened up several routes of trade and cultural exchanges that linked the major civilizations of Asia, Europe and Africa, collectively called the Silk Road by later generations. For thousands of years, the Silk Road Spirit-'peace and cooperation, openness and inclusiveness, mutual learning and mutual benefit'-has been passed from generation to generation, promoted the progress of human civilization, and contributed greatly to the prosperity and development of the countries along the Silk Road. Symbolizing communication and cooperation between the East and the West, the Silk Road Spirit is a historic and cultural heritage shared by all countries around the world."

The rather fuzzy term "the Belt and Road Initiative" allows to combine different regions/cultures, different modes of entry, different types of cooperation and different types of actions under one umbrella. From Chinese understanding the two pillars of "the Belt and Road Initiative" are the land routes labeled as "Silk Road Economic Belt" and the sea routes labeled as "21st-Century Maritime Silk Road" (chart 2, p. 24). The geographical description of the BRI region reads rather unprecise (NDRC, 2015): "The Belt and Road Initiative run through the continents of Asia, Europe and Africa, connecting the vibrant East Asia economic circle at one end and developed European economic circle at the other, and encompassing countries with huge potential for economic development. The Silk Road Economic Belt focuses on bringing together China, Central Asia, Russia and Europe (the Baltic); linking China with the Persian Gulf and the Mediterranean Sea through Central Asia and West

Asia; and connecting China with Southeast Asia, South Asia and the Indian Ocean. The 21st-Century Maritime Silk Road is designed to go from China's coast to Europe through the South China Sea and the Indian Ocean in one route, and from China's coast through the South China Sea to the South Pacific in the other. On land, the Initiative will focus on jointly building a new Eurasian Land Bridge and developing China-Mongolia-Russia, China-Central Asia-West Asia and China-Indochina Peninsula economic corridors by taking advantage of international transport routes, relying on core cities along the Belt and Road Initiative and using key economic industrial parks as cooperation platforms. At sea, the Initiative will focus on jointly building smooth, secure and efficient transport routes connecting major sea ports along the Belt and Road Initiative. The China-Pakistan Economic Corridor and the Bangladesh-China-India-Myanmar Economic Corridor are closely related to the Belt and Road Initiative, and therefore require closer cooperation and greater progress." Originally, academics, media and even politics accepted "BRI" as an overarching acronym for the geographically widespread activities. More recently, the acronym "Belt and Road Initiative" has gained popularity.

By taking the current status of the global political and economic landscape as point of departure, the envisaged multipolar, peaceful world as well as "the global free trade regime and the open world economy in the spirit of open regional cooperation can definitely be classified as far distant vision. This also holds for the intension that" countries along the Belt and Road Initiative may fully coordinate their economic development strategies and policies. From an economic point of view, BRI seems to enrich the basic idea of regional trade agreements with some Chinese characteristics such as a core-peripheral shape, high flexibility and an invisible political agenda. Not surprisingly, the network idea (*guanxi*) as the basic organizational principle of the Chinese society is mentioned as an applicable instrument: BRI should function as "all-dimensional, multi-tiered and composite connectivity networks Anyhow, BRI is competing with other regional investment projects (Szczudlik, 2016a).

Last but not least, cultural and environmental aspects round up the political and economic dimensions of the BRI initiative. In view of the political and military conflicts in the "Belt and Road Initiative" region, it seems to be unrealistic to expect that countries "enhance cultural exchanges; encourage different civilizations to learn from each other and flourish together; and promote mutual understanding, peace and friendship among people of all countries. Needless to say, that the growing complexity of the whole BRI approach increases the distance between vision and action.

Cooperation priorities

The realization of the visions behind BRI needs bilateral policy cooperation between China and each BRI country. The large number of MoUs cannot hide the fact that the institutional structure od BRI is weak. Intergovernmental cooperation is the only mentioned form. The document does not give any clear indication which kind of institutional framework should guarantee mutual responsibilities to implement multi-level intergovernmental macro policy exchange and communication mechanism, fully coordinate economic development strategies and policies, and jointly provide policy support for the implementation of practical cooperation and large-scale projects. The NDRC document (2015) aims to apply the cooperation approach to the following key area

Facilities connectivity

"On the basis of respecting each other's sovereignty and security concerns, countries along the Belt and Road Initiative should improve the connectivity of their infrastructure construction plans and technical standard systems, jointly push forward the construction of international trunk passage ways, and form an infrastructure network connecting all sub-regions in Asia, and between Asia, Europe and Africa step by step. At the same time, efforts should be made to promote green and low-carbon infrastructure construction and operation management, taking into full account the impact of climate change on the construction. The specifically Chinese interests become clearly visible by highlighting the importance of cooperation to ensure the security of oil and gas pipelines, build cross-border power supply networks and power-transmission routes, and cooperate in regional power grid upgrading and transformation. Another major focus is the facilitation of land, sea and air transportation which is essential for maintaining the competitiveness of Chinese exports in traditional markets as well as for successfully winning new markets. The project of an "Information Silk Road" is even more ambitious as a large number of countries along the Belt asnd Road are far behind the international standard in information and communication technologies.

Unimpeded trade

Besides improvements in the logistics of trade another boost to Chinese exports and investment should be achieved by the reduction of barriers to trade as well as the exploration of new modes of investment cooperation. Concrete measures that are mentioned for discussion with countries along the Belt and Road Initiative range from opening free trade areas, industrial parks, cross-border economic cooperation zones to cooperation in conserving eco-environment, protecting biodiversity, and tackling climate change. The document devoted just half a sentence to the welcome of companies from all countries to invest in China without announcing concrete measures that faciliate FDI in China. It should be noted that in 2017 the OECD's FDI Regulatory Restrictiveness Index (OECD, 2017) ranked China third behind the Philippines and Saudi Arabia with repsect to all types of FDI restrictions. In contrast, it is aimed to support localized operation and management of Chinese companies to boost the local economy.

Financial integration

Despite recent progress in the internationalization of the Chinese currency, the implementation of a currency stability system, investment and financing system and credit information system in Asia as well as the development of an Asian bond market have to overcome numerous economic and non-economic difficulties as similar attempts have shown in other regions of the world. It is recognized that financial integration needs close cooperation in financial regulation and crisis management. Last but not least, besides the meanwhile established international financial institutions Asian Infrastructure Investment Bank (AIIB) and the New Development Bank (NDB, established by the BRICS countries), the national Silk Road Fund-founded in 2014 as a state-owned investment fund and initially endowed with 40 million USD-should finance infrastructure projects along the Belt and Road Initiative. The relatively comprehensive and detailed catalogue of financial measures to be taken may serve as an indication that the Chinese government is aware of significant credit and even political risks when it comes to the implementation and advancement of the BRI initiative.

People-to-people bond

To an increasing extent, Chinese investment in large-scale infrastructure projects in several Southeast Asian countries had been exposed to massive public protests.[1] Dialogues with and between people in countries along the Belt and Road Initiative should inform about the initiative, but also contribute to create a welcoming behavior and trust to people on the ground. The Chinese government recognizes the necessity to establish intensive, ongoing, diversified and multi-level communication platforms. The bundle of proposed measures ranges amongst others from granting 10,000 government scholarships to the countries along the Belt and Road Initiative every year, holding cultural years, promoting inbound and outbound tourism in Asia-the latter by facilitating tourist visa applications-and support countries along the Belt and Road

---

[1]　In March 2018 the German news channel DW reported that Filipinos resist the China-funded dams because it will destroy both the source of life and livelihood of the indigenous people based in the area where part of the New Centennial dam is beeing built. DW, 14 March 2018, available at: https://www.dw.com/en/filipinos-resist-china-funded-dams-amid-beijings-growing-clout-in-southeast-asia/a-42973170

Initiative in their bid for hosting major international sports events. Cooperations between cities, NGOs and think tanks should provide a low-level institutional framework which captures the wider community.

According to the above mentioned official BRI document (NDRC, 2015), the key function which the initiative should fulfill is "to promote the connectivity of Asian, European and African continents and their adjacent seas, establish and strengthen partnerships among the countries along the Belt and Road Initiative, set up all-dimensional, multi-tiered and composite connectivity networks, and realise diversified, independent, balanced and sustainable development in these countries. Without doubt," connectivity became a trend, but its explanatory power how the five major fields of activities are interlinked is relatively low (figure 1).

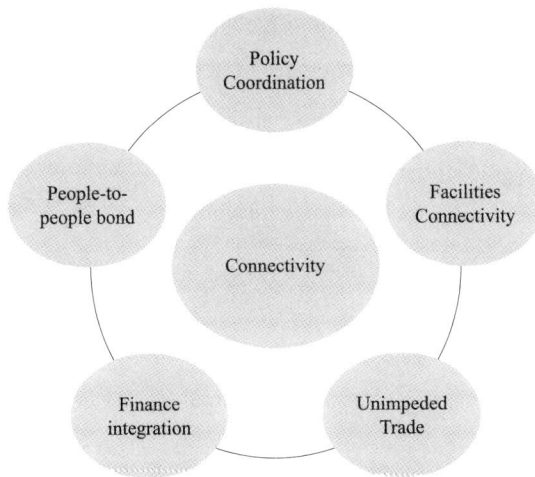

Figure 1. Connectivity and its approaches in the BRI Initiative
Source: Hongjian, 2016.

Cooperation mechanisms

The Chinese government is aware that the success of the BRI initiative strongly depends on the cooperation mechanisms. On the one hand it is envisaged to make full use of the existing multilateral cooperations mechanisms such as the Shanghai Cooperation Organization (SCO), ASEAN Plus China

(10+1), Asia-Pacific Economic Cooperation (APEC), Asia-Europe Meeting (ASEM), Asia Cooperation Dialogue (ACD), Conference on Interaction and Confidence-Building Measures in Asia (CICA), China-Arab States Cooperation Forum (CASCF), China-Gulf Cooperation Council Strategic Dialogue, Greater Mekong Sub-region (GMS) Economic Cooperation, and Central Asia Regional Economic Cooperation (CAREC), 16+1. Furthermore, existing forums, fairs, exhibitions should be enriched by BRI-related activities. On the other hand existing bilateral cooperation mechanisms should be strengthened by extending their scope of actions. It is well-known that the Chinese governance system is characterized by a complex multi-level and multi-dimensional network of committees which offers a suitable platform for BRI-related cooperation. Last but not least, the proposal to set up an international summit forum on the BRI initiative demonstrates the great importance which China's leadership pays to this initiative. It is worth mentioning that the participating political leaders of the Belt and Road Initiative Forum on International Cooperation in Beijing on 15 May 2017 stated in their Joint Communique that enhancing the connectivity between Asia and Europe has top priority, but it is also open to other regions such as Africa and South America.[1]

Domestic relevance

From an inward-looking point of view the BRI initiative is considered as an instrument of China's regional policy. BRI-related activities should strengthen interaction and cooperation among the eastern, western and central regions, and comprehensively improve the openness of the Chinese economy. For example, Xinjiang Uygur Autonomous Region should make use of its geographic advantages and its role as a window of westward opening-up by deepening its relations with Central, South and West Asian countries. As as core area on the Silk Road Economic Belt, Xinjiang's location makes it a key

---

[1] XINHUANET, 15. May 2017, Full text of the Joint Communique, available at: http://www. xinhuanet.com/english/2017-05/15/c_136286378.htm

transportation, trade, logistics, culture, science and education center. Provinces in the Northeast should benefit from Russia's far east region by pushing forward the construction of an Eurasian high-speed transport corridor linking Beijing and Moscow. The regions in Southwestern China should benefit from ASEAN neighbors by establishing an international corridor which also serves as an important gateway connecting the Silk Road Economic Belt and the 21st-Century Maritime Silk Road. The latter will provide new economic incentives for China's coastal regions, and Hong Kong, Macao, and Taiwan. It is expected that further opening up "motivate these areas to carry out deeper reform, create new systems and mechanisms of open economy, step up scientific and technological innovation, develop new advantages for participating in and leading international cooperation and competition, and become the pace-setter and main force in the Belt and Road Initiative, particularly the building of the 21st-Century Maritime Silk Road. It is also aimed to "make proper arrangements for the Taiwan region to be part of this effort. China's emerging inland cities such as Chongqing, Chengdu, Wuhan, Zhengzhou, Xi'an should play an important role in terms of railway transport and port customs clearance for the China-Europe corridor, cultivate the brand of China-Europe freight trains and construct a cross-border transport corridor connecting the eastern, central and western regions.

To sum up the document: It corresponds to the self-conception of China's leaders believing to speak for others: "Though proposed by China, the Belt and Road Initiative is a common aspiration of all countries along their routes. This far-reaching intention is to the detriment of precise time tables, mutual responsibilities, plans of activities. Or, as Chou and Bryant (2015) put it: "[The document] is relatively light on specifics, though it does make frequent reference to such catchphrases as cooperation, harmony, openness, and inclusivity." The wider range of opinions is rounded off by Chen's (2015) perception that "China's vision is no less impressive than the geographic scope. The Belt and Road Initiative will not only enhance 'five connections'-trade, infrastructure, investment, capital and people-it will create a community with 'shared interests, destiny and responsibilities.' China hopes the network will become two wings of Asia, with China at the head of this flying eagle."

4. The BRI Initiative: From vision to reality

As mentioned above, the BRI Initiative was for the first time presented in 2013, whereas the official document was published in 2015. The latter not only looks to the future but also addresses achievements in the meantime. Particularly noteworthy are the marketing activities in terms of visits of China's leaders to 20 countries followed by signing MoUs of cooperation on the joint development of the Belt and Road Initiative with some countries, and on regional cooperation and border cooperation and mid- and long-term development plans for economic and trade cooperation with some neighboring countries. Last but not least, a number of key cooperation projects in such fields as infrastructure connectivity, industrial investment, resource development, economic and trade cooperation, financial cooperation, cultural exchanges, ecological protection and maritime cooperation had been promoted under the umbrella of the BRI initiative.

A more detailed study of the aforementioned BRI document might give the impression that almost any type of China's political, economic, social, cultural, environmental measures on any governmental level fits to the BRI inititiative. This makes it difficult to compile a comprehensive list of BRI-related activities, to systemize clusters of activities and finally to evaluate the overall result. This even applies in the light of the short time span of around five years. The dimension of the BRI initiative becomes clear when comparing the USD 1 trillion earmarked for investment with the inflation-adjusted USD 130 billion of the Marshall Plan which had been allocated to Europe after WWII. However, it must taken into account that the former amount is a rough estimation. There is neither a concrete timetable for spending this amount nor a concrete number of countries which can apply for funding projects. In principle, the BRI initiative is open to engagement with all countries as well as international and regional organizations (State Council). Based on the official website on the Belt and Road Initiative hosted by the Chinese State Information Center, the Belt and Road Initiative website of the HKTDC[1] lists 75 countries under the umbrella of the BRI inititiatve (as of August 2018). Main partner countries include the ten ASEAN member states, most countries in Central and Eastern Europe, the Russian Federation, South Korea, Mogolia, India, Pakistan, Kazakhstan.

Financing

The funding of BRI-related projects is provided by three new institutions: The Chinese Silk Road Fund, established at the end of 2014 with a capital of USD 40 billion, the Asian Infrastrucutre Investment Bank (AIIB), established in December 2015 with an authorized capital of USD 100 million, and the New Development Bank (NDB), put into force in July 2015 with an authorized capital of USD 100 million. The latter two are multilateral development institutions. As of July 2018, the AIIB is headed by China and supported by 66 member countries and 21 prospective member countries[2]. The NDB was founded by the BRICS countries. It is noteworthy that infrastructure projects in BRI countries are to an increasing extent financed/co-financed by private capital. Furthermore, partnerships between Chinese and foreign state-owned development banks expand the financial scope for infrastructure projects. Several Chinese state-owned banks with specific tasks such as the Export-Import Bank of China are indirectly involved into the BRI initiative by financing foreign trade and investments. Finally, it should be noted that especially the Eurasian region has been prior to the BRI initiative an important field of activities for the World Bank, the Asian Development Bank and the

---

[1]   HKTDC, available at: https://beltandroad.hktdc.com/en/country-profiles
[2]   AIIB, available at: https://www.aiib.org/en/about-aiib/governance/members-of-bank/index.html

European Bank for Reconstruction and Development. AIIB and NDB differ only slightly in their principles of financing. The former aims to fund only financially, environmentally and socially viable projects, the latter imperatives are sustainability, pragmatism, innovation and speed of execution. The AIIB has to develop assessment instruments which allow to avoid trade-offs between the three requirements of the projects to be financed. Especially the NDB has to fight against the perception that its decisions are China-dominated.

Until the end of 2017, the AIIB approved 23 projects and invested a total of USD 4.22 billion and mobilized private cofinancing of USD 566 million.[1] There is no reliable information from Chinese officials on the financial resources which are necessary to realize the BRI vision or which China is willing or able to invest into this initiative. Esteban and Ortero-Iglesias (2015: 5) note that "even the figure of almost US$4 trillion amassed by China in its currency reserves pales into insignificance in the context of the US$21 trillion some international experts reckon it would cost to make the new Silk Road a reality, or the US$8 trillion the Asian Development Bank thinks Asia will need to invest on infrastructure before 2020. Inevitably, in the light of the sums being mooted, the Chinese authorities have made it clear that the plan does not rely on donations, but rather investments made in accordance with market criteria. From this perspective it is envisaged that both States and participating companies as well as private international investors will be able to provide financing for the project via a number of different routes. It should not be ignored that a growing complexity of financing increases the risk of inefficient investments. It is too optimistic to expect that all participating countries can rely on functioning governance mechanisms which guarantee efficient allocation of foreign capital. As Estban and Ortero-Iglesias (2015: 5) put it: "It hardly needs to be said that several of the States involved in the project do not exactly shine when it comes to good governance; on the contrary, they suffer from high levels

---

① AIIB, available at: https://www.aiib.org/en/news-events/news/2017/annual-report/highlights. html

of corruption and a political class that has a proprietorial attitude towards the State. This fits to an information published by the Financial Times[1] (9 May 2016) that "Chinese officials privately admit they expect to lose 80 per cent of their investment in Pakistan, 50 per cent in Myanmar and 30 per cent in central Asia." By testing the debt vulnerabilities of over 60 BRI countries, Hurley et al (2018) identify eight countries[2] where BRI appears to create the potential for debt sustainability problems, and where China is a dominant creditor in the key position to address those problems.

Motives

The first step to bring order into an overview on BRI activities is the uncovering of the BRI motives. The real motives reveal themselves by interpreting the official BRI document in the context of China's economic development path as well as in its geo-political ambitions. Three recurrently mentioned motives can be detected from the daily increasing number of statements, reports, analysis on the BRI Initiative, namely, first, to contribute to the development of the wider region surrounding China, second to support China's "new normal" growth model[3], third to strengthen China's geo-political position.

Regional motives

Although the superficial study of the above described BRI document suggests that the initiative has significant overlaps with China's African

---

[1]   FINANCIAL TIMES, 9 May 2016, available at: https://www.ft.com/content/e83ced94-0bd8-11e6-9456-444ab5211a2f

[2]   Djibouti, Maldives, Laos, Montenegro, Mongolia, Tajikistan, Kyrkyzstan, Pakistan.

[3]   Economists inside and outside China expect growth rates in the range of 6-7 percent over the next 10 years (Amighini, 2015; CAI, 2014; YANG, 2015). Harvard's Economic Complexity Growth Projection published on 3rd May predicts that this growth is likely to continue to slow to 4.9% annually for the coming decade (available at: http://atlas.cid.harvard.edu/rankings/growth-projections/)

development aid model, however, at some points there will be reference that China does not intend to follow the often observed resource-exploiting and destroying development strategy. The expected stimulus on economic growth in the BRI-countries should include a noticeable sustainability component. This should demonstrate that China wants to support these countries in avoiding negative consequences of its hitherto prevaling resource-intensive growth model. Sanwal (2016) criticised that the initiative is "consciously not adopting the development-cooperation model based on aid. Instead, it relies on a state strategy implemented by corporate investments and catalysed by the USD 40 billion Silk Road Fund."

Some expectations on the effects of BRI measures read themselves as a simplified version of the classical trade theory: "China aims to promote the flow of capital, goods and commodities across the region. If the plan is successful over the coming decades, the countries in the region 'will form a highly effective, efficient and socially developed region like the EU…The region will become highly converged economically rather than be in conflict.'"[①] Economic convergence in the Asian region is expected to contribute to greater political stability which reduces the vulnerability of China's far-distant energy imports. Territorial disputes in the South China Sea render China's maritime trade routes vulnerable.

Economic motives

The economic drivers are threefold. First, China is experiencing a worrying downturn in economic activity. Second, its growing dependence from foreign energy (mainly caused by the shutdown of environmentally harmful and hazardous coal mines) requires save land and maritime transport routes. Third,

---

① Quote of Li Daokui, Dean of Schwarzman College at Tsinghua University, Beijing, cited in World Economic Forum, the Belt and Road Initiative Signals China's Economic and Strategic Objectives, 28 June 2016, available at: www.weforum.org/press/2016/06/one-belt-one-road-initiative-signals-china-s-economic-and-strategic-objectives/

especially the backward regions in central and western China are expected to catch-up with the coastal areas when being connected with near and far distant countries.

For more than 30 years China pursued an investment-led growth model supported by an opening-up policy towards foreign investments and exports. This strategy has produced outstanding high economic growth, but seems to reach to its limits, partly due to the impact of the global financial crisis on China's economy. The decreasing external demand was replaced by domestic investment resulting in an investment ratio of up to 45% (Zhang, 2016: 3) The recently declining growth rates signal several negative effects of the investment- and export-driven model, amongst others overcapacities in manufacturing and infrastructure, decline of competitiveness in manufacturing due to increasing wages, growing functional and regional income inequality, inefficient credit intensity, deteriorating envionment. The 13th Five-Year Plan[①], formally adopted by the National People's Congress on March 14, 2016, demonstrates the leadership's recognition of the need to rebalance the economy into a sustainable growth path which is labelled as China's "new normal" phase. The turnaround had been already announced in 2013 at the Chinese Communist Party's Third Plenum. The 60 measures set in the *"Decision on Several Major Questions About Deepening Reform"*[②] aimed to boost the country's transition from dominant export-oriented low-tech manufacturing and excessive infrastructure investment to higher-value manufacturing and increasing private consumption. The BRI initiative is obviously considered as a project which supports the intentions of the 13th Five-Year Plan. Several concrete BRI projects are explicitly listed in the 13th Five-Year Plan (table 1).

---

① Kennedy and Johnson (2016) provide a detailed overview on the 13th Five-Year Plan.
② The English short version is available at: http://www.china.org.cn/china/third_plenary_session/2013-11/16/content_30620736.htm

Table 1. Selected BRI projects listed in the 13th Five-Year Plan

Plan	Purpose	Project	Province (prefecture)
Yangtze River Economic Belt	To build a "high-quality" transportation corridor	Shipping centre	Hubei (Wuhan)
		Upgrade of Yichang-Anqing channel	Hubei (Yichang/Anqing)
		Regional shipping logistics centre	Jiangsu (Nanjing)
		Shipping centre	Chongqing
		Construction of Zhoushan River transportation service cener	Zhejiang
the Belt and Road Initiative	Crossborder trade and investment	Develop Fujian into the core area of 21st-Century Maritime Silk Road	Fujian
		Develop "pivot" cities of the 21st-Century Maritime Silk Road	Fujian (Fuzhou, Quanzhou), Guangdong (Zhanjiang, Guangzhou), Guangxi (Beihai), Hainan (Haikou)
		Shanghai Co-operation Organisation (SCO) logistics park	Jiangsu (Lianyungang)
		China-Kazakhstan Logistics Co-operation Base	Jiangsu (Lianyungang)
		Develop Xinjiang into the core area of the Silk Road Economic Belt	Xinjiang
The development of special regions	Cross border trade and investment	Promote Guangxi as an "international channel" towards Asean	Guangxi
		Promote as a "pivot of cooperation" with Northeast Asia	Heilongjiang, Inner Mongolia, Jilin
		Changchun-Jilin-Tumen Development and Opening-Up Pilot Zone	Jilin, Liaoning
		Promote Tibet as an "international channel" towards South Asia	Tibet
		Promote Xinjiang as a "window" towards the west	Xinjiang
		Promote Yunnan as a "radiation centre" towards South Asia and South-east Asia	Yunnan

Source: Xinhua
Source: ECN, 2016: 5.

It goes without saying that BRI fits into China's "going out" strategy, but it differs considerably from its first phase of the "invite-in" policy as well as from its second phase of export-led policy (Heiduk and Holslag, 2011). As shown in table 1, BRI is an integral part of China's new development model outlined in the 13th Five-Year Plan. According to Johnson (2016: 5) the most frequently mentioned contributions are, first, "the opportunity to help absorb China's massive excess capacity that the increasingly over-leveraged Chinese economy simply can no longer sustain. Second, BRI-related projects can provide a lifeline to large state firms overburdened with debt by allowing them to gain access fresh capital from state banks that might otherwise have to deal with a large wave of nonperforming loans that could precipitate a financial crisis. Third, BRI can be viewed as providing the leadership with a semi-controlled laboratory to test the ability of the larger industrial state-owned enterprises (SOEs) to meet the leadership's call for developing themselves into internationally competitive global champions." Finally, Johnson adds that "BRI should help to overcome China's struggle with developing its chronically underperforming regions by integrating them into a holistic, externally oriented development program." More recently, the deteriorating competitiveness of China's manufacturing powerhouses, especially the Guangdong Province, demands a move away from the low-tech manufacturing of parts and components. To a certain degree, BRI projects may contribute to reverse the Asian production networks. Cheap and fast regional transportation networks, improved domestic infrastructure financed by Silk Road Fund or AIIB in nearby countries such as Myanmar, Laos, Cambodia, Vietnam are important preconditions to outsource Chinese low-tech production to these countries and to upgrade its own manufacturing basis.

Chinese analysts point to further aspects which are related to BRI or interpret the same aspects differently. LI and XU (2015) argue that "the main domestic driving force of the BRI strategy is a need to reduce foreign exchange reserves and to transfer excess capacity. However, the three principles of foreign exchange reserves are security, liquidity, and profitability, with security as the most important. Considering that the investment environment in Silk Road countries is not as developed as the environment in Europe and the U.S., the return on investment is likely to be low. Some investments may even become bad debts. It's a serious violation of the principles of foreign exchange reserves management to have these funds become bad debts. China needs to avoid this by all means. As for the question of excess capacity, let's take the steel industry as an example. Even if the demand for steel from Silk Road countries equals the demand of China's domestic railway consumption (itself an impressive figure), China still could not solve the problem of excess steel. In 2014, steel consumption for domestic railway construction totaled 21 million tons; the volume of excess steel reached 450 million tons. That massive discrepancy can't be solved by transferring materials to other countries. In this case, shutting down the factories may be the only solution, even if it is painful." Many analysts are pessimistic that neither BRI projects nor domestic shut-down of (ste-owned) companies will eliminate wasteful overcapacities. The resistence of SOEs against reforms, the local politicians who benefit from local SOEs, the central government that fears riots by dismissed workers are some arguments against a timely and sufficient reduction of overcapacities. There are even warnings to BRI coutries that the export of China's overcapacity via infrastructure projects those countries may create the same problems that China faces now. Based on an analysis of 95 infrastructure projects in China, Ansar et al (2016: 384) conclude that infrastructure investment does not lead to economic growth. "There is an even more detrimental boomerang effect of overinvestment in infrastructure. Unproductive projects carry unintended pernicious macroeconomic consequences: sovereign debt overhang; unprecedented monetary expansion; and economic fragility…China is not a model to follow for other economies-emerging or developed-as regards infrastructure investing, but a model to avoid."

Geopolitical motives

It is not surprising that in Europe the majority of comments on the BRI initiative focus on the economic effects, whereas publications in the U.S.A. reflect more often on its political dimension. Johnson (2016: 5), an Asian affairs specialists at the Washington based Center for Strategic & International Studies, views the BRI Initiative as a very personal "product" of Xi Jinping's foreign policy agenda: "It would be difficult to understand the leadership's vision of BRI in the absence of a thorough review of the Chinese Communist Party's (CCP) evolving foreign policy canon…There is little doubt that President Xi views BRI as the signature foreign policy theme of his leadership tenure and the practical embodiment of his 'China Dream' for promoting national rejuvenation and cementing the country's place as a leading world power." Finally, Johnson acknowledges the geostrategic component of BRI, but considers it as overstated, especially from observers in the USA. Anyhow, the impact of the BRI initiative on US interests in Asia is an intensively discussed issue. Political scientists, e.g. Wallace Cheng (2015), argue that the BRI Initiative is a response to US pivot to Asia. Chou and Bryant (2015) go even further by assuming BRI as a project to support China's global dream: "While there are clear supporters of this Sinocentric project, a chorus of critics have already expressed concerns that Xi's bold vision for the New Silk Road points to more than a 21st century revival of an ancient Chinese feat which altered the course of civilizations. With Xi's 'The Belt and Road Initiative' (BRI) initiative, as *The Wall Street Journal* columnist Jeremy Page has warned, China may be giving rise to a sinocentric 'New Asian Order". It's the 'Chinese Dream' gone global."

It does not surprise that such kind of geopolitical motives are not shared by Chinese politicians, academics and media. The former Foreign Minister LI Zhaoxing (2015) stated that "the 21st Century Maritime Silk Road is a fine example of China's neighborhood policy of 'closeness, sincerity, shared prosperity and inclusiveness'. There is no hidden agenda here, and there is no intention to use the 'Belt and Road Initiatives' as a means to spread China's sphere of influence, still less to violate other countries' sovereignty. That is to say, China will continue to firmly uphold its maritime rights and interests, safeguard the global and regional maritime order, work earnestly to provide public goods and ensure a harmonious ocean environment."

An important question refers to the selection of countries which build a stable geopolitical power with China as the center. LI and XU (2015) point to the political risks of the BRI strategy which result from the fact that "many countries along the land and maritime Silk Road routes suffer from political instability, serious corruption and/or the threat of terrorism. How to find political stable countries with economic potential that are willing to cooperate with China? This should be a major research question for the BRI strategy. We can loosely categorize Silk Road countries into four groups: small and medium-sized countries; countries that have territorial disputes with China; countries that are sub-regional powers; and countries that could potentially act as 'pivot states' (meaning they are reliable partners for China and reach a certain threshold of national power). Countries in this last group are the key to the BRI strategy."

In Europe, the BRI Initiative did not attract comparable attention like in Southeast and Central Asia. Countries which host terminal stations of BRI railroads make the economic effects a subject of official statements and information. On the level of the EU, a recently published Briefing of the European Parliament (2016) has rather informative character than analytical content. It is significant to note that the sub-title characterizes BRI as a Chinese regional integration initiative. This could be interpreted that the EU sees itself in a passive or even excluded role (see also chapter IV). This might be explained by several major challenges which BRI puts on the EU. Casarini (2015: 1) points to the risk that "a scramble for Chinese money could further divide EU member states and make it difficult for Brussels to fashion a common position vis-a-vis Beijing. Furthermore, China's economic penetration into Europe may lead—if not properly managed—to a populist backlash as well as a strain in relations with Washington." A study for the TRAN Committee of the European Commission (Steer, Davies, Gleave, 2018) show that the EU is still at the very beginning to develop an economic BRI strategy. Basically, it recommends to use the framework of the "Connectivity Platform" to seek greater clarity on the geographical and project scope of the BRI initiative.

Critics

Critical comments on the BRI Initiative come from different directions and refer to institutional, content-related and financial aspects.

From an economic point of view, one of the main challenges is the frictionless interlocking of BRI-related measures with measures to switch from the former investment-led growth of BRI measures with measures of the new consumption-led model. There are doubts that the latter are suited for fulfilling China's BRI commitment to cooperate on a win-win basis with its Asian partner countries. A further slowdown of China's growth rate may reduce the pull-effect of its demand for products from other Asian countries.

Another critical aspect of the current BRI program refers to the lack of a clear governance and management structure. According to official statements, e.g. from the People's Bank of China (2015), BRI projects should be financed on the basis of market-oriented principles resulting in adequate returns of investment. There are doubts that Chinese SOEs which are intended to play a prominent role in implementing BRI projects are capable (and even willing) to orient their management strategies on making profits. Johnson (2016: 22) stresses the risks that companies may hunt for BRI-themed projects without having sufficient experience in foreign markets. "If companies stumble in the markets where they have rushed in, there will be ramifications for them and the financial institutions that have underwritten their misadventures. Failing to assess risks appropriately may mean that the serious domestic preparations the central government has been trying to make for the project risk has been wasted. This is especially so given that BRI is more a sweeping vision than an operational blueprint." This leads to critics that there are no plans so far how to organize the two pillars of the BRI Initiative under one institutionalized umbrella. The dozens of high-level government meetings and rather imprecise assignments of responsibilities are probably not sufficient to make full use of the benefits of the invested funds. It goes without saying that the complexity and fuzziness of government-internal coordination mechanisms in China (which include also local and city governments) pose an unlikely manageable challenge to administrators, bankers, company leaders who are involved in the implementation of BRI projects. In addition, the external coordination of multiple-country projects could also prove difficult, namely in cases where countries lack experience in implementing and managing large-scale cross-border infrastructure projects.

Besides criticism on economic and institutional aspects of BRI there are also concerns on possible political consequences. Chou and Byant (2015) critically question the implication of BRI for the geopolitics of democracy by pointing to "the fear that countries under Beijing's sphere of influence may willingly or otherwise learn to see the appeal of autocracy, further shunning democracy in the process and precipitating what is known as a reverse-wave of democratization." The Indian analysist Sanwal (2016) raise the question "whether Asia will have two poles, as it has had throughout history, or will India remain at Asia's periphery as a regional power?" Furthermore, he questioned the BRI concept of connectivity, which offers clear strategic advantages for China, contrasts sharply with existing treaty-based integration concepts where the geographical scope, partner countries, strategy, principles and rules are clearly defined at the outset.

Johnson (2016: 22/23) summarizes the critics on BRI to the point by stating that there are "too many eggs in one basket" and "political imperatives outweigh economic pragmatism".

Finally, it should be mentioned that the Chinese side demands a clear position on BRI from European countries and institutions: LIU (2017: 4) stated that "to understand the real attitude of Europe towards the initiative, the official declarations of the European countries are far from enough. Therefore, it is necessary to analyze the motives behind European responses and the potential of the bilateral cooperation between the two sides."

The geography and economics of the BRI initiative

The BRI investments are estimated to affect the lives of 4.4 billion people and generate in around 900 projects USD 2.1 trillion in gross production (Hofman, 2015). As of June 2018, the HKTDC Resource Portal on the Belt and Road Initiative lists 90 implementation plans and cooperation agrements.[1]

From a conceptual perspective, the BRI initiative is split into two regions. The first is the "Silk Road Economic Belt" which streches westward from Xinjiang Province into Central Asia and Europe. The second is the "21st Century Maritime Silk Road" which connects China with Southeast Asia, the Subcontinent, the Middle East, Western Africa, and ultimately Europe. LI Zhaoxing (2015), former foreign minister, summerized the two legs of BRI as the "two wings of Asia" and added: "To fly high, we need both wings to be powerful." Build on already existing transport routes between inland hubs and ocean ports, this rough bipartition is refined into six geo-economic corridors. China expects from the two east-west corridors (China-Europe) improved access to European markets, from the four north-south/southwest corridors the reversal of regional production networks, the access to natural resources (oil and gas), and, last but not least, new connections between the Maritime Silk Road and land routes via access to ports in the Indian Ocean, the Bengal Sea and the Mediterranean Sea. One of the flagship projects is aiming to establish an intermodal sea-rail transportation route labelled as China-Europe Land-Sea Express Route. From the perspective of EU-China relations, the New Eurasia Land Bridge Economic Corridor including the Land-Sea Express Route. Forms

---

[1] HKTDC, Implementation Documents, available at: http://china-trade-research.hktdc. com/business-news/article/The-Belt-and-Road-Initiative/The-Belt-and-Road-Initiative-Implementation-Plans-and-Cooperation-Agreements/obor/en/1/1X3CGF6L/1X0A3857.htm

the core of a modern China-Europe Silk Road. Since the regular weekly cargo service began in 2012, the number of the origin and destination cities as well as the frequency of services increased rapidly. Currently, trains are running in three major train routes. All these new rail routes offer rail-to-rail freight transport, as well as the convenience of "one declaration, one inspection, one cargo release" for any cargo transported. (HKTDC, 2018b).

Xi Jinping's visits to countries in the Middle East (LI and ZHENG, 2016) and Africa (Tiezzi, 2018) are mostly crowned by the signing of official cooperation documents on the BRI initiative. Despite various conflicts, China expects to benefit when being involved into oil and gas exploration and exploitation. It can be concluded that the original geography of BRI experienced a fast expansion beyond the Eurasian continent.

5. China-Europe connectivity

On 8 May 2014, China's state-owned XINHUA New Agency started a series on China's New Silk Road which included a map indicating the originally planned land route of the Silk Road Economic Belt as well as the 21st Century Maritime Silk Road (Tiezzi, 2014). The map shows that the former route will begin in Xi'an (also the starting point of the ancient Silk Road), pass Lanzhou, Urumqi, Khorgas (border city with Kazakhstan). On its way to Istanbul it runs through Central Asia, Iran, Iraq and Syria. After crossing the Bosporus Strait it reaches Europe, where Bulgaria, Romania and the Czech Republic are transit countries before reaching the city of Duisburg in Germany which is connected by ship on the river Rhine with Rotterdam (The Netherland). A further land route to Venice will create a link between the Silk Road Economic Belt and the Maritime Silk Road. The latter will begin in Quanzhou, hit Guangzhou, Beihai and the island of Hainan, then passing the Malacca Strait. From Kuala Lumpur, the Maritime Silk Road heads to Kolkata, reaches Africa in Nairobi. After sailing round the Horn of Africa, the route moves through the Red Sea into the

Mediterranean Sea, with a stop in Athens' port of Pireus before meeting the land route in Venice. Evidence for the real existence of the Silk Road Economic Belt is provided by the China-Europe freight train network. With respect to the connectivity of the 21st Maritime Silk Road with Europe, the takeover of the Piraeus port by the Chinese SOE COSCO is the most prominent case so far. Dock workers opposed the deal by a one month strike.

By comparison with BRI projects in other corridors, the China-Europe connectivity is by far the most developed. From an economic point of view, this can be explained by China's current interest to improve the competitiveness of its manufacturing of parts and components in Europe by using cargo trains as a fast, reliable, secure and flexible transportation mode. The European automotive industry benefits from an increased competition between Chinese and Eastern European suppliers. In electronics, European OEMs benefit from fast and flexible component delivery.

Freight train routes, tourism, high-level dialogues

It may surprise that politics is not a dominant issue in China-Europe connectivity. One reason might be the longstanding intensive diplomatic relations between China and the EU as well as between China and European countries. Already in 1978, the EEC and China signed a bilateral trade agreement indicating that trade and economic cooperation dominates the relations from China's opening-up on. The 1985 Agreement on Trade and Economic Cooperation had been upgraded to a Partnership and Cooperation Agreement. The EU-China 2020 Strategic Agenda for Cooperation, adopted in 2013, paved the way for negotiations on an EU-China Investment Agreement. The EU-China Summit in 2015 resulted in an declaration which connected China's BRI Inititiative with EU's Investment Plan for Europe ("Juncker Plan").[1] The Declaration lists a wide range of new types of dialogues, financial

---

[1] European Commision (2016): EU-China Summit, *Press Release*, Brussels, 29 June 2015, availableat: http://europa.eu/rapid/press-release_IP-15-5279_en.htm.

cooperations and platforms. In September 2015, an BRI-related MoU on connectivity established the EU-China "Connectivity Platform". As the first non-EU country, China announced its contribution to the Juncker plan. It is envisaged to adopt a coordinated approach on infrastructure planning through matching BRI projects with EU's Trans-European Transport Network[1] (TEN-T). On top of the working agenda is the selection of pilot projects, the improvement of "connectivity" in fields such as customs proceedings and border crossing (Baron, 2016). Furthermore, an expert group should develop financing mechanisms. It is significant to note that the cooperation refers to projects in the EU and neighborhood as well as in China. The draft list of projects include amongst others the Budapest-Belgrade railway and several railway routes in China. Another focus of BRI's connectivity approach is the development of the EU-China people-to-people dialogue. Activities include the EU-China High-level People-to-People Dialogue which had been established as one of the three pillars of EU-China relations[2] even before the launch of the BRI Initiative (WANG, 2016). Another focus of connecting people is the development of China's outbound and inbound tourism. In order to stimulate inbound tourism, China launched in 2015 the "Year of Silk Road Tourism". At the EU-China Summit in June 2017, the European Investment Fund and the Silk Road Fund signed a Memorandum of Understanding that outlines new strategic cooperation to support equity investment across Europe. Once operational the China-EU Co-Investment Fund is expected to provide EUR 500 million to support growing companies in Europe.[3] In July 2018, the 3rd Chairs' Meeting of the EU-China Connectivity Platform resulted in an action plan which amongst others envisage to support the implementation of infrastructure

---

[1] For an overview on TEN-T see the public portal, available at: http://ec.europa.eu/transport/infrastructure/tentec/tentec-portal/site/en/abouttent.htm

[2] The first pillar is the High-Level Economic and Trade Dialogue, the second pillar the High-Level Strategic Dialogue.

[3] European Investment Fund, 02 June 2017, available at: http://www.eif.org/what_we_do/equity/news/2017/eib_silk_road_fund_initiative.htm

corridor development in the relevant countries and regions along the route. A jointly conducted "EU-China Railway Corridor Study" should define the most appropriate railway corridors, identify bottlenecks, identify and prioritize the missing links to improve the capacity and efficiency of rail corridors (European Commission, 2018).

Among the five different types of connectivity (Figure 1), the achievements in trade facilitation is most visible by the extension freight train routes, the frequency of trains and the volume of transported goods. One of the first freight train service (known as Yixinou Railway) started in 2011 and connects Chongqing and the German city of Duisburg via Kazakhstan, Russia, Belarus, Poland. The train needs 14-16 days for the 11.100 km which is 20 days shorter than by ship. The success of this land conncection has motivated a growing number of other Chinese cities to launch railway routes to European cities. The dynamics of the opening of new routes makes it difficult to provide an instructive and accurate picture of the China-Europe railway network. It is estimated that at the beginning of 2018 more than 60 cities in China, Central Asia, the Middle East and Europe are connected under the umbrella of the Silk Road Economic Belt (Shepard, 2018). According to China Railway the China-Europe rail network connects 43 Chinese cities and 42 destinations in 14 countries. Major Chinese hubs of origin are Chengdu, Chongqing and Zhengzhou, whereas major European destination hubs are Duisburg and Hamburg in Germany. Numerous cities in Central and Eastern Europe compete as destinations in the China-Europe rail network such as Łódź in Poland, Pardubice in the Czech Republic and Košice in Slovakia. There is evidence that the network is approaching the limits of its capacity. Especially Khorgos on the China-Kazakhstan border and Małaszewicze on the Belarus-Poland border are exposed to congestions due to a considearble increase in processed containers (Goh and Goettig, 2018). As a consequence, the Łódź-Chengdu train route could be redirected via as transit route through the Russian enclave Kaliningrad, then re-routing to Lithuania and finally continuing on the Trans-Siberian railway in order to avoid Malzewicze.[①] It is expected that the total number of China-Europe train trips will exceed 4000 in 2018 (Figure 2). With respect to the freight, Xinhua (2016) notes that "from Harbin in northeast China, Yiwu in the east, Wuhan and Changsha in central China, cargo trains carry IT equipment, automobiles and other products to Poland, Germany, Czech Republic and Spain, and bring the best of Europe to Chinese customers." The Łódź-Chengdu trains mostly carry foodstuffs.[②] Trains from Europe to China still have to contend with the problem of low load factors. Das (2016) points to a number of challenges to improve the competitiveness of the freight routes, especially to reduce the freight costs. Different railway gauges urges frequent switch of trains and increase the overall traveling time. Unnecessary delays due to non-standard customs procedures reduce the efficiency of border crossings. More general, there is a lack of a harmonized regulatory framework in the transportation industry. Pratesh (2016) puts these challenges under the headline of "institutional connectivity".

NUMBER OF TRAIN TRIPS

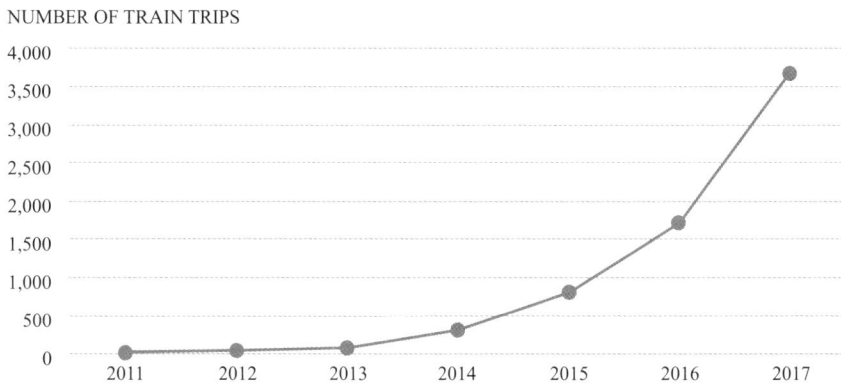

Source: China Railway Express

J. Wu, 25/06/2018　　　　　　　　　　　　　　　　　　　　　🌐 REUTERS

Figure 2.　Number of China-Europe train trips, 2011-2017
Source: tmsnrt.rs/2txkLZJ (citied in Goh and Goettig, 2018).

---

① RailFreight, 17 October 2017, available at: https://www.railfreight.com/corridors/2017/10/17/new-rail-freight-services-between-europe-china/
② Polish Ministry of Foreign Affairs, available at: http://www.msz.gov.pl/en/p/msz_en/news/chengdu__rail_link_with_lodz_a_chance_for_food_industry

In order to underline that all China-Europe freight lines are part of the Silk Road Economic Belt, the Chinese government and the China Railway Corporation unified the routes under the China Railway Express brand (Xinhua 2016).

The growing railway freight volume gives reason to assume that BRI positively affect the EU-China trade. Herrero and XU's simulation exercises (2016) predict that EU countries could be clear winners of the BRI Initiative. In contrast, their conclusion may surprise that a China-initiated free trade area within the BRI area will not result in benefits for the EU, but for Asia. There is evidence that the imbalance between European inbound freight train load and European outbound freight train load may even increase EU's trade deficit with China.

There is evidence that the People-to-People Dialogue as one pillar of the BRI connectivity approach plays a more important and successful role in the China-Europe corridor than in other BRI corridors. The China-Europe mass tourism records high growth rates in both directions due to higher frequency on main flight routes as well as opening of new flight routes. A study of Goldman Sachs (2015) estimates that the number of Chinese tourists to Europe will increase from 10 million in 2015 to 22.5 million in 2025 which would exceed the Chinese tourists to the USA by more than four times. According to the Ctripairline ticket sales data, Europe was the second most popular destination for Chinese tourists in 2017, accounting for 9.3% of the total surpassing the USA as top non-Asian destination.[1] The most popular destinations in Europe are France, Italy, Spain and Germany.

BRI and CEE16+1

Finally, it should be noted that China aims to connect its 2012 established CEE16+1 Initiative with its BRI Initiative. The geographical location of the CEE region predistine it as a bridge between Asia and (Western) Europe. In order to fulfill this function, the CEE region needs to offer a sufficient

[1] Ctrip (2018), available at: https://www.chinatravelnews.com/images/201801/4103dfd 7b458c94a.pdf

and efficient transportation infrastructure which could be one of China's BRI priorities for investment in CEE. Furthermore, the role of CEE as near-shore manufacturing hub for western European industries may also gain attractiveness for the fast growing Chinese MNEs. The Chinese government has obviously recognized the importance of the CEE region, while the 16 CEE countries did not develop a region-wide BRI strategy. Matura (2016) points to the fact that BRI may give more substance and content to the 16+1 cooperation, but this needs more active input from the 16 CEE countries. So far, they are hesitant to grab more actively the chances which an integration of BRI into the 16+1 agenda offer. "CEE countries are geographically predestined to be part of BRI, and the looming project of connecting the port of Piraeus with Budapest through Macedonia and Serbia is one of the first examples of how BRI and 16+1 may eventually merge together. Meanwhile China is considering to relocate some of its industrial or manufacturing capacities into foreign countries to rebalance its domestic economic structure and its foreign trade. Central and Eastern Europe is a region which might be able to attract such kind of Chinese investment, and transportation corridors of BRI may offer a particularly good chance" (Matura, 2016). Instead of a common 16 CEE BRI agreement with China, countries obviously prefer to negotiate bilateral agreements (Table 2). Hungary and Serbia had been the first 16+1 countries that start negotiations with China on BRI and signed MoUs in 2014 (Table 2). Macedonia and Slovenia are the only countries which did not sign a BRI-related MoU with China. Belarus, Moldovia and Ukraine are non-16+1 countries which signed BRI-related agreements with China. Other European countries with BRI-related agreements are Germany, Greece, Ireland, the Netherlands.

Table 2. China's BRI-related agreements with 16+1 countries

Country	Relation to EU	Agreement	Topic
Albania	Candidate country, 2014	MoU, 2017	Construction (motorway)
Bosnia and Herzegovina	Membership application accepted in 2016	2 MoUs, 2017	BRI cooperation; trade, education

Continued Table

Country	Relation to EU	Agreement	Topic
Bulgaria	Member	2 MoUs, 2015,2016	Construction; port+harbor cooperation
Croatia	Member	2 MoUs, 2016, 2017	Port+harbor; BRI cooperation
Czech Republic	Member	Several MoUs, 2015, 2016, 2017	Jointly promoting BRI; financial, industrial, health cooperation
Estonia	Member	Agreement, 2017	Education cooperation
Hungary	Member	Several MoUs, 2014, 2015, 2017	Promoting BRI; SMEs; R&D; Belgrade-Budapest railway
Latvia	Member	2 MoUs, 2016	BRI cooperation; port+harbor cooperation
Lithuania	Member	MoU, 2016	Port+harbor industrial park cooperation
Macedonia	Candidate country, 2005	-	-
Montenegro	Candidate country, 2010	MoU, 2015	Construction (motorway)
Poland	Member	Several MoUs, 2015, 2016, 2017	BRI cooperation; investment in logistics infrastructure; customs clearance; block trains
Romania	Member	MoU, 2015	Joint development of Silk Road Economic Belt
Serbia	Candidate country, 2012	Several MoUs, 2014, 2015,2017	Jointly promoting BRI; Belgrade-Budapest rw; telecom, trade, agriculture, financial coop.
Slovakia	Member	MoU, 2015	Jointly promoting BRI
Slovenia	Member	-	-

Source. Steer Davis Gleave, 2018.

Kuzma (2016:14) identified the following shortcomings in the China-CEE BRI cooperation: "[First] CEE countries would like to see more Chinese attention to large Greenfield investment and not just predominantly investments in branding companies. [Second] On the other side Chinese partner face the lack of willingness on the part of CEE partners to carry out more coordination task (which is sometimes even condradictonary replaced by competition). CEE states "are used to have competed for direct investments from developed countries for years. [Third] Chinese companies are sometimes inexperienced in pursuing these model of cooperation. [Fourth] More tailored made financial models for BRI investments in CEEC."

The only China-Europe flagship transportation and infrastructure project which needs multilateral cooperation is the China-Europe Land-Sea Express route. The sea route starts in one of China's east coast ocean ports[①] and ends in the Greek port of Pireas. In April 2016, the Chinese shipping company COSCO acquired 67% of the Piraeus Port Authority (PPA)[②] and took over its management. Container traffic in creased from 3.47 million TEU in 2016 to 3.69 million TEU in 2017.

The efficiency of the European land route significantly depends on the an high-speed rail link between Piraeus and Hungary's capital city Budapest. The already existing spatial connectivity is suboptimal due to a missing institutional connectivity. The 1.100 kilometer rail route starts in Greece-a member state of the European Union, then passing through two non-EU countries (Macedonia and Serbia) and entering Hungary, again an EU member state. In 2013, China agreed with Serbia and Hungary to support financially the 350 kilometer route between Belgrade and Budapest. The travel time will be reduced from eight hours to three hours with an maximum speed of 160 km/h. On the occasion of the 16+1 Summit in Sofia on 7 July 2018, the Serbias's Prime Minister announced an agreement with China that the modernization of a part of the Serbian route is contracted and financed by Chinese SOEs with a USD 1.1 billion loan. It is interesting to note that the ceremonial launch of the work took place already on 28 November 2017. As long as Hungary did not fullfil the EU

① In July 2018, the PPA signed an MoU with Qingdao Port Group aiming to establish a strategic cooperation in fields such as know-how and information exchange, personnel training, protection of the environment (PPA press release, 24 July 2018, available at: http://www.olp. gr/en/press-releases/item/4041-memorandum-of-understanding-mou-between-ppa-sa-and-qingdao-international-port-group
② The deal is divided into 51% at the signature of the acquisition and 15.7% in January 2021 with the completion of the planned investment.

rules which require to open a competitive tender, the Hungarian part of the rail way project is under EU review. The Hungarian part of the train route is still under EU review. At the 16+1 Summit in Budapest on 28 November 2017, Hungary announced it would publish a procurement tender for its section of the line, after a probe by the European Commission said the original design was not in line with EU rules.[1] According to a statement of the Hungarian Ministry of Foreign Affairs and Trade-published on 8 June 2018, two Hungarian-Chinese joint ventures submitted valid applications. It is also stated that he Budapest-Belgrade high-speed railway line must be completed by the end of 2023 at the latest.[2]

Some remarks on BRI and Poland

Poland is considered the leading country in Central and Eastern Europe which will almost automatically terminate its leading role as China's cooperation partner in 16+1 dialogues. The first 16+1 Summit took place in Warsaw in 2012. The institutional weakness, economic and political diversity, EU- and non-EU membership may be the reason that CEE countries push forward also their bilateral relations with China. Besides the above mentioned Hungary, Poland is the most prominent example. In June 2016, on the occasion of Xi Jinping's visit to Poland, six Polish-Chinese cooperation agreements had been signed which partly address the China-Poland cooperation in BRI projects (PAIiIZ, 2016). Furthermore, in 2016 Poland joint as the first CEE country the Asian Infrastructure Investment Bank (AIIB) followed by Hungary in 2017. This may open opportunities for Polish companies to be involved in infrastructure projects in Asia. From the Polish point of view, BRI is considered "in symbiosis" with Poland's "Plan for Responsible Development" (Plan na Rzecz Odpowiedzialnego Rozwoju). A further sign of the significance of BRI

---

[1]   EUobserver, 29 November 2017, available at: https://euobserver.com/eu-china/140068

[2]   Hungarian Minister of Foreign Affairs and Trade, 29 November 2017, available at: http://www.kormany.hu/en/ministry-of-foreign-affairs-and-trade/news/the-budapest-belgrade-high-speed-railway-line-must-be-completed-by-the-end-of-2023-at-the-latest

for the Polish-China relations is the opening of the Warsaw office of the China Council for the Promotion of International Trade (CCPIT) during Xi Jinping's visit.

In the short run, it is to be expected that Łódź as the final stop of the freight railway line (run by the Polish PkP Cargo company) which starts in Chengdu is the main beneficiary in Poland. According to PiiIZ, Łódź would like to develop a logistic and techno-park for Chinese projects. Gdańsk expressed its interest to be a part of the 21st Martime Silk Road by building an external port in the city to provide services for Chinese cargo. Warsaw, European terminal of the Suzhou-Warsaw freight route, serves as a multimodul distribution hub for products that are manufactured or processed in the wider Shanghai-Hangzhou-Suzhou region. This freight service is also offered by the Polish PKP Cargo company. In 2015, the company started a new Zhengzhou-Hamburg weekly scheduled block train along the trans-Kazakh West Corridor. Małaszewicze, border city to Belarus, plays an important role in the China-Europe railway network as multimodul distribution and logistic center for several freight rail services. In recent years, transport and logistic companies such as DHL or DB Schenker have expanded their presence at this border city. "The Małaszewicze site, which DHL is consistently expanding as a gateway to and from Asia, plays a special role in this connection due to its strategically important geographic location."[1]

From a broader perspective, Szczudlik (2016b) notes that BRI offers chances to increase Polish exports to China, attract investment and improve infrastructure. But so far, no significant project has been launched within the BRI framework. She warns for too high expectations and recommends to assess the Chinese declarations carefully. A major concern of the Polish government seems to be the question in how far Polish companies benefit from Chinese infrastructure projects. It is intended to invite Chinese investors to participate

---

[1] DHL (2016): DHL expands connections between Asia, Europe and North Africa, *Press Release,* 29 June 2016, available at: http://www.dhl.com/en/press/releases/releases_2016/all/logistics/dhl_expands_connections_between_asia_europe_and_north_africa.html

in the government's plan to establish a "Central Communication Port" close to Warsaw which should serve as a transportation hub combining multi modal transports such as air, rail and road (Devonshire-Ellis, 2018).

A sketchy proposal for an analytical framework for the Silk Road Economic Belt railway transport network

The large number of China-Europe train routes raises the question how to guarantee the efficiency of the China-Europe land bridge. One of the challenges that BRI puts on economics is the development of an analytical framework for optimizing a long distance rail lines network including the efficient investment in transport and logistics infrastructure. Literature on the interdependence between trade and the spatial distribution of transport infrastructure (e.g. Felbermayr and Tarasov, 2015) suggest that national planning of the transport infrastructure leads to a inefficiently low global investment in infrastructure. This holds especially for an area where trade crosses many borders.

The transport structure of the Silk Road Economic Belt raises three questions: Firstly, what is the optimal capacity of the railway network? Second, which geographical route fits best to which type of traded goods? Third, does each route exploit the potential benefits and avoids unnecessary losses? Hereinafter, the focus is on the latter question.

The maps on existing railway lines show four types of cities, namely, originating city, destination city, (potential) stopover city, border crossing cities. In most cases, the latter do not contribute to the overall benefit of the railway line. They cause costs without generating profit often due to insufficient demand. In addition, border stations usually need a special infrastructure. The costs of border crossing are part of the total distance costs. If the train does not stop on the route-except on borders-the starting and end points create gains from interaction between these two cities under the assumption that the train carries load in both directions. These gains can be increased if the two cities function as intermodul distribution hubs. Assuming that there are several cities along the train route with a potential to increase the overall gains, it is beneficial to include these cities as stopovers. Cities where stopover costs are higher than gains should be excluded. Improvements of the institutional framework such as free trade agreements or special economic zones, can increase the overall gains. As for the geographical course of the train route, the Silk Road Economic Belt is structured in corridors which indicates a certain flexibility in determining the course of the railway route. Besides these economic criteria the topographic and geologic composition must also be included into the analysis.

The gravity approach is best suitable for analyzing this simple model (figure 3). Although the gravity approach is the "work horse" in empirical studies on trade between countries, some studies apply it to trade relations between cities (e.g. Onyemechi et al, 2014). Country studies face the problem to proxy distance, where the distance between capital cities is often used as solution. Studies on the city level face the problem of data on city-to-city trade.

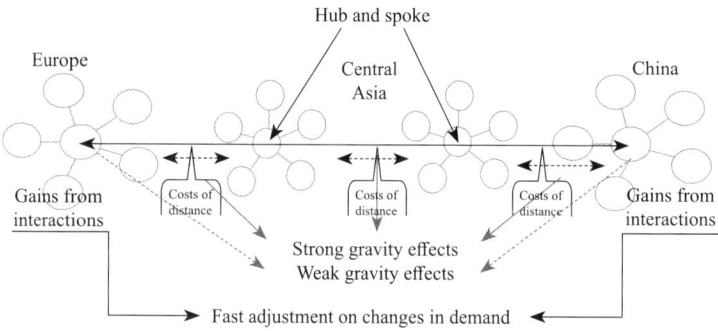

Figure 3. Trade between cities, geographical distance and barriers of trade
Source: Own.

Interactions (e.g. trade) between two cities are a function of the size of these cities and the distance between them. Hub-and spoke systems at both ends of the routeincrease the interactions. The larger the cities, the higher is the probability of the existence of complementarities and synergies. Furthermore, evidence suggests that distance and interactions are linked inversely. The more countries are included, the higher the costs of trade barriers. Under certain conditions, stopovers increase the total gains. Depending on the relations between the cities, e.g. sister city agreement, partnership agreement, the pure trade-focused analysis can be extended by including other interactions which may also create benefits.

The gravity approach suggests the following hypothesis on the gains of international trade between cities located in different countries and connected by a long distance railway route:

1. Trade flows (in and out of the city) related to the size of the city

Hyp 1a: Trade flows are positively correlated with the size of the city.

Hyp 1b: Ex and Im are symmetric when the city size correlation is high.

2. Trade flows related to the location of cities

Hyp 2a: Cities in the center of countries or on domestic transportation nodes create higher gains of intercity trade than border cities.

3. Trade flows related to the geographical distance between cities

Hyp 3: Trade flows are negatively correlated with geographical distance: Gravity effects are weaker between Chinese and European cities than between stopover cities as well as between origin/destination cities and stopover cities.

4. Trade related to the cultural distance (measured by the share of populationwith ethnic identity)

Hyp 4: Trade flows are negatively correlated with cultural distance.

5. Trade flows related to the institutional environment

Hyp 5a: Trade flows are negatively correlated with the number of border crossings.

Hyp5b: Trade flows are positively correlated with free trade areas, special economic zones, transit agreements, city partnerships/sister city agreements.

6. Trade flows related to complementary activities

Hyp 6: Trade flows are positively correlated to two-way FDI, investment in infrastructure and financial arrangements.

In its simple form, the gravity model may be expressed as follows:

$$T_{ij} = kP_iP_j/d_{ij}^a$$

where T_{ij} is the interaction (trade) between the cities i and j; P_i, P_j is the size of the population ini and j; d_{ij} is the distance between i and j; k is a sklar constant which allows to differentiate between the relative volume of trade; the exponent a expresses special features of trade which are related to distance.

In view of the probably large gap between necessary and available trade data, the empirical tests might face serious challenges.

6. Conclusion

Undoubtedly, BRI is by far the economically best-endowed, geographically most widespread and politically most ambitious single-country initiative after WWII. Its missing institutional foundation, non-binding character and fuzzy connectivity approach as well as its short observation period may explain why there are neither widely accepted perceptions or evaluations on this initiative, nor sound academic discussions and analysis. Within the less than five-year period, an ever growing number of official statements, from positive to negative ranging opinions, but few in-depth economic analysis had been published all around the world. A far longer period is necessary to measure economic, political and social effects and to differentiate them according to the five W-questions (why, which, where, when, who). It is realistic to expect that actions and reactions to a considerable extent also depend on BRI-independent global, regional and domestic developments. Anyhow, at the current stage three critically questioning statements should replace tested conclusions. First, an unilateral announced, but globally effective initiative of a country aspiring to regain its status of the "Middle Kingdom" (Zhongguo) can not claim to be widely accepted. LI and XU (2015) point to three questionmarks which the BRI initiative faces on its way from vision to reality: "First, how should China assess the United States' 'rebalance to Asia' is it containment or hedging? Second, how can China gain recognition and cooperation from countries along the Belt and Road Initiative? Third, how can China avoid economic and political risks as much as possible?" Evidence suggests that a number of countries in the Asian BRI region are keen to take advantage from the initiative's economic promises, but continue to rely on USA's security umbrella. Voices are unmistakable that warn of a loss of political independence. Second, BRI creates new economic interdependences where the distribution of welfare gains is not necessarily equal, even if China intends to create win-win situations. For every infrastructure project it has to be examined whether it is based on commercial or political logic. This is closely related to the question who decides on the selection, assessment, implementation, control, financial conditions of infrastructure projects. A Chinese dominance may lead to hostile behavior of parts of the population, not only against China but also against national/local governments. Even researchers in government-near institutions warn that many small and medium-sized countries are worried that economic dependence on China will lead to a flood of Chinese immigrants as well as an increase in domestic corruption (LI and XU, 2015). Third, BRI as an instrument of developingChina's backward regions has to be questioned considering the geographic size, the low potential of spillover effects from cities to hinterland, the uncertainty of a long-term stable and economically sufficient connectivity to BRI countries/regions abroad. The latter question is partly related to the efficiency of the railway routes on the Silk Road Economic Belt.

Summarizing the dominant echo on Xi Jinping's BRI Initiative, a geographical differentiation is clearly visible. In China, party cadres, think tanks and media praise BRI as an important pillar for China's further economic transformation as well as for its global political ambitions. The US feels that its scope of actions in "rebalancing to Asia" is unexpectedly disturbed by China. Southeast Asian and Central Asian countries consider BRI as a welcome gift which replaces missing own development efforts and, in some cases, help to stabilize the political regime. In the EU, BRI is considered as a project which promotes trade and investment and therefore fits into the core competence of EU's politics and core strategies of European companies. A look over all countries involved in BRI shows, that similar civic protests that could be observed against CETA and TTIP are rather exceptional.

Finally, it should be noted that the historical Silk Road and the BRI initiative do not have much in common. The former was characterized by trade, cultural and technological learning based on balanced exchange. The latter is a unilateral initiative where trade is unbalanced and leveraged infrastructure projects may create in some countries risks of excessive debt. The promise of a win-win situation needs careful planning based on criteria such as local and regional efficiency, social value sustainability, transparency, and first and foremost mutual trust. As long as countries in Europe and especially the European Union have concerns regarding political motivations behind the BRI initiative, it will be difficult to compare this initiative with the old Silk Road. Xi Jinping's promise not to interfere in the internal issues of other countries needs to be verified by a soft connectivity strategy. The long-term success of the BRI initiative as an important part of EU-China relations will significantly depend on an agreement including implementation mechanisms of a Europe-wide spatial, socio-economic and legal connectivity plan.

References

AIIB: Approved Projects, (2016). Available at: http://euweb.aiib.org/html/2016/PROJECTS_1010/163.html.

Alessia Amighini, "China's Economic Growth.Heading to a 'New Normal'". in: Alessia Amighini and Axel Berkovsky (eds), *Xi's Policy Gamble: The Bumpy Road Ahead*, ISPI Report, pp. 2015, p.49-64, Instituto Per Gli Studi Di Politica Internazionale, Milano, available at: http://www.ispionline.it/it/EBook/XiPolicyGambles.pdf.

Atif Ansar, Bent Flyvbjerg, Alexander Buidzier, and Daniel Lunn, "Does Infrastruicture Investment Lead to Economic Growth or Economic Fragility? Evidence from China", *Oxford Review of Economic Policy,* 2016, 32(3): 360-390.

Alain Baron, "1st Working Group Meeting of the EU-China Connectivity Platform, European Commission", 2016, available at: http://ec.europa.eu/transport/sites/transport/files/themes/international/european_neighbourhood_policy/european_eastern_partnership/doc/tenth-eastern-partnership-transport-panel/eu-china_connectivity_platform_by_dg_move.pdf.

Christopher I. Beckwith, *Empires of the Silk Road-A History of Central Eurasia from the Bronze Age to the Present*, Princeton, NJ: Princeton University Press, 2009.

Fang CAI, "Labor Trends and China's Potential Growth under the New Normal", paper presented at the conference "Key Issues Concerning China's Growth and Reform", 11-12 October 2014, Pudong: Shanghai Press Group.

Nicola Casarini, "Is Europe to Benefit from China's Road and Belt Initiative?", *IAI Working Papers,* 2015, 15/50, Instituto Affari Internazionali, Rome.

Mark Chou and Octavia Bryant, "Will China Promote Autocracy Along its New Silk Road?", *Carnegie Ethics Online,* 14 December 2015, available at: https://www.carnegiecouncil.org/publications/ethics_online/0112.

Hongjian CUI, "The Belt and Road Initiative and its Impact on Asia-Europe Connectivity", China Institute of International Studies-CIIS, 2016. available at: www.ciis.org.cn/english/2016-07/21/content_8911184_2.htm

Son Daekwon, "Xi Jinping Thought Vs. Deng Xiaoping Theory", *The Diplomat,* 25 October 2017, available at: https://thediplomat.com/2017/10/xi-jinping-thought-vs-deng-xiaoping-theory/.

Ram Upendra DAS, "Asia-Europe Connectivity-Current Status, Constraints, and Way Forward". IN: Anita Prakash (ed.), *Asia-Europe Connectivity Vision 2025: Challenges and Opportunities*, An ERIA-Mongolia Government Document, Jakarta: Economic Research Institute for ASEAN and East Asia, 2016, pp. 45-52.

Chris Devonhsire-Ellis, "Poland's EU Infrastructure Cash Windfall A Boom for Chinese Contractors ?", *The New Silk Road Project,* 9 June 2018, available at: https://www.thenewsilkroadproject.com/writing/2018/6/9/polandseu-infrastructure-cash-windfall-a-boom-for-chinese-contractors.

Romain Duval, Kevin C Cheng, Kum Hwa Oh, Richa Saraf and Dulani Seneviratne, "Trade Integration and Business Cycle Synchronization: A Reappraisal with Focus on Asia", *IMF Working Paper,* 2014, No 14/52, Washington: International Monetary Fund.

ECN (2016): China's 13th Five-Year Plan-Opportunities for Finnish Companies, *sponsored by Tekes,* Beijing: The Economist Corporate Network Asia.

Elizabeth C. Economy, "When Will the Jury Be In on the AIIB?", *Asia Unbound,* council on Foreign Relations, July 1, 2016, available at: http://blogs. cfr.org/asia/2016/07/01/when-will-the-jury-be-in-on-the-aiib/.

Vadim Elisseeff, *The Silk Roads-Highways of Culture and Commerce*, Paris: Berkhahn Books, 2000.

Mario Esteban and Miguel Ortero-Iglesias, "What are the Prospects for the Chinese-ledSilk Road and Asian Infrastructure Investment Bank", *ARI 23/2015,* Elcano Royal Institute, Madrid.

European Commission (2018): Meeting Minutes of the 3rd Chairs' Meting of EU-China Connectivity Platform, available at: https://ec.europa.eu/transport/ sites/transport/files/2018-07-13-chairs-meeting.pdf.

European Parliament (2016): the Belt and Road Initiative: China's Regional Integration Initiative, *Briefing,* July 2016, European Parliamentary Research Service.

Gabriel J. Felbermayr and Alexander Tarasov, "Trade and the Spatial Distribution of Transport Infrastructure", *CESifo Working Papers*, No 5634, 2015. Center for Economic Studies and Ifo Institute, Munich.

Financial Times, sources are listed in footnotes.

Michael D. Frachetti1, Evan Smith1, Cynthia M. Traub and Tim Williams "Nomadic Ecology Shaped the Highland Geography of Asia's Silk Roads", *Nature,* Vol. 543: 193-198, 2017.

Peter Frankopan, "Ancient Silk Road Was also Founded on Tax and Credit", *Financial Times,* May 9, 2016, available at: http://www.ft.com/cms/ s/2/e824f0fe-0bd8-11e6-9456-444ab5211a2f.html#axzz4FDjerT6X.

Brenda Goh and Marcin Goettig, "In Europe's East a Border Town Strains Under China's Silk Road Train Boom", *Reuters,* 27 June 2018, available at: https://www.reuters.com/article/us-china-europe-silkroad-insight/in-europes-east-a-border-town-strains-under-chinas-silk-road-train-boom-idUSKBN1JM34M.

Goldman Sachs, *The Chinese Tourist Boom*, New York, 2015.

Valerie Hansen, "The Impact of the Silk Road Trade on a Local Community: The Turfan Oasis, 500-800". In: E.de La Vaissière (ed), *Les Sogdiens en Chine, Ecole française d'Extrême-Orient*, 283-309, 2005.

Guenter Heiduk and Jonathan Holslag, "China's Opening-up in the 1980s and 1990s". IN: Guenter Heiduk and Agnieszka McCaleb (eds.), *China's Choices after the Current Economic Crisis: going Global, Regional*, National, pp 11-26, 2011. Warsaw: Warsaw School of Economics Publishing.

Guenter Heiduk and Agnieszka McCaleb, "What Motivates China's Cities To Establish Partner Agreements With Cities In Asia*?"* In: *Dimensions of Regional Processes in the Asia-Pacific Region*, edited by Bogusława Drelich-Skulska, Anna H. Jankowiak, Szymon Mazurek, Research Papers of Wroclaw University of Economics Nr 413, pp. 52-61, 2015.

Alicia García-Herrero and Jianwei XU, "China's Belt and Road Initiative: Can Europe Expect Trade Gains?", *Working Paper,* 5-2016, Brussels: Bruegel, 2016.

Jonathan E. Hillmann, "The Rise of China-Europe Railways", Center for Strategic and International Studies, 6 March 2018, available at: https://www.csis.org/analysis/rise-china-europe-railways.

HKTDC (2018a): Economic and Trade Information on China, *China Trade Research,* 16. July 2018, available at: http://china-trade-research.hktdc.com/business-news/article/Facts-and-Figures/Economic-and-Trade-Information-on-China/ff/en/1/1X000000/1X09PHBA.htm.

HKTDC (2018b): The Belt and Road Initiative, *HKTDC Research,* 3 May 2018, available at: http://china-trade-research.hktdc.com/business-news/article/The-Belt-and-Road-Initiative/The-Belt-and-Road-Initiative/obor/

en/1/1X3CGF6L/1X0A36B7.htm.

Bert Hofman, "China's the Belt and Road Initiative: What We Know Thus Far", *World Bank Blog,* 12 April 2015, available at: http://blogs.worldbank.org/eastasiapacific/china-one-belt-one-road-initiative-what-we-know-thus-far.

John Hurley, Scott Morris and Gailyn Portelance, "Examining the Debt Implications of the Belt and Road Initiative from a Policy Perspective", *CDG Policy Paper,* No 121, 2018. Center for Global Development, Washington, DC.

IMF (2018): People's Republic of China, Country Report No 18/240, July 2018, Washington, DC: International Monetary Found.

IMF (2016a): The People's Republic of China, *IMF Country Report*, No 16/2016, Washington, DC: International Monetary Fund.

IMF (2016b): Factsheet-Review of the Special Drawing Right (SDR) Currency Basket, Sept. 30, 2016, Washington DC: International Monetary Fund.

Christopher K. Johnson, "President Xi Jinping's 'Belt and Road Initiative'- A Practical Assessment of the Chinese Communist Party's Roadmap for China's Global Resurgence", *CSIS,* 2016, Washington DC: Center for Strategic & International Studies.

Scott Kennedy and Christopher K. Johnson, *Perfecting China, INC. - The 13th Five-Year Plan*, Washington, DC: Center for Strategic & International Studies, 2016.

Parag Khanna, "China's Infrastructure Alliances". In: WEF (ed.), *Geo-Economics with Chinese Characteristics: How China's Economic Might is Reshaping World Politics*, 2016, pp 15-17, Geneva: World Economic Forum.

Vojko Kuzma, "Some Views, Remarks and Geopolitical Thoughts about BRI and '16+1' Initiative", Ministry of Foreign Affairs Slovania, 2016. available at: http://eregion.eu/attached-documents/5254/.

Jean-Pierre Lehmann, "The New Silk Road: A Visionary Dream for the 21st Century", FORBES, May 27, 2015, available at: http://www.forbes.com/sites/jplehmann/2015/05/27/the-new-silk-road-a-visionary-dream-for-the-21st-century/#73be238e5039.

Xue LI and Yanzhuo XU, "How Can China Perfect its 'Silk Road' Strategy?", *The Diplomat,* 9 April 2015, availabel at: http://thediplomat. com/2015/04/how-china-can-perfect-its-silk-road-strategy/.

Xue LI and Yuwen ZHENG, "The Future of China's Diplomacy in the Middle East", *The Diplomat,* 26 July 2016, available at: http://thediplomat. com/2016/07/the-future-of-chinas-diplomacy-in-the-middle-east/.

Zhaoxing LI, "Join Efforts to Build Two Wings of Asia", *China Daily USA,* 13 February 2015, available at: http://usa.chinadaily.com.cn/ opinion/2015-02/13/content_19578869.htm.

Zuokui LIU, "Europe and the "Belt and Road Initiative: Responses and Risks", *Working Paper,* No 2017-7, Institute of European Studies, Chinese Academy of Social Sciences, Beijing.

Jushua J. Mark, "Silk Road, *Ancient History Encyclopedia",* 2014. available at: http://www.ancient.eu/Silk_Road/.

Tamas Matura, "Europe Needs to Take Full Advantage of the 16+1 Cooperation and BRI". IN: Islam, S. (ed.), EU-China Relations, New Directions, New Priorities, *Discussion Paper,* 2016, Friends of Europe, available at: http://www.friendsofeurope.org/media/uploads/2016/07/EU-CHINA_BOOK_inside_WEB.pdf.

NDRC (2015): Vision and Actions on Jointly Building Silk Road Economic Belt and 21st-Century Maritime Silk Road, National Development and Reform Commission, available at: http://en.ndrc.gov.cn/ newsrelease/201503/t20150330_669367.html.

Annalee Neewitz, "New research Changes Our Understanding Of Who BuilT Ancient Silk Roads", *Ars Technica,* 3 December 2017, available at: https://arstechnica.com/science/2017/03/new-research-reveals-origins-of-the-ancient-silk-road/.

Theo Notteboom, "The New Silk Road (BRI): Looking Beyond China-Europe Rail Services", 2018, Ghent University, Belgium, available at: http:// www.law.ugent.be/gandaius/gpv/marsympo/10-NotteboomT.pdf.

OECD (2017): FDI Regulatory Restrictiveness Index, available at: https://

stats.oecd.org/Index.aspx?datasetcode=FDIINDEX#.

Chinedum Onyemechi, Chinemerem, C.Igboanusi and Anthony Ekene Ezenwa, "International Trade Flow Analysis Using the Gravity Model-The Nigerian Conondrum", *International Journal of Latest Research in Science and Technology*, 2014, 3(4): 181-185.

PAIiIZ (2016): Visit of Chinese President: Poland China Business Forum, 20 June 2016, Polish Information and Foreign Investment Agency, available at: http://www.paiz.gov.pl/20160620/visit_of_Chinese_president_Poland_China_Business_Forum.

People's Bank of China (2015): The Silk Road Fund Enters into Operation, 26 February 2015, available at: http://www.pbc.gov.cn/english/130721/2810708/index.html.

Anita Prakash (ed.), Asia-Europe Connectivity Vision 2025: Challenges and Opportunities, *An ERIA-Mongolia Government Document,* Jakarta: Economic Research Institute for ASEAN and East Asia.

Mukul Sandaal, "China's the Belt and Road Initiative: A New Model for Global Governance", *IDSA Comment*, 2016, Institute for Defense Studies and Analyses, available at: http://www.idsa.in/idsacomments/china-one-road-one-belt-initiative_msanwal_290916.

Wade Shepard, "The Hidden Economic Rationale of China-Europe Rail", *Forbes,* 22 March 2018, available at: https://www.forbes.com/sites/wadeshepard/2018/03/22/the-hidden-economic-rationale-of-china-europe-rail/#449a046640d1.

State Council The People's Republic of China: The Belt and Road Initiative, available at: http://english.gov.cn/beltAndRoad/.

Steer Davies Gleave (2018): Research for TRAN Committee: The New Silk Route-Opportunities and Challenges for EU Transport, European Parliament, Policy Department for Structural and Cohesion Policies, Brussels.

Alexandr Svetlicinii, "China's Belt and Road Initiative and the Eurasian Economic Union", Eurasiasn Studies, 1st April 2018, available at: http://greater-europe.org/archives/4605.

Justyna Szczudlik, "Many Belts and Many Roads: The Proliferation of Infrastructure Initiatives in Asia", *Policy Paper,* No 7(148), The Polish Institute of International Affairs, Warsaw, 2016a.

Justyna Szczudlik, "Three Years of the Silk Road: Successes and Challenges", *PISM Bulletin,* 71(921), The Polish Institute of International Affairs, Warsaw, 2016b.

Shannon Tiezzi, "China's Belt and Road Initiative Makes Inroads in Africa", *The Diplomat,* 31 July 2018, available at: https://thediplomat. com/2018/07/chinas-belt-and-road-makes-inroads-in-africa/.

Shannon Tiezzi, "China's 'New Silk Road' Vision Revealed", *The Diplomat,* 9 May 2014, available at: http://thediplomat.com/2014/05/chinas-new-silk-road-vision-revealed/.

Shuaihua Cheng, "China's New Silk Road: Implications for the US", *Yale Global Online,* 28 May 2015, available at: http://yaleglobal.yale.edu/content/ china%E2%80%99s-new-silk-road-implications-us.

Shichen WANG, "China's People-to-people Diplomacy and its Importance to China-EU Relations: A Historical Institutionalism Perspective", *Journal of China and International Relations,* 2016, 4(1): 1-19.

Andrew Williams, "China-Europe Rail: The Road Less Travelled", *Automotive Logistics,* 12 April 2016, available at: http://automotivelogistics. media/intelligence/china-europe-rail-the-road-less-travelled.

Tim Winter, "the Belt and Road Initiative, One Heritage: Cultural Diplomacy and the Silk Road", *The Diplomat,* 29 March 2016: available at: http://thediplomat.com/2016/03/one-belt-one-road-one-heritage-cultural-diplomacy-and-the-silk-road/.

Willy Lam Wo-lap, "Getting Lost in 'the Belt and Road Initiative' ", *Hong Kong Economic Journal,* April 7, 2016, available at: http://www.ejinsight. com/20160412-getting-lost-one-belt-one-road/.

Peter Wolff, "China's 'Belt and Road' Initiative-Challenges and Opportunities", 2016. Bonn: German development Institute.

Harry X.WU, "China's Geo-Economic Power". In: WEF (ed.), *Geo-*

Economics with Chinese Characteristics: How China's Economic Might is Reshaping World Politics, pp 7/8, 2016, Geneva: World Economic Forum.

Xinhua, "China-Europe Freight Rail Route Boosts Silk Road Trade", 18 June 2016, available at: http://news.xinhuanet.com/english/2016-06/18/c_135447251.htm.

Yao YANG, "A New Normal, but with Robust Growth: China's Growth Prospects in the Next 10 Years", 2015. available at: https://www.brookings.edu/wp-content/uploads/2016/07/tt20-china-growth-prospects-yao.pdf.

Longmei ZHANG, "Rebalancing in China-Progress and Prospects", *IMF Working Paper,* 2016*,* WP/16/183, Washington, DC: International Monetary Fund.

The Implications of Brexit for China-EU Economic Relations

Agniezska McCaleb

Abstract

The United Kingdom's (UK) decision to leave the European Union (EU) means reformulating their political and economic relationships. The type of divorce between the EU and the UK either "soft" or "hard" will have significant repercussions for their relationships with other major global partners such as China. The EU-China relations are based on trade and investment but also encompass such key areas as infrastructure investments, energy and climate change, as well as research and development. Both the EU and China economies are facing challenges for the former related with Brexit and eurozone governance and for the latter with slowing economic growth and transition to new economic model based on inclusive growth, innovation, and green development. Without the UK, that has been the largest recipient of Chinese outward FDI in the EU and is home to many world's top universities, the EU's stance in relations with China may be weakened. As for China with the departure of the UK it loses a supporter within the EU that was open towards China's economic goals (free trade agreement, market economy status, investment agreement). Thus, China may face more protectionist attitude of the EU that dominates in the continental Europe. With much yet unknown about the details of Brexit the paper attempts to analyze the possible implications of Brexit for China-EU economic relations.

Introduction

The aim of the paper is to identify how Brexit will impact the economic relations of the EU and China, especially in the areas of trade, investment, R&D and energy cooperation.

The EU has become China's largest trading partner, and China is the EU's second-largest export market and main source of imports. But besides trade in goods other areas of economic relations are under-developed such as trade in services, levels of foreign investment or cooperation in technological innovation. For example, the level of foreign direct investment does not match the size of the two economies or their trade in goods (García-Herrero et al., 2017, p).

Both the EU and China economies are facing challenges for the former related with Brexit and eurozone governance and for the latter with slowing economic growth and transition to new economic model based on inclusive growth, innovation, and green development.

On 23 June 2016 in a referendum the British decided to leave the EU which resulted in debates as to the EU's and UK's relations with their major economic partners. Without the UK, that has been the largest recipient of Chinese outward FDI in the EU and is home to many world's top universities, the EU's stance in relations with China may be weakened. As for China with the departure of the UK it loses a supporter within the EU that was open towards China's economic goals (free trade agreement, market economy status, investment agreement). Thus, China may face more protectionist attitude of the EU that dominates in the continental Europe. On the other hand, China's foreign policy has changed recently from support of multipolar multilateralism to focus on bilateral relations with nation-states (Knodt et al 2015). With much yet unknown about the details of Brexit the paper attempts to analyze the possible implications of Brexit for China-EU economic relations, focusing on trade, investment, as well as R&D and energy cooperation.

The paper is organized as follows. The next part discusses the impact of Brexit on trade and investment relations between the EU and China. The third part, analyzes the cooperation in R&D between EU and China and the role that UK plays in it. The fourth part is dedicated to relations between the three entities in energy. The final part concludes with implications of Brexit on the discussed areas of economic engagement between the EU, the UK and China.

1. Post-Brexit EU-China trade and investment *

The future commercial relationships between the EU, the UK and China depends on the relative role of the UK and the remaining EU Member States in trade with China. The United Kingdom is China's second largest export destination in the EU; imports from China constitute 7% of the UK's total imports. The share of the UK in trade of goods constituted 16.7% in 2015 (Mackiewicz, McCaleb 2018). In this respect the UK followed Germany and was on par with the Netherlands. It these terms the position of the UK is important. The UK's exports to China as a share of the whole EU's placed it on the third position in 2015 with 9.2%, while Germany, EU's leader in exports to China, reached the share of above 42% (Mackiewicz, McCaleb 2018). This considerable disproportion is indicated as a confirmation of the unused potential of Great Britain, which can be reduced by greater freedom in shaping trade regulations after Brexit. (Mackiewicz, McCaleb 2018). In 2016, for UK China ranked 5th in trade. But for the UK the goal is to enter China with its services. "The UK had a surplus of £1.6bn on trade in services with China in 2016, the largest being travel services." (BBC 2018). The analysis done by Mackiewicz and McCaleb (2018) shows that possible free trade agreement between the UK and China will have little impact on trade in goods as trade restrictions have little impact on these flows. As for the UK, the country is blocked in proceeding with any trade-related agreements till it finalizes its exit terms with the EU.

---

* This part draws on Mackiewicz M, McCaleb A (2018 forthcoming). The impact of Brexit on foreign direct investment and trade relations between the United Kingdom and China.

Free trade agreement between the UK and China would be beneficial to China located exporters to UK as the OECD findings show that China supplies the UK market mainly by trade as opposed to the USA, France, the Netherlands and Japan that do it by trade and sales by foreign affiliates (OECD 2017).

The EU without the UK will still be one of key export markets for Chinese goods. It provides the EU with maintained strong position in holding China to rules-based trade (promoted so strongly by Brexit supporters) related with granting China the status of market economy once Chinese products' prices reflect their true value (Tobin 2018). The trade-related issues that await solving between the EU and China concern market economy status, protection and enforcement of intellectual property rights (China is the world's number one source of counterfeited products which aggravated with online sales; in 2016 80% of seized counterfeited goods originated from China, European Commission 2018), free trade agreement that is contingent of market economy status and IPR protection, anti-dumping. As to the latter, EU introduced new anti-dumping rules that remove the extant distinction between "market and non-market economies" for calculating dumping. The new rules require to prove the existence of a "significant market distortion" between a product's sale price and its production cost (Xinhua 2017).

China's Go Global Policy introduced in 2000 provided a start to rapidly growing outward foreign direct investments (OFDI) which currently make China the second largest FDI source in the world only after the United States (WIR 2017). Europe became a key target of Chinese investment which in 2015 amounted to over 30 million euro, double the size of Chinese OFDI in the United States (Institute for Security & Development Policy 2017). The EU is attractive to Chinese FDI seeking mainly strategic assets such as brands, technology, know-how, R&D infrastructure, distribution channels, which allow Chinese firms to enhance their competitiveness in the global and domestic markets. The benefit has been also the access to the EU market which is the number one recipient of Chinese exports and the largest market in the world. At the end of 2016, the highest growth in the value of Chinese investment transactions compared to the annual average in the period 2013-2015 for the

EU-28 was registered in industrial machinery and equipment, ICT, utilities, transport and infrastructure (see figure 1). Recent takeovers carried out by Chinese companies such as Midea's (Chinese producer of consumer appliances) acquisition of Kuka, German robotics manufacturer considered a national champion, started to raise concerns across the old EU countries over the loss of their most competitive assets. It could result in the EU's imposing screening and in the end restrictions on some investment coming from China (Cerulus and Hanke 2017). The investment agreement between the EU and China providing equal access to markets and protection of investment has been negotiated for a long time and there are no signs it will happen any time soon.

Figure1. Chinese Investors Target High-Tech, Services and Infrastructure Assets Distribution of Chinese OFDI in the EU-28 by industry 2016; Bubble size represents total investment 2000-2016.

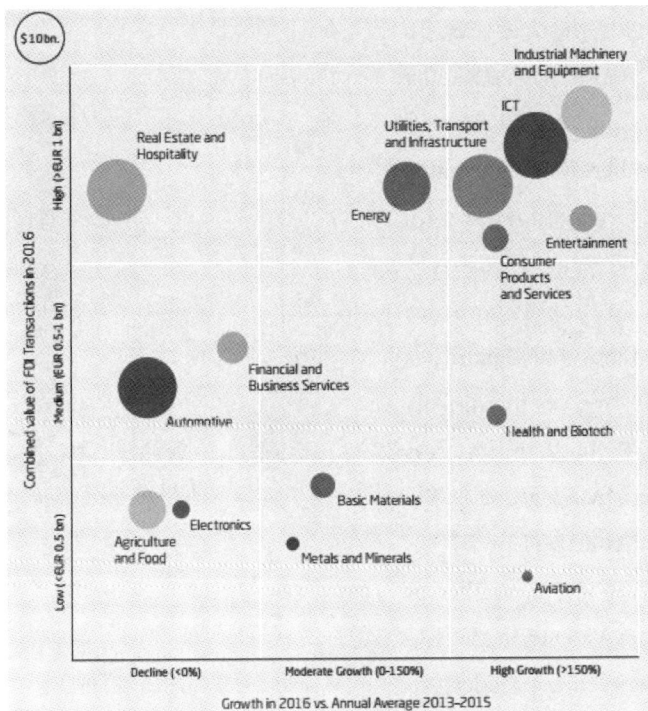

Figure 1
Source: Hanemann, Huotari 2017.

The UK has been the largest recipient of Chinese outward FDI, followed by Germany (see figure 2). Chinese investment in the UK has been mostly related with real estate (44% of the value of deals between 2012 and the first half of 2016), energy (7%), finance (8%), healthcare (5%), agriculture, technology and entertainment industries (see figure 3, Kynge 2017). Chinese interest in the British real estate is a related with search for safe placement of their assets. In the fiscal year 2016-2017, the number of Chinese FDI projects and the number of newly created jobs increased compared with the previous year. But 2015-2016 had higher number of safeguarded jobs which indicates more M&A type of investments (see figure 4). In 2016, in terms of Chinese M&As globally the UK ranked fourth (Liu 2017). When looking at the number of Chinese M&A deals in the EU the UK has been the leader (18 months by the end of June 2016 there were 80 announced deals

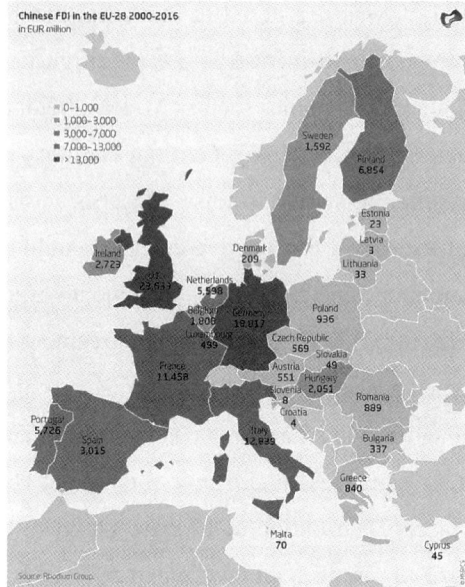

Figure 2. Chinese FDI in the EU-28, 2000-2016.
Source: Hanemann, Huotari 2017.

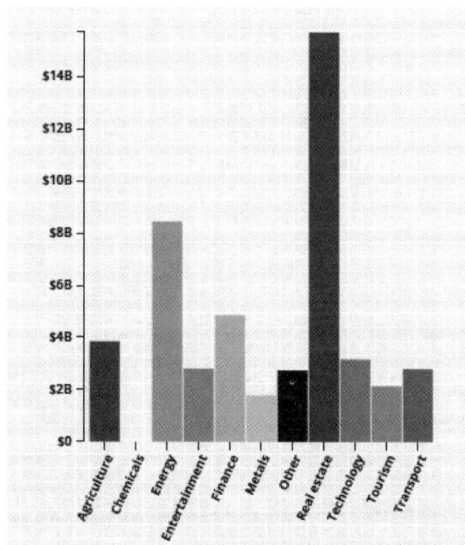

Figure 3. Chinese Foreign Direct Investment and Construction Contracts in the UK by sector, 2005-2017
Source: American Enterprise Institute and the Heritage Foundation 2017.

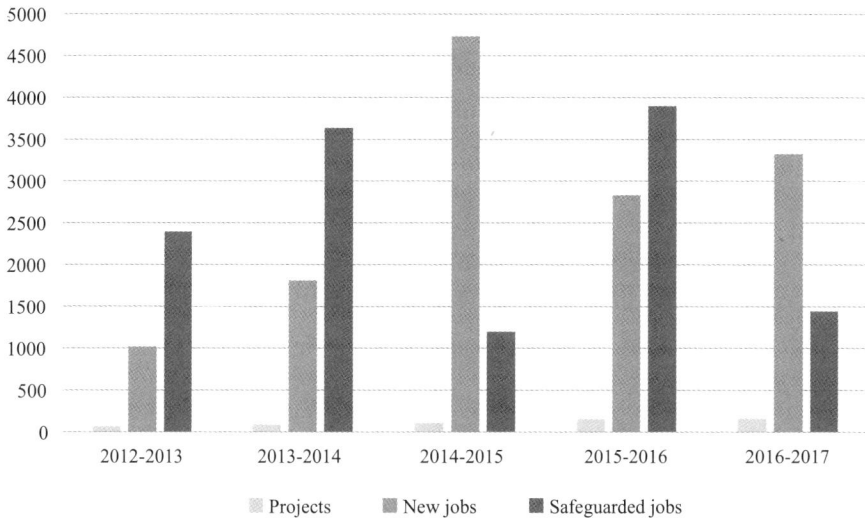

Figure 4. Chinese foreign direct investment in the UK: number of projects, new jobs created and safeguarded jobs, 2012-2017.
Source: Own calculations based on UK Trade and Investment Inward Investment
Reports for various years.

while for Germany only 67, IMAA Institute 2017) implying strong interest in strategic-assets and much lesser in market expansion through FDI (Clegg, Voss 2012). In spite of the Chinese government's restrictions on outward FDI introduced at the end of 2016 which was motivated by decreasing Renminbi and foreign exchange reserves the number of Chinese FDI projects in the UK in 2016-2017 increased year-on-year (Davies 2017, Ernst&Young 2017). The possible explanation is that these projects were related with access to already mentioned strategic assets related with key strategic industries that are not included in China's OFDI restrictions and receive support from the government. Strategic assets Chinese firms invest in the UK include renowned UK brands such as House of Fraser, MG Rover, Pizza Express, and Weetabix (Voss 2017), advanced specialized knowledge such as nuclear plant, Hinckley Point C or R&D center set up by Sinovet in 2015 that deals with animal health R&D and aims at specialized clusters (UK Trade&Investment 2015).

The above information indicates that Brexit could affect to some extent the decisions to invest in real estate which value may be affected by depreciation of pound. On the other hand, British firms became cheaper for Chinese businesses as the British pound lost value from the day of referendum of 9.43 Chinese Renminbi to 8.97 in May 2017 and 8.76 in November 2017. During that time Euro increased in value by more than 5% thus making the Euro priced assets more expensive for Chinese investors (Voss 2017). Some Chinese investments in the UK related with strategic asset seeking should not be greatly affected if they do not require employment of foreign staff, cooperation with the EU agencies or participation in research funded by the EU. In case of establishment of R&D centers the attractiveness of the UK may be affected by post-Brexit limitations to mobility when it will be more difficult and probably costly to hire highly skilled researchers from the EU-27. The number of newly announced M&A deals dropped by 20% in the first six months of 2017 compared with the same period in 2016 (Hanemann et al 2017). Such slowdown in Chinese corporate FDI might be explained by waiting for further devaluation and better deals. But if Chinese investors look for advanced assets related with wider EU cooperation then they may shift their interests towards alternative assets with the EU-27. Chinese market-seeking firms that target the whole EU market will most probably lose interest in the UK and choose other locations with similar characteristics such as Ireland with English language and similar laws.

2. R&D, Science and Technology cooperation

The scientific cooperation between the EU and China started in December 1998 with signing of a Science & Technology Cooperation Agreement which was renewed for the third time in December 2014. In 2012 a joint declaration on High Level Innovation Cooperation Dialogue was issued with the aim to enhance the level and intensity of research and innovation relations with China through establishment of a forum for discussing innovation policies and systems, responding to framework conditions and initiating new joint R&I projects (European Commission, 2017). Majority of the EU member states signed bilateral science and technology agreements with China's Ministry of Science and Technology. The EU research programs such as the current Horizon 2020 are a platform for cooperation with China for small EU countries with insufficient research funding such as the new members from the Central and Eastern Europe.

During the 13th meeting of the Joint Steering Committee of the EU-China Agreement for Scientific and Technological Cooperation, on 29 March 2017, the EU and China agreed to continue promoting closer cooperation based on mutual benefit. The two sides agreed to develop a package of joint flagship initiatives to be launched in 2017, targeting areas such as food, agriculture and bioeconomy, the environment, climate and sustainable urbanization, surface transport, biotechnologies and biomaterials, and aviation(UK Research and Innovation 2017). The scientific cooperation between the EU and China has been based on co-funding mechanism launched in December 2015 where financing is provided by the Ministry of Science and Technology to China based entities that participate in joint projects with the EU partners within Horizon 2020 (DG Research and Innovation 2018). Under FP7 (2007-2013) the EU contribution to retained proposals has been steadily decreasing (DG Research and Innovation 2015). In Horizon 2020 (2014-2020) the number of Chinese participations in the EU framework program was smaller due to the new Horizon 2020 rules excluding China-based entities (together with those from the other BRICM countries) from automatic funding. It also resulted in reduced contribution by the EU (figure X). This situation has been partially amended in WP 2016/17 with several Horizon 2020 programs dedicated to cooperation with China (European Commission, 2017). The co-funding mechanism has been criticized as being rather restrictive and uncertain for Chinese participants (Liu and Yi 2016). When comparing Horizon 2020 with FP7, under Horizon 2020 by October 2017 Chinese organizations participated 255 times in 117 signed grants under collaborative, MSCA and ERC actions while under FP7 respectively 651 times in 413 signed grants. As to obtained funding, under Horizon 2020 Chinese entities obtained direct funding amounting to 3 million euros while 26.7 million euros was non-EU budget of China's beneficiaries; under FP7 respective numbers were 53.5 million euros from the EU budget and 20.5 million from non-EU funding (European Commission, 2017, p 6). The numbers show declining interest of the EU in scientific cooperation with China or at least in the extent of provided funding.

As to research areas in which Chinese participants have been the most active throughout FP6, FP7 and Horizon 2020 we can observe stable focus on: Food, Information and Communication Technologies as well as Secure Societies, and Environment (including Climate change) (table 1). Under Horizon 2020 Chinese participants were also active in Societies and Energy (table 1).

Table 1. Participation of China in FP6, FP7 and Horizon 2020 by main research areas.

FP6	FP7	Horizon 2020
information society technology (29%)	Food	Food
Sustainable development, global change and Ecosystem (19%)	Agriculture and Biotechnology	Societies (Secure societies-Protecting freedom and security of Europe and its citizens)
food quality and safety (7%)	Information and Communication Technologies	ICT
	Environment (including Climate change)	Energy
		Environment
		Health

Source: Own compilation based onArnold *et al.*, 2008, p 24; DG Research and Innovation 2015; European Commission, 2017, p 7.

The EU member states cooperating most actively with Chinese entities in research projects are Germany, UK and France. Within FP5 and FP6 in terms of projects with at least one Chinese participant, the leading EU countries that had the highest number of Chinese participants were Germany (12% of total), the UK (11%), France (9%) (Arnold et al., 2008, p 24).

The UK's science and research is strongly outward oriented where big portion of R&D budget (17%) comes from abroad, especially when compared to other EU innovation leaders such as Germany or Sweden for which the share of foreign financing is three times lower. This indicates the UK's relative dependence on foreign funding when compared to other EU countries (Weresa 2018). The UK is overall a net contributor to the EU but in case of research it is net recipient (Brooker and Chonaill, 2015) as it contributes around 11% to the EU research budget and receives around 16% of that funding (House of Lords, 2016a, p. 7, after Weresa 2018). The UK benefits from the EU funding mainly through the EU Framework Programs (Weresa 2018). In the period 2007-2013 the EU framework program financing amounted to 3% of the UK's total R&D expenditures (Royal Society 2015). In FP7 the UK was number one recipient of EU funding for health that amounted to 17% of the total EU contribution (Royal Society 2015).

The EU membership is related with benefits from access to important scientific networks, funding, free movement of researchers, but also from the easy transfer of materials such as blood and tissue that are necessary in health research or access to information as the EU facilitates shared access to bio banks and data sharing across Member States (Brooker and Chonaill, 2015, p xi). If Brexit means no access to EU R&D funding the universities would suffer the most as significant share of FP7 funds in the UK was granted to universities (71%) (Weresa 2018).

If Brexit means limitations to mobility of people it would be disadvantageous to the UK's research base which relies to significant extent on talent coming from other EU member states. In 2014/2015, 16% of academic staff in the UK came from other EU member states (The Royal Society, 2016, p 8). There is also the strategic value of EU membership which refers to the ability of countries, especially innovation leaders in their fields, to lead and influence respective policies created at the EU level (Brooker and Chonaill,

2015, p x). It is expected that in the long-run the UK after Brexit may follow the path of Switzerland with decline in participation and financial benefits from the EU research programs (Weresa 2018; Brooker and Chonaill, 2015). In the light of the above facts, Brexit poses a threat to the UK's global research position by disconnection with vital networks, people and substantial funding. The UK's research areas supported by EU funding must find alternative source of funding to maintain their muli-centre and multi-disciplinary research. Brooker and Chonaill (2015) suggest it could be achieved by "buy-in" scheme where UK would contribute to the EU research funding and this way UK researchers could apply, participate and receive funding from the EU. In case such option is not possible another source of funding could be China's research funding institutions. Such scenario is highly likely as Chinese institutions seem disappointed with Horizon 2020.

A signal towards such closer cooperation between is the UK-China Joint Strategy for Science, Technology and Innovation Cooperation launched on 6 December 2017. The Joint Strategy outlines priority areas for collaboration including life sciences, food security, renewable energy and environmental technologies reflecting China's goals related with achievement of sustainable development (HM Government 2017).

For the development of collaboration in innovation and R&D between the EU and China, the Chinese researchers who studied in Europe are especially important. Limiting collaboration in R&D between the EU and the UK will negatively influence the EU's access to vast number of Chinese researchers who studied in the UK and naturally have personal contacts there. Brexit in this case means loss of these existing networks for EU research programs in which the UK will most likely be less engaged. Thus, Brexit will decrease the attractiveness of the UK as research partner disconnected from networks and funding. At the same time the position of the EU as global research leader will be affected by the loss of one of the most innovative member state. Thus, Brexit may negatively impact the EU-China cooperation in research and innovation where some of the projects are likely to be carried out by teams outside of the

EU S&T programs. At the same time other EU member states with similar innovative capacities should be expected to fill the void after the exit of the UK. When looking at innovative capacities by technology the UK is challenged by Netherlands in medical technology, computer technology, civil engineering, basic materials chemistry, by France in pharmaceuticals, organic fine chemistry in, by Germany in electrical machinery, apparatus, energy, and transport (table 2). The UK is strong leader in biotechnology with no significant competitor within the EU (table 2).

Table 2. The EU's leading recipients of EU Research, Development and Innovation funding within FP7 and China, by Patent Applications by Top Fields of technology (share of country's total patent applications) in 2002-2016.

	UK	Germany	France	Netherlands	China
Pharmaceuticals	7.28	3.55	5.31		5.04
Medical technology	6.23	4.20	3.76	6.38	
Computer technology	6.05		5.13	7.11	6.45
Organic fine chemistry	5.73	4.53	6.28	3.81	
Civil engineering	5.09		3.62	3.92	
Measurement	5.05	5.28	4.47	4.92	5.95
Electrical machinery, apparatus, energy	4.58	7.35	5.61	6.21	6.70
Biotechnology	3.92				
Basic materials chemistry	3.91	3.62		4.24	4.24
Transport	3.88	8.77	8.69		
Mechanical elements		6.30			
Engines, pumps, turbines		5.60	4.08		
Machine tools		3.80			4.29
Digital communication			4.94		6.12
Audio-visual technology				8.62	
Optics				4.68	
Semiconductors				4.14	
Materials, metallurgy					4.18
Food chemistry					4.15
Other special machines					4.04

Source: Own elaboration based on WIPO, http://www.wipo.int/ipstats/en/statistics/country_profile/, 6.02.2018

Table 3. The UK' research specialization compared with China's strategic emerging industries

UK's specialization based on WIPO patent applications (2002-2016)	China's 13th FYP supporting emerging industries overlapping with UK's specialisation	EU-China S&T Cooperation Agreement's flagship initiatives launched in 2017
Pharmaceuticals		
Medical technology	precision medicine	
Computer technology	next generation information technology, intelligent systems	
Organic fine chemistry		
Civil engineering		sustainable urbanization
Measurement		
Electrical machinery, apparatus, energy	high-end equipment and materials, high-efficiency energy storage and distribution systems, efficient energy conservation	
Biotechnology	biotechnology	biotechnologies and biomaterials, agriculture and bioeconomy, environment, climate
Basic materials chemistry		
Transport	new-energy vehicles, next generation aviation equipment, smart transportation	surface transport, aviation

Source: Own compilation based on WIPO (2018) and China's National Development and Reform Commission's 13th Five Year Plan (2016).

3. Energy cooperation

EU and China are the world's largest importers of resources relying to great extent on external sources of energy mainly from the Middle East and Russia, which makes them vulnerable to changes on international energy markets. This situation results in their competition for world energy resources but at the same time pushes them towards cooperation on resolving the issue of energy security. China and the EU respectively represent approximately 22% and 12.5 % of global energy consumption (Europa 2017). China's fast economic growth over the last four decades has posed a challenge for the country in terms of high resource needs, heavy pollution and mass urbanization with cities which are to great extent unsustainable. Thus, China in energy cooperation aims at resolving its domestic problems by promoting renewable and low carbon solutions. Accordingly, China has launched domestic reforms on energy with ambitious goals to achieve by 2020: "Increasing the share of non-fossil fuel in primary energy consumption to 15%, Increasing the proportion of natural gas to at least 10%, keeping the percentage of coal consumption below 58%." (Liu 2017b). These reforms already achieved impressive results as in 2016 China ranked number one in the world in terms of investment in green energy sector (Hui 2017).

As has been discussed in the previous part in terms of R&D cooperation with the EU, China is especially interested in environment, climate change and energy. The EU energy cooperation with China dates back to 1981 when DG Energy visited China, but it gained importance only in 2012 with the launch of EU-China High-level Energy Meeting. During this meeting two institutions were set up, namely EU-China Urbanization Partnership and the EU-China Strategic Energy Consumer Partnership (Zhang 2017). The EU-China energy cooperation has been carried out through sectorial dialogues since 1994. The last EU-China Energy Dialogue took place during the EU-China Summit in 2017 marking its importance to both sides (Europa 2017). Priority areas of cooperation include: renewable energy, smart grids, energy efficiency in buildings, clean coal, nuclear energy, energy legislation (Europa 2018b). The latest document setting the framework for energy cooperation between the EU and China is EU-China Energy Roadmap (2016-2020) (Europa 2016). The Roadmap focuses on energy supply: sourcing, production and distribution, which includes: renewable energy sources, power grid sector, fossil fuels, nuclear safety, as well as energy demand: consumption, demand side management, energy efficiency. The Roadmap provides for exchange of best practices in areas of energy regulation, demand and supply analysis, energy crisis, and nuclear safety, as well as grid design and the integration of renewable energy into the electricity grid. The two parties aim at fostering trade and investment in renewables with the goal of enhancing competition and lowering costs, but also improving trade and investment conditions in the energy sector as a whole.

The energy cooperation between the EU and China has not been smooth however resulting in growing distrust between the two sides. The reasons for that were multifold. Firstly, the issues related with artificially low prices of efficient light bulbs, rare earths exported by China and subsidized solar panels. China also opposed to include aviation in the EU Emissions Trading System (Preston et al 2015). Secondly, unresolved controversies on intellectual property rights (Knodt et al 2015). It is said that in China the law on scientific and technological progress states that when research funds are received from the Chinese government it means that it is the one acquiring ownership of the technology resulting from the research (European Commission 2018). Thirdly, the long history of EU-China energy dialogue is not reflected in the current network which is not dense and decentralized. Both sides' energy structure is fragmented with energy issues being part of multiple agencies which makes cooperation inefficient. China perceives EU as important source of renewable energy development and an advanced norm-setter. But according to Knodt et al (2015) the Chinese are less interested in cooperation with the EU than EU actors as they prefer cooperation on bilateral basis with individual member states. Fourthly, according to Zhang (2017) some EU-China energy institutions are not working properly. For example, some institutions have their statutory goals but do not implement them, such as urbanization forum that was planned to be annual forum but in fact has not been organized annually. Furthermore, currently there is a lack of one high-level decision making institution and high level representation as the EU-China Energy Dialogue is attended only by energy officials. In addition, mutual perceptions and lack of trust play a role. The Chinese consider EU partners as not reflexive in seeking compromise or changing their stand point while the EU actors lack trust towards Chinese partners (Knodt et al, 2015, p 24). Knodt et al (2015) point out that Chinese are no more interested in following what others create but want to have an influence on these aspects internally and globally.

An important step in energy cooperation between the UK and China has been investment in Hinckley Point C nuclear project. During Xi Jinping visit in the UK in October 2015 a deal between China General Nuclear Power Corp (CGN) and Electricite de France SA (EDF), lead investor in Hinckley Point, was signed. CGN obtained one third of shares. It is the first new nuclear plant in UK since 1995. Other nuclear plants are old and are being phased out. The Hinckley Point C was thought by CGN as the first nuclear plant in a string of projects carried out in the UK. Hinckley Point C however is troubled as it never worked. It is French technology which has not yet worked in other locations either such as Finland and Normandy, where it has been three times over time and over budget. Moreover, Austria is in the process of suing European Commission for signing off the Hinkley deal as it argues it should not have obtained the state aid which is permitted only in exceptional cases while the nuclear energy belongs to the past and it should not be supported (Watt 2017).

The result of Brexit is the UK decision to withdraw from the European nuclear regulator Euratom which promotes nuclear energy related research and consistent safety standards. UK's leaving Euratom means it has to sign its own nuclear treaties with individual countries, which would delay construction of nuclear plants in the UK, including the Hinckley Point C (The Week 2017). The UK would have to provide for its nuclear non-proliferation safeguards commitment which means either establishing own independent agency or transfer these responsibilities to the British Office for Nuclear Regulation. But Brexit will also entail leaving the single market which would hinder delivery of nuclear infrastructure (The Week 2017). As of now, these possible Brexit outcomes mean for Chinese energy investors unpredictable environment with no access to resources available at the EU level such as the ability to cooperate and participate in formulation of standards at Euratom. Such cooperation with nuclear technology leaders and influence on industry standards in the EU would allow to build reputation for Chinese firms on the global stage (the way

Huawei did in telecommunications, see Drahokoupil, McCaleb, Pawlicki and Szunomár, 2017). Chinese nuclear energy companies could shift their interest towards other EU leaders in nuclear heat production. In 2016, out of the EU 14 member states having nuclear plants the ones with highest level of nuclear heat production were France, Germany, UK, Spain and Sweden (Europa 2018). On the other hand the UK is attractive partner for China in other energy issues. In 2017, the UK for the first time generated more electricity from renewable (wind, solar, hydro, and biomass) and nuclear energy than from gas and coal (Ward 2018). UK has made significant progress saving money due to demand reduction and smart management (Hilton 2018). These areas remain possible for the future cooperation between the UK and China.

4. Conclusion

Brexit, depending on type of divorce between the EU and the UK, already has an impact on their relations with the major partners. Both the EU and the UK became weaker on international stage due to Brexit. At the same time, Brexit negotiations shift EU leaders focus on developing relations with China, among other issues.

With UK being supporter of China within the EU-28 after Brexit London and Beijing will get even closer with possible free trade agreement signed. Example is the City of London which has established a "green finance centre" with a Chinese entity to fund sustainable development projects such as development of new city near Beijing called Xiongan but also projects within Belt and Road initiative (South China Morning Post 2018). On the other hand, the EU without the UK's softer approach towards China, on the issues of free trade agreement, market economy status, and investment agreement, may take stiffer approach to relations with China. The EU introduced new method of calculating dumping. In October 2017, Brussles declared it will investigate foreign investment in strategic sectors. If investments are restricted in sensitive areas such as advanced technologies it may mean hindered FDI by Chinese in the EU after Brexit. The uncertainty caused by Brexit as to possible effects it may have on cooperation with entities in the UK may withhold Chinese firms from investing in the UK until Brexit process is finalized.

Brexit means EU should be prepared for less interest of China in energy cooperation as China will focus on bilateral relations. For the UK Brexit means that China will maintain its interest in some areas of energy cooperation that do not rely on external actors such as nuclear energy as the UK still possesses attractive technology and know-how related to energy efficiency solutions and city management. In February 2017, China's NDRC announced a catalogue, as part of implementation of the 13th Five Year Plan (2016-2020), of strategic emerging industries that maintains the key position of new energy industries. It includes new energy vehicles, energy-saving and environmental protection industries but also related services which encompass research, standardization and financial services (Ban and Hou 2017). China's drive towards new energy and environmental protection has been pushed also by the Chinese public that since 2000 has been more aware of environmental harm resulting in increased number of complaints to Environmental Protection Bureau in period 1990-2006 annually by 450% and more public protests (Munro 2014). These facts mean China should maintain or even strengthen its cooperation in new energy with the UK.

References

Erik Arnold, Sylvia Schwaag Serger, Sophie Bussillet and Neil Brown, "Evaluation of Chinese participation in the EU Framework Programme", (February 2009). http://www.eurosfaire.prd.fr/7pc/doc/1246969355_china_fps_final_07_03_2009.pdf.

Victor Ban, "China Names Latest 'Strategic Emerging Industries'". 2017. https://www.globalpolicywatch.com/2017/03/china-names-latest-strategic-emerging-industries/, 12.03.2018.

BBC (2018). http://www.bbc.com/news/uk-42821084, 22.03.2018.

Danel Boffey, "EU scorns UK's 'pick and mix' approach to trade post-Brexit". https://www.theguardian.com/politics/2018/mar/07/uks-brexit-red-lines-will-limit-depth-of-future-trade-deal-eu-guidelines, 22.03.2018.

Daniel Brooker, Siobhán Ní Chonaill, "Scoping the impact of UK membership of the EU on UK health research", Ebook by RAND, 2015. https://www.rand.org/pubs/research_reports/RR565.html.

Laurens Cerulus and Jakob Hanke (2017). "Enter the Dragon: Chinese investment in crisis-hit countries gives Beijing influence at the European Union's top table". https://www.politico.eu/article/china-and-the-troika-portugal-foreign-investment-screening-takeovers-europe/, 30.03.2018.

CGN (2017). http://en.cgnpc.com.cn/encgn/c100035/2017-12/19/content_61eb093d9bd64b35a03e83c1f595fe32.shtml, 3.03.2018.

European Commission, "Roadmap for EU-China S & T cooperation"|, (October 2017), pp. 1-23. http://ec.europa.eu/research/iscp/pdf/policy/cn_roadmap_2017.pdf.

Rob Davies, "*China to rein in outward investment as domestic growth stalls*", 2016. https://www.theguardian.com/business/2016/dec/26/china-to-rein-in-foreign-investment-as-domestic-growth-stalls, 11.11.2017.

Jan Drahokoupil, Agnieszka McCaleb, Peter Pawlicki and Agnes Szunomár, "Huawei in Europe: strategic integration of local capabilities in a global production network". In book: *Chinese investment in Europe: corporate strategies and labour relations*, Publisher: European Trade Union Institute, Editors: Jan Drahokoupil, 2017, pp.211-229.

Ernst & Young Global Limted, (2017), *EY: China's outbound investment in 2017 is expected to steadily slow down; Chinese enterprises should concentrate on the quality of their investments to achieve stable development*, http://www.ey.com/cn/en/newsroom/news-releases/news-2017-ey-china-outbound-investment-is-expected-to-steadily-slow-down, 11.11.2017.

Europa (2016). EU-China Roadmap on energy cooperation (2016-2020), https://ec.europa.eu/energy/sites/ener/files/documents/FINAL_EU_CHINA_ ENERGY_ROADMAP_EN.pdf, 1.03.2018.

Europa (2017). EU-China Energy Dialogue: clean energy in an international context, https://ec.europa.eu/energy/en/news/eu-china-energy-dialogue-clean-energy-international-context, 1.03.2018.

Europa (2018). Nuclear energy statistics, http://ec.europa.eu/eurostat/ statistics-explained/index.php/Nuclear_energy_statistics, 3.03.2018.

Europa (2018b). International cooperation: China, https://ec.europa.eu/ energy/en/topics/international-cooperation/china, 15.03.2018.

European Commission (2017). EU-China Summit: moving forward with our global partnership, http://europa.eu/rapid/press-release_IP-17-1524_en.htm, 5.03.2018.

European Commission (2018). Report on the protection and enforcement of intellectual property rights in third countries, http://trade.ec.europa.eu/doclib/ docs/2018/march/tradoc_156634.pdf, 24.03.2018.

Alicia García-Herrero, K.C. Kowk, Liu Xiangdong, Tim Summers and Zhang Yongsheng, (2017) 'EU-China Economic Relations to 2025 Building a Common Future EU-China Economic', *Report*, Sptemper 2017. https://www. chathamhouse.org/publication/eu-china-economic-relations-2025-building-common-future.

Thilo Hanemann and Mikko Huotari (2017), "Record flows and growing imbalances. Chinese Investment in Europe in 2016", *Report*, 2016, Mercator Institute for China Studies. https://rhg.com/research/record-flows-and-growing-imbalances-chinese-investment-in-europe-in-2016/.

Isbel Hilton, "Isabel Hilton on UK-China cooperation on clean energy", 2nd February 2018, https://eblnews.com/video/isabel-hilton-uk-china-cooperation-clean-energy-320207, 3.03.2018.

Hui LIU, "China and the UK to bolster energy cooperation", *China Daily,* 23.11.2017. http://www.chinadaily.com.cn/world/cn_eu/2017-11/23/ content_34886382.htm, 2.03.2018.

IMAA Institute (2017). Plotting A New Course: The Impact Of Brexit On

M&A Activity, https://imaa-institute.org/plotting-new-course-impact-brexit-ma-activity/, 24.03.2018.

Institute for Security & Development Policy (2017). China and Europe's Investment Clash, http://isdp.eu/china-europe-investment-regulation-clash/, 8.02.2018.

Michèle Knodt, Nadine Piefer and Suet-Yi Lai, "Perceptions and Challenges of China-EU Energy Cooperation". Mainz: Chair of International Relations, Working paper, No.10, 2015, Johannes Gutenberg University. https://international.politics.uni-mainz.de/files/2012/10/MPIEP-10_CEDI-WP-1.pdf.

Chelsea Battle, "Strong growth for top Chinese investments in UK", *China Invests Overseas, CIO,* 03.16.2017. https://www.ft.com/content/262d1258-0725-11e7-97d1-5e720a26771b, 11.11.2017.

Cecily Liu, "Chinese companies will continue to look for UK investments", *China Daily*, 30.06.2017. http://www.chinadaily.com.cn/business/2017-06/30/content_29942193.htm, 11.11.2017.

Liu Xiaoming, "Stronger China-UK Energy Cooperation Paves the Way for Building A Community of Shared Future: Keynote Speech by H.E. Ambassador Liu Xiaoming at the UK Energy", 27.01.2017. http://www.chinese-embassy.org.uk/eng/ambassador/dsjhjcf/2017remarks/t1434442.htm, 2.03.2018.

Neil Munro, "Profiling the victims: public awareness of pollution-related harm in China". *Journal of Contemporary China*, 2014, 23(86), pp. 314-329.

Bernice Lee, Nick Mabey, Felix Preston, Antony Froggatt and Siân Bradley, "Enhancing Engagement Between China and the EU on Resource Governance and Low-Carbon Development", Research Paper, June 2015. https://www.chathamhouse.org/publication/eu-china-cooperation-engagement, 1.03.2018.

The Royal Society (2016) 'UK research and the European Union The role of the EU in international research collaboration and researcher mobility', p. 38. Available at: https://royalsociety.org/~/media/policy/projects/eu uk-funding/phase-2/EU-role-in-international-research-collaboration-and-researcher-mobility.pdf.

The Week (2017). Hinkley Point 'will cost public double the amount it should', http://www.theweek.co.uk/60778/hinkley-point-will-cost-public-double-the-amount-it-should, 13.03.2018.

Damian Tobin, "Why the UK won't get a better trade deal with China outside the EU", *Report,* 31.01.2018. https://theconversation.com/why-the-uk-wont-get-a-better-trade-deal-with-china-outside-the-eu-90981, 22.03.2018.

UK Trade & Investment (2015), *UKTI Inward Investment Report 2014 to 2015* (Online viewing), https://www.gov.uk/government/publications/ukti-inward-investment-report-2014-to-2015/ukti-inward-investment-report-2014-to-2015-online-viewing, 02.11.2017.

Hinrich Voss, (2017), "China's outward FDI to Europe after Brexit", *China Policy Institute: Analysis*, *Report,* 26.05.2017. https://cpianalysis.org/2017/05/26/chinas-outward-fdi-to-europe-after-brexit/, 16.10.2017.

Holly Watt H, "The long read Hinkley Point: the 'dreadful deal' behind the world's most expensive power plant", The Guardian, 2017. https://www.theguardian.com/news/2017/dec/21/hinkley-point-c-dreadful-deal-behind-worlds-most-expensive-power-plant, 13.03.2018.

World Investment Report (2017). Investment and the Digital Economy. http://unctad.org/en/PublicationsLibrary/wir2017_en.pdf, 8.02.2018.

World Nuclear Association (2017). Nuclear Power in the European Union, http://www.world-nuclear.org/information-library/country-profiles/others/european-union.aspx, 3.03.2018.

Chao Zhang, "The EU-China Energy Cooperation: An Institutional Analysis", *Report*, EIAS, 2017.http://www.eias.org/wpcontent/uploads/2016/03/ EIAS_Briefing_Paper_EU_China_Energy_Cooperation_2017.02.pdf, 5.03.2018.

China's investments and infrastructural expansion in Central and Eastern Europe[*]

Ágnes Szunomár

Abstract

Chinese companies have increasingly been targeting Central and Eastern European (CEE) countries in the past one and a half decade, while diplomatic relations are also on the rise. This development is quite a new phenomenon but not an unexpected one. On one hand, the transformation of the global economy and the restructuring of China's economy are responsible for growing Chinese interest in the developed world, including the European Union. On the other hand, CEE countries have also become more open to Chinese business opportunities, especially after the global economic and financial crisis with the intention of decreasing their economic dependency on Western (European) markets. Disappointment coming from the slower-than-expected catching-up processes to Western Europe also resulted in these countries' turning towards the East. Therefore, this chapter examines China's growing presence in Central and Eastern Europe through China's investments as well as infrastructure-related projects in the CEE region as the latter represents a rather new type of Chinese economic expansion and might also show the limits of current Chinese strategies in CEE, at least in the countries of the European Union.

---

[*] This paper was written in the framework of the research project "Non-European emerging-market multinational enterprises in East Central Europe" (K-120053), supported by the National Research, Development and Innovation Office (NKFIH)

Introduction

In the past decade, China has increasingly been perceived in Central and Eastern Europe (CEE) as a country which could bring economic benefits to the region through developing trade relations, growing inflow of Chinese investment and recently also through infrastructure projects carried out by Chinese companies, financed from Chinese loans. Although when compared to China's economic presence globally or in the developed world, its economic impact on CEE countries is small but has increased significantly in the past decade. China is indeed pushing forward in the region: according to the Chinese Ministry of Commerce, China-CEE trade increased to 58.7 billion USD in 2016 (from 43.9 billion in 2010), while its investment in CEE countries has accumulated to more than 8 billion USD, covering industries such as machinery, chemical, telecom and new energy. This is quite a new phenomenon but not an unexpected one: on one hand, the transformation of the global economy and restructuring of China's economy are responsible for growing Chinese interest in CEE and, on the other hand, CEE also represents new challenges and new opportunities for China.

The above-mentioned trends together with the 16+1 summit of the 16 Central and Eastern European countries and China in late 2017 have drawn the attention of Western diplomats, scholars and media to these intensifying efforts and the potential implications on the EU or even globally. Therefore, this chapter examines China's growing presence in Central and Eastern Europe through China's investments as well as infrastructure-related projects in the CEE region as the latter represents a rather new type of Chinese economic expansion while might also show the limits of current Chinese strategies in CEE, at least in countries of the European Union. As most of these projects have not yet been finalized or started and are still under negotiation, we will focus on one of the most important project, that is the Budapest-Belgrade railway. This would be one of the first Chinese infrastructural projects of the Belt and Road Initiative on EU soil.

The chapter is structured as follows: the first section analyses the motivations of both China and CEE for building a stronger economic relationship. The second section shows the main trends and patterns of Chinese foreign direct investment in the CEE region. The third section gives a brief overview on Chinese infrastructure projects in Central and Eastern Europe, while section four focuses on the Budapest Belgrade railway project of the Belt and Road Initiative. In the Summary section, conclusions will be drawn in order to evaluate the recent developments of China-CEE relations.

1. Changing motivations on both sides

In 2000, the Chinese government initiated its "go global" (*zou chu qu*) policy aimed at encouraging domestic companies to become globally competitive. It introduced new policies to encourage firms to engage in overseas activities in specific industries, particularly in relation to trade. In 2001 this was integrated and formalized under the 10th five-year plan, which also echoed the importance of the "go global" policy (Buckley et. al. 2007). This policy shift was part of the continuing reform and liberalization of the Chinese economy and also reflected the Chinese government's desire to create internationally competitive and well-known companies and brands.

As China's economic growth has begun to slow, the economy is facing new challenges and its economic strategy is transforming. Furthermore, the country's global trade and investment position and strategies are altering as well. New challenges require new answers, particularly regarding the fact that China has chosen not to stimulate its economy by turning only inwards but by opting for diplomacy, trade and investment to broaden China's sphere of interest and business opportunities. In this way, it can promote economic relations, people-to-people links and political influence whilst strengthening the legitimacy of the ruling party and Xi Jinping. Thus, the focus on new directions, referred to as Beijing's "The Belt and Road Initiative" (*yi dai yi lu*) initiative, is the result of domestic politics, geopolitics and historical and economic reasons.

Relations between China and the CEE region date back to ancient times, when these regions were closely linked together over 2,000 years ago via the (old) Silk Road. Now, after a long break, the relationship is about to be revived through the (new) Silk Road. Naturally, there were also connections between China and CEE during the Cold War and in the 1990s. Some countries had better ties, while others were less friendly, but generally, the region had no special role from either the Chinese or CEE point of view. Attitudes gradually began to change after the millennium.

When the CEE countries became members of the European Union, China developed an interest in strengthening ties with them. The CEE's growth potential, institutional stability and market size attracted Chinese companies. In fact, Beijing sees Central and Eastern Europe not only as one of its new frontiers for export expansion but also as a strategic entry point for the wider European market. It chose this region because CEE countries have dynamic, largely developed, less saturated economies directly connected to the EU common market. Chinese corporations can significantly cut business costs by setting up in CEE countries and at the same time they can integrate into the EU industrial network, while there are fewer political expectations and economic complaints (or rather these are expressed more quietly) than in Western Europe.

Xi Jinping's 2009 vice-presidential tour to Europe signaled a real shift in the Chinese leadership's attitudes toward the Central and Eastern European region and marked the beginning of a new stage in bilateral relations. Xi made an extended tour of Europe, visiting Belgium, Germany, Bulgaria, Romania, and Hungary (and spent longer in Budapest). The tour was framed as a visit to consolidate and develop economic cooperation between China and these five countries but Xi's visit to Central and Eastern Europe was more about China's evolving "go-out" investment strategy. Another reason for this higher representation can be the diversification strategy because recently Chinese global investment strategy places great emphasis on the diversification in all respects. A good example for that is China's 16+1 initiative which provides a joint platform for all Central and Eastern European countries and China, as well as the Belt and Road Initiative, which provides more and more connections for Chinese businesses.

If we examine the motivations of the CEE, we see that their "eastern awakening" dates back to the same time. As China became a major player in the world economy and politics, CEE became more interested in developing relations with China. The economic and financial crisis was an additional impetus as CEE governments started to seek out new opportunities in their recovery from the recession (Szunomár, 2015). Before the crisis, many CEE countries had mixed feelings about closer economic ties with China. On the one hand, they actively wanted to attract Chinese investment, and were anxious about losing out on trade and business opportunities with China. On the other hand, there were fears about the reliability of Chinese firms or because of human rights. Today an increasing number of CEE countries have decided to cast aside their doubts and even the coolest relations (like Czech-Chinese relations) have entered a warmer period. CEE countries' disappointment coming from the slower-than-expected catching-up processes to Western Europe also resulted in these countries' turning towards the East, which is further reinforced by the current tendency of populism in the region. However, it is true that despite all of this, most CEE governments lack a unified strategy towards China or Chinese companies. Hungary is one of the few exceptions: in the spring of 2012 the government launched a new economic policy with special emphasis on its "Eastern opening" policy, formulated after and partly as a result of the crisis (Éltető-Szunomár, 2015).

2. Chinese investments in the CEE region: macroeconomic, institutional and political factors

Chinese outward investment to CEE-as well as trade volumes-has steadily increased in the last one and a half decades, particularly after 2004 and 2008.

2004 was the accession date of 8 CEE countries (Estonia, Latvia, Lithuania, Czech Republic, Slovakia, Poland, Hungary, and Slovenia) to the EU while 2008 is the year of the economic and financial crisis. The crisis has been indeed an additional impetus for both China and the CEE countries to strengthen their economic relations. CEE countries started to search for new opportunities in their recovery from the recession: we can observe increased interest of the CEE governments in boosting trade relations and attracting Chinese investors. In parallel, the crisis brought more overseas opportunities for Chinese companies to raise their share in the world economy as the number of ailing or financially distressed firms has increased all over Europe, including also CEE countries. China just took these opportunities, which can be one of the reasons of the wider sectoral representation of Chinese firms in CEE countries in recent years.

Overall, the role of Chinese capital in Central and Eastern Europe, compared with all the invested capital is still very small, but in the last few years this capital inflow accelerated significantly, especially after 2008. Similarly to trade relation, Chinese outward foreign direct investment is on the rise in every CEE countries but some of them stand out: the countries of the Visegrad Four (Czech Republic, Hungary, Poland and Slovakia), together with Romania, Bulgaria and Serbia are the most popular destinations (see Figure 1. and 2.) and usually receive more than 85 percent of total Chinese FDI to the whole CEE region.

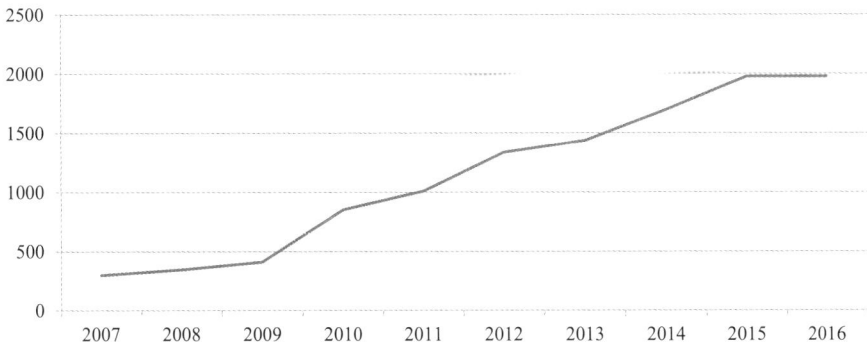

Figure 1. China's outward FDI stock in CEE, 2007-2016, million USD
Data source: MOFCOM/NBS, PRC

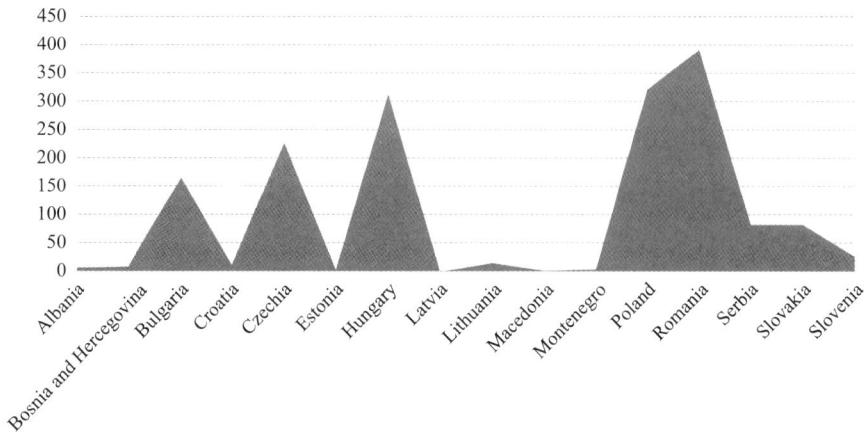

Figure 2. China's outward FDI stock in 16 CEECs, 2016, million USD
Data source: MOFCOM/NBS, PRC

In some cases, FDI amount is even far greater when taking into account cumulative data instead of national-home or host country-statistics, since a significant portion of Chinese investment is received via intermediary countries or companies, therefore it appears elsewhere in Chinese statistics. For example, according to the author's calculations, Chinese investment in Hungary by 2017 was around 3,5-4 billion USD[1], while official Chinese statistics showed less than 500 million USD.

When calculating the percentage share of Chinese FDI in selected CEE countries to all the invested capital, using UNCTAD's statistics on total inward FDI stock as well as MOFCOM data on Chinese FDI in selected four CEE countries, we found that only 0.22 % of total inward FDI were from China in the five most popular CEE host countries. The highest percentage is in Hungary: 0.4%, in other countries it is even lower (the lowest is in Poland with 0.17% in Poland). However, when using the data of China Global Investment Tracker (CGIT) instead of MOFCOM (see Figure 3.), as CGIT tracks back data

---

[1] More than 1.5 billion USD from that is the investment of the Chinese chemical company Wanhua, which acquired a 96 percent stake in the Hungarian chemical company BorsodChem through its Dutch subsidiary in 2010 and 2011 and later also invested in the development of BorsodChem. It is the largest Chinese investment in the CEE region so far.

to the ultimate parent companies, we found that 2.14% of total inward FDI in selected CEE countries were from China: the highest percentage is again in Hungary: 7.84%, while in Poland it is still below 1%.

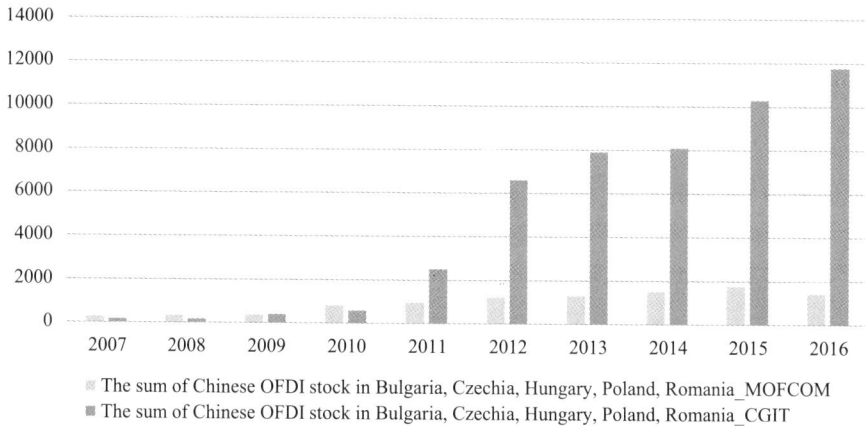

The sum of Chinese OFDI stock in Bulgaria, Czechia, Hungary, Poland, Romania_MOFCOM
The sum of Chinese OFDI stock in Bulgaria, Czechia, Hungary, Poland, Romania_CGIT

Figure 3. Comparing MOFCOM and CGIT statistics-China's OFDI stock in selected CEECs 2007-2016, million USD
Data source: MOFCOM/NBS, PRC and China Global Investment Tracker (CGIT)

Chinese investors typically target secondary and tertiary sectors of the selected countries. Initially, Chinese investment has flowed mostly into manufacturing (assembly), but over time services attracted more and more investment as well, for example in Hungary and Poland there are branches of Bank of China and Industrial and Commercial Bank of China as well as offices of some of the largest law offices in China, Yingke Law Firm (in Hungary in 2010, in Poland in 2012) and Dacheng Law Offices (in Poland in 2011, in Hungary in 2012). Main Chinese investors targeting these countries are interested primarily in telecommunication, electronics, chemical industry and transportation. Major investors are for example Wanhua, Huawei, ZTE Corporation, Lenovo, Sevenstar Electronics Co., BYD and Comlink.

Considering the motivation of Chinese investments in CEE countries, their economic integration into the EU has been the most important attractive factor especially in the manufacturing sector. Accessing the old EU-15 markets was the most important, while local markets were of secondary importance (market-seeking). EU membership of the CEE countries allowed Chinese investors to avoid trade barriers and the countries served as an assembly base due to the relatively low labour costs (efficiency-seeking, see McCaleb-Szunomár 2017). However, parallel with the increasing number of mergers and acquisitions in the region, strategic asset-seeking motives have become more and more important for Chinese MNCs in recent years. Therefore, Chinese investments are also motivated by the seeking of brands, new technologies or market niches that they can fill in European markets.

In addition to the traditional macroeconomic factors, institutions also play a role. An interesting aspects that is inducing investments in CEE is institutional stability (e.g., protection of property rights), which is in line with the findings of Clegg and Voss (2012, p 101) who argue that Chinese OFDI in the EU shows "an institutional arbitrage strategy" as "Chinese firms invest in localities that offer clearer, more transparent and stable institutional environments". The role of state subsidies and incentives should be also mentioned here as a potential attracting factor of Chinese FDI. Especially before EU membership, but also afterwards, governments and local authorities applied sometimes tailor-made incentives to attract large investors, such as customs free zones or special economic zones with support services, tax allowances, partial funding for employee training or the residence visa[1]. Recently Chinese firms became also attracted by privatization opportunities of state enterprises which provide access to technology (patents), brands, distribution networks, and manufacturing capacity for European markets.

Moreover, Chinese diaspora, which is an acknowledged attracting factor of Chinese FDI in the extant literature (e.g., Buckley et al., 2007) - is the largest in Hungary among CEE countries. As a result, Hungary received relatively bigger amounts of FDI in the past one and a half decade and earlier than others in CEE.

---

① Hungary is the only country in the region that introduced special incentive for foreign investors from outside the EU, which is a possibility to receive a residence visa when fulfilling the requirement of a certain level of investment in Hungary (300000 EUR)

Chinese companies also seem to pay more attention to the level of political relation: political gestures and measures are still important in developing relations with China. Hungary-which is one of the major recipients of Chinese OFDI in the CEE region-has had historically good political relations and earlier than other CEE countries. By contrast, the smaller amounts of Chinese investments in the Czech Republic or Slovakia can be explained by the colder political relations of the past years (see Fürst-Pleschová, 2010). However, the situation has changed and the bilateral relationship between the Czech Republic and China has improved significantly since the Czech Social Democratic Party (CSSD) went into power after the election in 2013. Along with the rapid improvement of the political relation, Chinese investments also started to rush into the country.

As presented above, Chinese investments have been flowing to the CEE region in recent years, however, this doesn't mean that all 16 CEE countries are receiving major amounts of Chinese FDI. EU member states, especially the Visegrad Four countries together with Romania and Bulgaria, of the group of 16 attract the majority of Chinese investment in the CEE region while others, such as the Western Balkans lag behind. The reason behind this representation is obviously the fact that Chinese companies are targeting the EU markets and would like to avoid trade barriers. Interestingly but understandably, the patterns of Chinese infrastructure projects in the CEE region are just the opposite: infrastructural projects are implemented rather in the non-EU states of this group, for example in the Western Balkans as-among other factors-strict EU rules and regulations not hamper these processes there, while other sources- such as EU structural funds in the EU member CEE countries-are not available or less accessible.

3. Belt and Road Initiative: Chinese-CEE relations in a new framework?

The Belt and Road Initiative is an example of economic and infrastructural collaboration covering the whole of Eurasia. In fact, the initiative is a set of instruments to facilitate connectivity in terms of trade, investment, finance and flows of tourists and students (Summers, 2015). Connected to this initiative, the "New Silk Road" project-the Silk Road Economic Belt and the 21st Century Maritime Silk Road-has become the cornerstone of China's public diplomacy. The Silk Road Economic Belt also provides opportunities for CEE countries that wish to participate in implementing the strategy.

There are already existing (i.e. not constructed under the Belt and Road Initiative) railway links between Chinese and CEE cities: the railway line from the Chinese city of Chengdu to Łodz in Poland has been in operation since April 2013, the line between Wuhan and Prague was launched in 2012(Liu, 2014), while in 2017 the first freight train has arrived to Budapest from Xian. In addition, there are some other rail links, which connects China with Western and Southern European cities such as Hamburg, Duisburg or Madrid, while crossing CEE countries, too.

When taking a closer look, a clear link can be found between China's Belt and Road Initiative and the 16+1 formation. Moreover, it seems to be more and more evident that 16+1 is becoming an inherent part of the Belt and Road Initiative strategy. On the one hand, the CEE region is a strategic area for Belt and Road Initiative and an infrastructure cooperation of this kind can also enhance relations between China and the CEE countries. Belt and Road Initiative guarantees the durability of the 16+1 initiative and can help to fill it with more content. On the other hand, as Turcsanyi (2016) highlights, China can also learn from the experiences of the 16 + 1 initiative so far and can use those in its broader Belt and Road Initiative strategy. Such experiences are, for example, that more effective communication ora clearer definition of goals could help in the future to avoid excessive expectations or doubts.

As can be seen in the Table 1, China is planning and negotiating several infrastructure-related projects in all the 16 Central and Eastern European countries: they are interested in building highways, constructing or reconstructing railways as well as building or expanding power plants (among others thermal, hydro, coal-fired as well as nuclear power plants).

**Table 1.   List of key Chinese projects-construction/reconstruction/acquisition/expansion-
under implementation or negotiation in 16 CEE countries**

Albania	Motorvays: 'Arber' (connecting Albanian Ionian Sea to the Bulgarian Black Sea) and 'Blue Corridor' (Adriatic-Ionian); industrial park in Durres; international airport in Tirana
Bosnia and Hercegovina	Stanari thermo power plant, Banovici thermal power plant, Tuzla coal-fired power plant, Banja Luka-Split motorway (potential)
Bulgaria	Motorways (potential): Varna-Burgas motorway, Ruse-Svilengrad motorway; investment in Kozloduy (potential)
Croatia	Banja Luka-Split motorway (potential)
Czechia	Temelín and Dukovany nuclear power plants (potential), football stadium Eden (acq. and reconstruction); Hodonin logistic centre (potential)
Estonia	China-Europe freight train network (potential)
Hungary	Belgrade-Budapest high-speed railway
Latvia	Yiwu-Riga 'Trans-Eurasian' railway connection; construction of Rail Baltica (potential), investment in airBaltic (potential)
Lithuania	development of the Xinjiang-Europe railway connection (potential); Kaunas combined heat power plant (potential)
Macedonia	Railway modernisation-Corridor X; two stretches on the motorways linking Kicevo-Ohrid and Miladinovci-Stip
Montenegro	Section of the European Motorway corridor XI (to Serbia); Renewal of the country's ship fleet; Investment in various energy projects / hydro power plant, thermal power plant (potential); Blue Corridor motorway project (potential)
Poland	Chengdu-Europe Express Rail; Jaworzno coal-fired power plant
Romania	Rovinari thermal power plant, Mintia-Deva T thermal power plant, Tarnita-Lapustesti hydro power plant, Cernavoda nuclear power plant; Dej, Setra and Clue photovoltaic power plant
Serbia	Danube bridge in Belgrade; Belgrade-Budapest high-speed railway; 350MW unit at Kostolac thermal power plant; Sections of the European motorway XI (to Montenegro), 3 industrial parks
Slovakia	Liaoning-Slovakia freight train service
Slovenia	Krško nuclear power plant (potential); Divača-Koper railway line (potential)

Source: author's own collection by using-among others-EBRD sources

China's motivations are easy to understand, as the New Silk Road project will allow them to expand their political and economic sphere of interest: once the alternative transport routes are completed they will be in a more favourable strategic position, they will have more and more alternative transport routes, they can reach their target markets easier and faster and they will be able to work off some of their industrial overcapacities accumulated in recent years. In addition, these projects may provide a reference for further Chinese investment in the broader region, especially in the more developed part of Europe.

Infrastructure development is indeed a hot topic in all CEE countries; however, there are other resources-for example EU funds-to finance them. therefore, a more interesting question is: what is it that motivates the CEE side in building infrastructure with Chinese companies? The importance of Europe, particularly Central and Eastern Europe, to the project was emphasized long ago by China and welcomed by several CEE countries, including Hungary. Hungary was the first European country to sign a memorandum of understanding with China on promoting the Silk Road Economic Belt and Maritime Silk Road, during Chinese Foreign Minister Wang Yi's visit to Budapest in June, 2015. The Hungarian government was very keen on the railway project and when it signed the construction agreement in 2014, Prime Minister Orbán called it the most important moment in cooperation between the European Union and China (Kesztehlyi, 2014).

China-during China's then Prime Minister Wen Jiabao's visit in Warsaw in 2012- offered a special credit line worth of 10 billion USD to the CEE region to be used for investments in infrastructure, modern technologies and the green economy. This credit line is available for the whole 16 CEE regions it is part of the 16+1 cooperation between these countries and China. However, later on it turned out that CEE countries, at least those part of the European Union cannot really use those funds as certain conditions of this funding opportunity-such as the necessary involvement of Chinese companies and materials-may go against EU rules, for example public procurement regulations. It seems that no significant progress has been made in this field so far and the conditions which attracted the worries of-among others-the European Union have not yet been changed.

Later on it turned out that the majority of Central and Eastern European countries are not even interested in the Chinese funding opportunity and haven't used the credit line it offered for the region. As Jakóbowski (2015) highlights, "companies and public institutions from EU states had access to more attractive forms of funding, including EU structural funds". As a consequence, the credit line was typically carried out in non-EU member states and used for infrastructural projects in the Western Balkans. Examples included-as stated in Table 1. - the construction of the Bar-Boljare motorway in Montenegro, of the Mihajlo Pupin Bridge in Belgrade and of the Stanari thermal power plant in Bosnia and Herzegovina.

It means that China's Belt and Road Initiative hasn't really been able to reach all of its goals so far in the CEE region as they couldn't enter the EU yet, although initial plans were included rail links to Western European markets. The construction of the Budapest-Belgrade railway would be a perfect case in this respect as it links a non-EU CEE country, Serbia with the EU member state Hungary, creates a connection between the Greek port of Piraeus and Western European markets for Chinese goods and at last but not at least, it provides a successful implemented Chinese infrastructure project on EU soil.

4. Entering the EU market with infrastructural projects: the case of the Budapest-Belgrade railway

The Chinese government often emphasizes that it treats Hungary as a hub for Chinese products in the European Union. Consequently, it expressed its interest in several infrastructure-related investment recent years, such as plans to transform Szombathely airport into a major European cargo base or develop the infrastructure of the Debrecen airport. The project to modernize the Belgrade-Budapest rail link is a recent example of both the Hungarian government's Eastern opening policy and China's Belt and Road Initiative. The aim is simple: to reduce travel time between Budapest and Belgrade to 2.5-3 hours, and to establish closer trade links by transporting Chinese goods-delivered by ship to the Chinese-run Greek port of Piraeus-to Western Europe via Serbia and Hungary[①]. The underlying motivations and potential outcomes are, however, more complex.

Map 1. Rail route between Piraeus and Budapest, via Skopje and Belgrade
Source: People's Daily Online. Available online: http://en.people.cn/n/2014/1218/c90883-8824383.html(accessed on September 15, 2017).

The geographic positions of Hungary and Serbia mean they are suited to handling the transit traffic between China and Europe and occupy an important role in implementing the Chinese grand strategy.[②] Consequently, at the end of 2014, the prime ministers of Hungary, Serbia, China and Macedonia signed an agreement in Belgrade at the third Central and Eastern Europe-China summit on the construction of a rail link between Budapest and Belgrade. Regarding

---

① The Shanghai-Piraeus route lasts for about 22 days, which is 10 days less than reaching the Rotterdam or Hamburg port. The Balkan Corridor of the New Silk Road starts from the Piraeus port and reaches Central Europe from the Aegean Sea via the existing Corridor X (Macedonia, Serbia and Hungary).

② See for example: "China-CEE cooperation gathers momentum," *Xinhua*, June 8, 2015. Available online: http://news.xinhuanet.com/english/2015-06/08/c_134308024.htm

practical issues, more than 85 per cent of the total cost of investment for the whole, 350-kilometre-long section will be financed from Chinese loan. According to recent estimates it will take between two and two and a half years to construct the track.

The reconstruction of a railway track on the Hungarian side is useful in itself-the current railway line there is relatively old and is in poor condition-but is it worth it for Hungary, if it is financed from Chinese loans, and will mostly likely be implemented by Chinese firm, potentially the China Railway Construction Corporation?

As a Hungarian journal summarized (Bodacz, 2017), the Hungarian section will cost 750 billion forints (around 3 billion USD). As mentioned above, of this, 85 percent will be financed from Chinese loans, with interest between 132 and 200 billion forints (500 and 800 million USD, respectively) and 15 percent by the Hungarian government. It means that the whole project will finally cost around 950 billion forints (3.7 billion USD). As the construction has been already delayed, it might take further years to start the construction. As a result, the first train could be launched in 2023 or 2024 (Vörös, 2018).

And the construction was indeed delayed by the European Commissionas the EU probe looked into whether it follows the European Union's procurement rules, stipulating that public tenders must be offered for large infrastructure projects and found that the design was not in line with EU regulations. At the end of November last year, after the two-day 16+1 summit in Budapest, the Hungarian Government finally published a procurement tender for its section of the line. Still, with or without tender, the construction will be definitely carried out by the already mentioned China Railway Construction Corporation since this tender presumably excluded other companies from starting off. According to the regulation of this tender, only those companies can apply that has such a big amount of revenue generated from railway construction that can only be met by Chinese, Russian, American or Indian companies. In Europe, such companies doesn't really exist, while Russian, Indian or American companies have not indicated their interest in the project yet.

So far it seems that Chinese engineers will be responsible for carrying out planning, land surveying and preparatory work, and Hungarians may play a role in converting the plans made with the Chinese software. The construction will also be done by Chinese contractors or subcontractors, which means mostly Chinese machines and Chinese workers in the construction process since the whole technology is also Chinese.

For now, it is likely that the only benefit Hungary can expect from the Budapest-Belgrade railway construction comes in the form of the transit fees which the country will get as soon as the travel begins on the railway line. Although the exact amount is not yet known, it will hopefully cover the loan repayments, at least parts of it. However, being a transit country is not the only option: Hungary could build support infrastructure along the railway line to serve as a logistics and/or assembly centre (since it already has experience in this field): Hungary could create factories, logistics centres and industrial or economic zones to attract Chinese (or other) investors. This strategy would not only better exploit the potential of the line but could create further jobs and manufacturing in the country. Unfortunately, such initiatives haven't been announced so far by the Hungarian Government.

Summary

As mentioned above, the enhancing cooperation between China and CEE is quite a new phenomenon but not an unexpected one. On one hand, the transformation of the global economy and the restructuring of China's economy are responsible for growing Chinese interest in the developed world, including the European Union. Here, China can benefit a lot from the EU's core and peripheral type of division. CEE for China represents dynamic, largely developed, less saturated economies, new frontiers for export expansion, new entry points for Europe and cheap but qualified labor. This adds up to less political expectations, less economic complaints, less protectionist barriers and less national security concerns compared to the Western European neighbors. On the other hand, CEE countries have become more open to Chinese business opportunities, especially after the global economic and financial crisis with the intention of decreasing their economic dependency on Western (European) markets. Disappointment coming from the slower-than-expected catching-up processes to Western Europe also resulted in these countries' turning towards the East, which is further reinforced by the current tendency of populism in the region.

The China-CEE relationship is experiencing a momentum, however, it shall not be interpreted as a strategic and influential alliance that could affect world politics or economy for several reasons.

First, when compared to China's economic presence globally or in the developed world, its economic impact on CEE countries is relatively small: CEE countries are highly dependent on both trade and investment relations with developed, mainly with EU member states while China represents a minor (although increasing) share here. From Chinese point of view, as far as trade or investment statistics are concerned, the CEE region is also far from being among the most important partners of China (within the EU, for example, Germany, the UK and France accounted for more than half of total Chinese investment value last year, while CEE region received less than five percent).

Second, China still has to learn a lot on how to do business with Europe, even if it is Central and Eastern Europe: it can be seen from its first infrastructure-building attempts in CEE that China tries to bring in the same package as in the developing world, Southeast Asia or Africa, not considering the different-and sometimes very strict-rules and regulations or standards of the EU. Therefore an interesting distinction can be made between Chinese foreign direct investment (FDI) and infrastructure projects in the CEE region: while the majority of FDI goes to EU member state CEE countries (11 of the 16) in order to take advantage of the skilled but relatively cheap workforce and to obtain the 'made in EU' label for products assembled or produced there, infrastructure projects are more prevalent in the non-EU CEE countries (5 of the 16) where strict EU regulations are not applicable. The latter case is well illustrated by the long-running plan of the Budapest-Belgrade railway, which would be built by Chinese constructor, mainly from Chinese credit. The Serbian side would have gladly started the construction works earlier, while the Hungarian side had to wait for the European Commission's approval.

Third, the CEE region itself is the main obstacle for the deepening of the relations as there are competing interests among the countries of the region with sometimes excessive expectations regarding what to expect from them and they lack the proper knowledge on how to deal with China. In addition, the 16+1 cooperation is also lacking proactive initiatives, plans or strategies from CEE side as well as consultation among each other before such summits: these 16 countries are rather wait for the Chinese side to offer or suggest something instead of proposing common ideas and use the synergies of the region.

Some Western Europeans fear that China may use its influence in the CEE region to frustrate some aspects of the EU's common China policy, but in reality, China's influence is far from being decisive, yet. As can be seen from above, in the current stage, the China-CEE cooperation is more like a new relationship with full of potentials. Exploiting such potentials will require further steps and careful-economic as well as political-considerations from both sides.

References

Bodacz Péter, "Kihagynák a magyar cégeket a több száz milliárdos óriásberuházásból". Magyar Nemzet, 10 May 2017, https://mno.hu/gazdasag/kihagynak-a-magyar-cegeket-a-tobb-szaz-milliardos-oriasberuhazasbol- 2398203.

Andrea Éltető, Ágnes Szunomár, "Ties of Visegrád countries with East Asia-trade and investment". Hungarian Academy of Science, Centre for Economic and Regional Studies, Institute of World Economics *Working Paper*, No. 215, 2015.

Ágnes Szunomár, "Blowing from the East". *International Issues & Slovak*

Foreign Policy Affairs, Vol. XXIV, No. 3/2015, pp. 60-78.

Peter J Buckley, Jeremy Clegg, Adam R Cross, Xin Liu, Hinrich Voss and Ping Zheng, "The determinants of Chinese outward foreign direct investment". *Journal of International Business Studies*, 2007, Vol.38, 499-518.

Jakub Jakóbowski, "China's foreign direct investments within the '16+1' cooperation formula: strategy, institutions, results". OSW Commentary, 2015. https://www.osw.waw.pl/en/publikacje/osw-commentary/2015-12-03/chinas-foreign-direct-investments-within-161-cooperation.

Christian Keszthelyi, "Belgrade-Budapest rail construction agreement signed", *Budapest Business Journal*, December 17, 2014.

Zuokui Liu, "Central and Eastern Europe in building the Silk Road Economic Belt," Institute of European Studies, Chinese Academy of Social Sciences, *Working Paper Series on European Studies,* 2014, Vol. 8, No. 3.

Agnieszka McCaleb and Agnes Szunomar, "Chinese foreign direct investment in Central and Eastern Europe: an institutional perspective". In: Chinese investment in Europe: corporate strategies and labour relations. ETUI, Brussels, 2017. ISBN 978-2-87452-454-7, pp. 121-140.

Tim Summers, "What exactly is 'the Belt and Road Initiative'", *The World Today* Vol. 71, No. 5, September 2015. Available online: https://www.chathamhouse.org/publication/twt/what-exactly-one-belt-one-road (accessed on October 1, 2015).

Richard Q. Turcsanyi, "China-CEE Cooperation in the 16+1 Platform and Its Role in the Belt and Road Initiative". In HUANG PING and LIU ZUOKUI. 2016. *China—CEE Cooperation and the "Belt and Road Initiative."* China—CEE Think Tanks Book Series. 2016. Beijing, China Social Science Press.

Zoltán Vörös, "Who Benefits From the Chinese-Built Hungary-Serbia Railway? -The details behind the project make it clear that China is the real winner". *The Diplomat*, 4 January 2018, https://thediplomat.com/2018/01/who-benefits-from-the-chinese-built-hungary-serbia-railway/.

Xinhua (2015): China-CEE cooperation gathers momentum," *Xinhua*, June 8, 2015. Available online: http://news.xinhuanet.com/english/2015-06/08/c_134308024.htm.

BRI and EU-China connectivity: European perceptions, aims and concerns[*]

Gustaaf Geeraerts

Abstract

BRI figures in the eyes of the EU as a potentially constructive initiative, to which it is ready to respond in a business-like manner and which it wants to further explore for opportunities leading to cooperation that genuinely serve the interests of both sides, while remaining alert to possible pitfalls and attempts by Beijing to get its way by employing divide and rule tactics among EU member states. BRI is not viewed as a giant leap forward, but rather as one in a series of steps that can possibly foster steadily close engagement with China. As the end point and focus of China's BRI initiative, the EU is well aware of its important role in the initiative. Therefore, the EU aims to take advantage of this opportunityon condition that the Chinese are willing to take into consideration its vital interests and conditions. In the end of the day, BRI is primarily about trade and investment. That is the foreign policy field in which the treaties have endowed the EU with exclusive competence. The main aim of this chapter is to explore the EU's perception, aims and concerns regarding the BRI initiative.

---

[*] This chapter was presented as a paper at the 5th Chengdu Roundtable *The Sustainability of China-EU Relations in the Changing World*, Sichuan University, Chengdu, May 22-23, 2017

1. European perceptions of BRI[1]

In September 2013, President Xi Jinping proposed the building of the New Silk Economic Belt during his visit to Kazakhstan, and in October of the same year in Indonesia, he proposed the building of the 21st Century Maritime Silk Road-now collectively called BRI.[2] Some four years later, the concept, scope, and nature of the initiative are still fluid, and the BRI narrative is likely to evolve over time. It is therefore not surprising that the true nature and purpose of BRI are subject to much speculation in Europe. Perceptions of what BRI is really all about and how feasible it is, diverge widely. Some observers "argue that the initiative, launched with a flourish by President Xi in 2013, is primarily about economics; others that it is principally about geo-politics. For some it is driven, like most Chinese foreign policy, by priorities and pressures close to home; for others, it is a visionary strategy for expanding China's sphere of international influence and establishing regional hegemony, while countering the US-led Trans-Pacific Partnership. Some think it is really about promoting the development of backward inland provinces; others that it is about exporting China's massive excess capacity in steel, cement and other industries. Then again, some think it is aimed at preventing instability in neighbouring Islamic states spilling over into the western province of Xinjiang, with its large and restive Muslim population. Still others see it as an extension of China's "Going Out" strategy, intended to promote outward investment that will also safeguard the country's dependence on extended supply lines of imported energy and raw materials. And some observers view BRI as little more than a slogan containing

---

[1] Recently a shorter acronym 'the Belt and Road Initiative' (BRI) seems to be gaining currency. In this article we stick with the orginal BRI acronym.

[2] Zhao Hong, "China's the Belt and Road Initiative: An Overview of the Debate", in *Trends in Southeast Asia*, No. 6, Singapore, 2016, p. 1. Available at: https://www.iseas.edu.sg/images/pdf/TRS6_16.pdf (accessed April 6, 2017).

very little real substance to date".[1] Still, a majority seems to be of the opinion that the main rationale behind BRI is found in the context of its economic and, as Chinese experts such as Wang Jisi see it, strategic purpose of pushing China's state apparatus to look beyond the rivalry with the United States in East Asia. The initiative is a means for China to invest its global foreign exchange reserves, to continue to grow and export its increasing excess capacity in the construction industries, in a context of slower growth at home and slower domestic investment.[2]

What stands beyond doubt is that BRI commands powerful high-level Chinese support and is backed by a large investment of political capital. It is no less than the personal signature initiative of President Xi, who has made clear that he regards it as central to his political legitimacy and as the tangible embodiment of his "China Dream" of rejuvenating the nation and its ruling Communist Party. Less clear is how the whole project is coordinated. Foreign diplomats have indicated that it is difficult to extract specifics about the initiative from Chinese officials and even to find out who is in overall control of it. Obviously, the projects involves a multiplicity of special interests, in addition to the plethora of different and often rival agencies and departments that are known to be involved in the country's policy-making process.[3] Seemingly, the initiative is being implemented "top-down by the State Council and the ministries (Commerce, Foreign Affairs, and the National Development and Reform Commission) via local governments and state-owned enterprises (such as the China State Construction Engineering Corporation, China Communications Construction Company, and China CAMC Engineering Co.), and some private businesses (such as the Sany Group), with input from

---

[1] Guy de Jonquières, "Xi Jinping's long road to somewhere? China's BRI initiative and how Europe should respond", *ECIPE Policy Brief*, No. 2, 2016, pp. 1-2.

[2] Mathieu Duchâtel et al., "Eurasian integration and the EU", in European Council on Foreign Relations (ed.), *Absorb and conquer: an EU approach to Russian and Chinese integration in Eurasia*, May 2016, p. 14.

[3] Guy de Jonquières, "Xi Jinping's long road to somewhere? p. 2.

academic and social institutions (such as universities and think-tanks). Silk Road research centres and working groups, companies, and banks are in the process of studying the risks, the feasibility, and the implementation of BRI".[1] With so many fingers in the pie, there has quite naturally been fierce competition to win government support for BRI projects but its political nature brings along the danger of serious misallocation of resources.

Some observers in Europe wonder whether China's BRI initiative is not overly ambitious. It has very broad geographical coverage as it seeks to strengthen infrastructure both on the westward land route from China through Central Asia and on the southerly maritime routes from China through Southeast Asia and on to South Asia, Africa, and Europe. China's involvement is expected to expand the region's economic prospects, particularly through access to large loans for infrastructure. This will enhance the scope for addressing infrastructure gaps and economic diversification. While countries within the New Silk Road Economic Belt, especially the five Central Asian countries, responded enthusiastically and positively to these measures, which are expected to contribute to Asian development and integration, Southeast and South Asian countries, on the other hand, expressed more concerns and reservations about the initiative.[2] Anyway, whether these initiatives can be a major solution to China's excess capacity problems remains to be seen. Much will depend on the overall macro-economic impact of these initiatives on China's demand.[3] At this moment, China accounts for, on average, 13.8 per cent of imports and 8.9 per cent of exports of the countries along BRI.[4] China accounts for more than 10 percent of total trade in 29 of them, and of more than

---

[1]   Mathieu Duchâtel et al., "Eurasian integration and the EU", p. 14.

[2]   Zhao Hong, "China's the Belt and Road Initiative: An Overview of the Debate".

[3]   Dollar, David. 2015. "China's Rise as a Regional and Global Power Enters a New Phase." *Order from Chaos. Foreign Policy in a Troubled World.* Available at http://www. brookings.edu/blogs/order-from-chaos/posts/2015/07/20-china-aiib-one-belt-one-road-dollar?rssid=chinas+economy (accessed May 12, 2015).

[4]   Mathieu Duchâtel et al., "Eurasian integration and the EU", p. 14.

20 percent in a further 13 countries. According to the International Monetary Fund (IMF), trade between China and the CCA (Caucasus andCentral Asia), for example, has increased tenfold from $5 billion in 2005 to almost $50 billion in 2014.[①] Over the years, China has the capacity to invest upto $35 billion more in the CCA region.

　　Finally, there is the question how far China can afford the substantial investment that BRI calls for. Though no firm figures have been given for its overall cost, some put it around $1 trillion.[②]The finance involved is potentially enormous.[③]The initiative will be supported by the $100 billion Asian Infrastructure Investment Bank (AIIB). China has also set up the Silk Road Fund of $40 billion, aimed at promoting private investment along BRI. Official foreign exchange reserves, the China Investment Corporation, the Export-Import Bank of China, and the China Development Bank all sponsor the fund. The China Development Bank is said to be investing over $890 billion into more than 900 projects involving 60 countries as part of its efforts to bolster the initiative. While these headline figures are impressive, as things stand now, the paid-in capital is much lower than authorised capital. On the other hand, doubts about China's investment capacity arising from its economic downturn are largely unfounded: China's mammoth trade surplus (now 6 percept of GDP) and the structural need to diversify, ensure that there is plenty of money available. China's BRI-related funds will be able to finance, year after year, as much as the World Bank and Asian Development Bank (ADB) combined, in the range of $20 billion per year.[④] Still, China's slowing growth rate, rapidly rising

---

① "Regional Economic Outlook-Middle East and Central Asia", *International Monetary Fund*, October 2015, availableat http://www.imf.org/external/pubs/ft/reo/2015/mcd/eng/pdf/mreo1015.pdf.

② "The new Silk Road", *the Economist*, 12 September 2015.

③ According to some sources the total estimated investment for BRI could be as high as $4-$8 trillion. See Gal luft, *It Takes a Road. China's the Belt and Road Initiative: An American Response to the New Silk Road*, Washington D.C., Institute for the Analysis of Global Security, 2016. Available at: http://www.iags.org/Luft_BRI.pdf (accessed April 6, 2017).

④ Mathieu Duchâtel et al., "Eurasian integration and the EU", p. 14.

debt, capital outflows, and deep structural problems, which its "deepening" reform policies try to tackle, all raise some doubts about its future trajectory.

2. EU's expectations, aims and strategy with regard to BRI

The architects of BRI have conceived it as a truly global enterprise, extending beyond Asia to Europe and also embracing Africa and even Latin America. The Chinese government has "sought to sell the initiative to European policymakers, at both EU and national level, as a shot in the arm for the region's economy that could revive its growth and restore its flagging dynamism by increasing levels of investment".[1]

While some in Europe buy into this, the overall appraisal is more tempered. Europe undoubtedly does need more investment. Fixed capital formation in the EU suffered a collapse after the global financial and Euro crises, from which it has yet fully to recover. However, there are doubts about how much BRI can offer in terms of a solution. Europe's problem is not lack of capital: it has enough of it. High savings levels in many countries, encouraged by the austerity policies imposed, voluntarily or involuntarily, on Eurozone members, have put substantial financial resources at their disposal. Europe's problem is that a substantial proportion is not used at home but is exported. In 2015, net lending to the rest of the world exceeded net borrowing in 23 of the EU's 28 member states and the Euro area was a net international creditor to the tune of 2.9 percept of aggregate GDP.[2]

Europe's problem is also not that it is short of the technology, knowledge, experience and engineering and management skills needed to undertake large-scale infrastructure projects and investment in a wide range of productive,

---

① Guy de Jonquières, "Xi Jinping's long road to somewhere? China's BRI initiative and how Europe should respond", p. 4.
② Ibid.

wealth-creating activities. By most measures, it remains far ahead of China, which actually needs what Europe has to offer rather more than the other way round. A common view in Europe holds that Beijing view BRI strategy as a way to catch up by acquiring abroad know how and assets essential to economic and industrial development that the country lacks.

As a report by the European Investment Bank concluded in 2013, investment in Europe is being held back, not principally by financial constraints, but by weak demand, by over-capacity generated by the chronic misallocation of capital that triggered the Euro crisis and by a climate of acute political and economic uncertainty.[1] Together, these have depressed prospective returns on investment and made owners and custodians of Europe's abundant pool of capital acutely cautious about committing it. The Juncker's plan main purpose is precisely to redress this situation.

The keys to Europe's economic revival and restoration of its self-confidence lie primarily in its own hands as was made clear in the Commission's communication *Europe 2020: A European Strategy for Smart, Sustainable and inclusive growth*.[2]Europe has to overcome its structural weaknesses. Even before the Great Recession, there were many areas where Europe was progressing far less than the rest of the world. Europe's average growth rate has been structurally lower than that of its main economic partners, largely due to a productivity gap that has widened over the last decade. Much of this is due to differences in business structures combined with lower levels of investment in R&D and innovation, insufficient use of information and communications technologies, reluctance in some parts of our societies to embrace innovation, barriers to market access and a less dynamic business environment.[3] Moreover,

---

[1] Guy de Jonquières, "Xi Jinping's long road to somewhere? China's BRI initiative and how Europe should respond", p. 4.

[2] European Commission, *Europe 2020. A Strategy for Smart, Sustainable and Inclusive Growth*. COM(2010) 2020, Brussels: European Commission.

[3] European Commission, *European Competitiveness Report 2012*. Commission Staff Working Document, SWD(2012) 299 final, Brussels: European Commission.

Europe's employment rates are still significantly lower than in other parts of the world. Finally there is the problem of an ageing and shrinking population. The combination of a smaller working population and a higher share of retired people will place additional strains on Europe's welfare systems. If Europe is to regain its vitality and competitiveness, it will have to redress the imbalances it has build up since the seventies and which the establishment of the Monetary Union in 1999 only appears to have aggravated.

While China's integration into the global economy has been beneficial for Europe, China's growing economic clout has also raised serious challenges to Europe's economic security.[①] Competitively priced imports from China have added to the pressure on the European economy to adjust to new sources of global competition, in particular in traditional low value-added manufacturing. Moreover, Chinese products compete with EU products not just at home but in emerging markets in Asia, Africa and Latin America. While such competition is inevitable and poses an important incentive to European competitiveness, it is clear that Europe needs to develop and consolidate its areas of comparative advantage in high value and high-tech design and production through constant innovation. The more so as China's research efforts are developing rapidly and China is moving up the value chain into traditional areas of EU expertise. As China develops its technological resources, the economic complementarity between China and Europe is dwindling. Recent research at the Brussels Institute of China Contemporary Studies has revealed that the complementarity index for European and Chinese exports dropped from 85 per cent in 2000 to 65 per cent in 2010. In other words, while the overlap in Sino-European exports was only 15 per cent in 2000 it has moved up to 35 per cent in 2010.[②]

---

① Gustaaf Geeraerts and and Weiping Huang, "The Economic Security Dimension of the Eu-China Relationship: Puzzles and Prospects", in Emil Kirchner, Thomas Christiansen and Dorussen Han (eds.) *Security Relations between China and the European Union from Convergence to Cooperation?*, Cambridge, Cambridge University Press, 2016, pp. 187-208.
② Jonathan Holslag, "Unravelling Harmony: How Distorted Trade Imperils the Sino-European Partnership", *Journal of World Trade*, (2012), No. 46, pp. 221-238.

Faced with the prospect of a slow economic recovery and the fall-out of the sovereign debt problem, political forces in Europe asking for turning the Sino-EU relationship into a level playing field have become stronger.[1] Through better market access, European exporters should be well placed to increasingly sell their products on the rapidly expanding Chinese consumer market.[2] While China continues to be regarded as a promising export market and destination for investment, the image of China as a fierce and unfair competitor is definitely on the rise. A contentious issue here is the poor access to the Chinese services market, a sector in which the EU is particularly strong. Unlike the other G20 countries, China is very restrictive about direct investment in the modern services such as finance, telecom, media, and logistics. Whilst total bilateral trade in goods reached €435 billion in 2012, trade in services, is still about ten times lower at €49.8 billion and remains an area full of potential if China were to open its market more. Voices demanding China to take up greater responsibilities in redressing bilateral trade imbalances and supporting a sustainable global economy are growing louder and sounding more determined. A growing part of the European business community feels thwarted about China's trade barriers, currency policy, and enforcement of intellectual property rights. Calls for more assertive trade policies are resounding all the more loudly throughout the lobbying corridors in Brussels and the capitals of EU member states.

All this resonates keenly in the Joint Communication *Elements for a new EU strategy on China*[3], which maps out the European Union's relationship with China for the next five years and definitely implies a strategy of pragmatic conditional engagement. It identifies major opportunities for

---

[1] Denise Prevost et al., *EU-China Trade Relations*. Brussels: European Parliament, 2011.
[2] Rafael Leal-Arcas, "European Union-China Trade Relations: Difficulties, Possible Solutions, and the Way Forward", in Jan van der Harst and Pieter Swieringa (eds.) *China and the European Union. Concord or Conflict?*, Maastricht: Shaker Publishing, 2012, pp. 129-45.
[3] European Commission & High Representative of the Union for Foreign Affairs and Security Policy, *Elements for a new EU strategy on China*, JOIN(2016)30 final, Brussels, 22.6.2016.

the EU's relationship with China, in particular with the aim of creating jobs and growth in Europe as well as vigorously promoting a greater opening up of the Chinese market to European business, thus contributing to the first priority of President Juncker's Commission. Opportunities mentioned include concluding a comprehensive agreement on investment, a Chinese contribution to the Investment Plan for Europe, joint research and innovation activities, as well as connecting the Eurasian continent via a physical and digital network through which trade, investment and people-to-people contact can flow. Looking further ahead, broader ambitions such as a deep and comprehensive Free Trade Agreement can be considered once a comprehensive investment agreement between the two sides has been concluded and reforms that level the playing field for domestic and foreign companies have been implemented. In this regard, China must make significant, time-bound and verifiable cuts in industrial over-capacity, notably in the steel sector, to prevent negative consequences from unfair competition. Further strengthening the effectiveness of the EU's Trade Defence Instruments, notably through the swift adoption of the Commission's Trade Defence Instruments modernisation proposal of April 2013, is key. Meanwhile, the EU will continue to support China's economic and social reform programme through its many dialogues with China so that the country can reap the full benefits of market-led reform, including by eliminating state-induced economic distortions and reforming state-owned enterprises. The communication also stresses forcefully that the EU should work cohesively and effectively as a coherent block to achieve its ambitions in its relationship with China.

Against this backdrop BRI figures in the eyes of the EU as a potentially constructive initiative, to which it is ready to respond in a business-like manner and which it wants to further explore for opportunities leading to cooperation that genuinely serve the interests of both sides, while remaining alert to possible pitfalls and attempts by Beijing to get its way by employing divide and rule tactics among EU member states. BRI is not viewed as a giant leap forward, but rather as one in a series of steps that can possibly foster steadily close engagement with China. As the end point and focus of China's BRI initiative, the EU is well aware of its important role in the initiative. Therefore, the EU aims to take advantage of this opportunity on condition that the Chinese are willing to take into consideration its vital interests and conditions. In the end of the day, BRI is primarily about trade and investment. That is the foreign policy field in which the treaties have endowed the EU with exclusive competence. It is also the one in which China has the keenest interest and is currently the requesting party. Chinese companies are increasingly looking overseas to acquire the technology, management know how, marketing expertise and brands that they need to grow profitably.[1] At the same time, Beijing is keen to diversify its more than $4 trillion of foreign exchange reserves away from low-yielding paper securities and natural resources into more productive industrial and commercial assets.[2]

The EU's take on BRI is clearly realistic. As one observer puts it: "the EU has little choice but to try to work with China. It lacks the superpower status, the strategic stake and the political and military influence in Asia that lead many in the US to view China as a threat. It also has little to lose by trying to engage more deeply with China. Seeking to build bridges and make common cause in areas of mutual benefit mayor may not pay off politically and economically in the longer term. But setting its face against China would not insulate Europe from the aftershocks if the country suffered serious economic setbacks or entered a period of political and social turbulence. Whatever happens, China's economy is simply too big and too deeply integrated with the rest of the world, and the country's global impact too great, to be ignored."[3]

---

[1]   Philippe Le Corre and Alain Sepulchre, "Why China is investing heavily in Europe", in *South China Morning Post*, 15 May 2016. Available at http://www.scmp.com/comment/insight-opinion/article/1944491/why-china-investing-heavily-europe (accessed July 27, 2016).

[2]   Guy de Jonquières, The European Uninions's China Policy: Priorities and Strategies for the New Commission", in *ECIPE Policy Brief*, No. 3, 2015, p. 3.

[3]   Guy de Jonquières, "Xi Jinping's long road to somewhere? China's BRI initiative and how Europe should respond", p. 5.

3. BRI and the EU-China connectivity platform: state of play

China and the EU both have significant economic interests in BRI, particularly increased market access and the developmental potential of countries along BRI. According to Chinese estimates, the number of middle-class consumers in the regions serviced by BRI will reach three billion by 2050, and BRI will create $2.5 trillion in trade among the 65 countries and involve over four billion people.[①] The Chinese economy continues to slow and must undergo substantial restructuring. Therefore, as China's economic system transitions away from a reliance on manufacturing, ensuring both short and long-term profit-making opportunities outside its borders are essential for China and are among the key drivers of BRI. Europe, meanwhile, wants to make its economic recovery following the Great Recession permanent and more robust. While China hopes that cooperation will facilitate the transfer of advanced technology eastward, the EU expects European countries to benefit from BRI as recipients of investment and expertise, which can contribute to economic development and stability, especially on Europe's less developed periphery. Conveniently, the EU's new economic strategy prioritizes the development of various types of infrastructure in the EU and its neighborhood. A $315 billion Investment Plan for Europe (IPE) has been put on the tracks to facilitate the strategy. Significant overlap exists between the pillars and objectives of the IPE and BRI related investment in infrastructure, improved connectivity and development of advanced technology. In particular, the domains of digital technology and clean energy are at the heart of both initiatives. Importantly, the IPE is driven by the European Fund for Strategic Investment (EFSI), which aims to enlist contributions from non-EU and private sector sources.

While Europe has been slow in its response to China's BRI initiative

---

① Guy de Jonquières, "Xi Jinping's long road to somewhere? China's BRI initiative and how Europe should respond", p. 15.

the pace and interest are picking up. The launch of a so-called "connectivity platform" at the 17th EU-China Summit has kick-started a much-needed exchange on synergies between China's ambitious vision of an inter-connected world and Europe's multi-billion euro investment plan to boost jobs and growth. The EU-China Summit Joint Declaration 2015 highlights the two parties' mutual interest in the Chinese Silk Road projects, as well as the Chinese will to support Juncker's Investment Plan for Europe. Besides the Connectivity Platform, the declaration introduces a range of tools to improve EU-China relations in several areas, the EU-China High Level Economic and Trade Dialogue, cooperation in the AIIB, EU-China Economic and Financial Dialogue, and the possibility of a EU-China Investment Agreement. Interestingly, the decision taken at the 17th EU-China summit to set up a "connectivity platform" seems to indicate that the EU is determined to take the lead in shaping Europe's participation in BRI projects.

The 5th High Level Economic and Trade Dialogue meeting on 28 September 2015 led to a number of outcomes that confirm the EU-China connectivity's momentum. Following the conclusions of the EU-China summit, the EU and China representatives re-affirmed the strong interest in each other's flagship initiatives, namely the Investment Plan for Europe (IPE) and BRI, and discussed synergies between these initiatives. The High Economic and trade Dialogue (HED) has identified the following practical avenues for mutually beneficial co-operation. First, the two sides agreed to set up a joint working group to increase cooperation between the EU and China on all aspects of investment. The working group will include experts from China's Silk Road Fund, the Commission, and the European Investment Bank (EIB). Second, the European Commission and the Chinese government signed a Memorandum of Understanding on the EU-China Connectivity Platform to enhance synergies between China's BRI initiative and the EU's connectivity initiatives such as the Trans-European Transport Networks (TEN-T). The Platform will promote cooperation in areas such as infrastructure, equipment, technologies and standards. This will create multiple business opportunities and promote employment, growth and development for both sides, and it will be done in cooperation with the EIB.

During the 18th EU-China Summit leaders from both sides took stock of progress on a first list of projects on connectivity, linking EU priorities under the Trans-European Transport Networks (TEN-T) and the European Fund for Strategic Investment (EFSI) with Chinese priorities under the Belt and Road Initiative. In this context China's contribution to the EFSI was also discussed. Apparently, Brussels was successful in persuading China to sink money into a EU-controlled fund over which Beijing has no direct say. At the 18th EU's annual summit with China, premier Li Keqiang made an initial investment of about two billion euros in a financing vehicle linked to the European Union's 315-billion-euro European Fund for Strategic Investments. The deal that was first discussed a year ago should be a success for European Commission President Jean-Claude Juncker. The latter faced skepticism in 2014 when he proposed the fund because EU governments are putting in only seed money. While China already invests billions of euros in Europe, Beijing hopes that by putting money into a European Union-controlled infrastructure fund, it can avoid past pitfalls of operating alone in Europe and still generate strong returns as China seeks to reduce its reliance on massive exports. The investment also marks a deepening of Sino-EU economic ties, after European governments signed up to the Chinese-led Asian Infrastructure Investment Bank (AIIB), despite Washington's displeasure.[1]

The 6th HED, held in October 2016 in Brussels, appears to confirm the connectivity momentum.[2] Both parties covered the need to see significantly improved market access for EU companies as well as a level playing field for business and investment. The EU handed over a list of the key concerns on

---

[1] Robin Emmott, "Beijing to make good on investment pledge at EU-China summit, *Reuters*, 10 July 2016. Available at http://www.reuters.com/article/us-china-eu-idUSKCN0ZQ12K (accessed July 12, 2016).

[2] European Commission, "EU and China discuss trade, investment, overcapacity and cooperation on states aid control at the 6th High-level Economic and Trade Dialogue", *Press release*, 18 October 2016. Available at: http://europa.eu/rapid/press-release_IP-16-3441_en.htm (accessed April 14, 2017).

market access and encouraged China to provide a list of their key concerns. The EU and China agreed to work together on addressing structural market access problems to ensure that the key barriers affecting both sides are eliminated. Both sides agreed to review progress at the Joint Committee on Trade in 2017. Furthermore, the HED welcomed the growth in two-way investment flows and took stock of the negotiations towards a bilateral investment agreement between the EU and China. Vice-Premier Ma Kai and Vice-President Katainen encouraged the negotiating teams to reach broad agreement as soon as possible on the core provisions needed for the exchange of market access offers, and proceed with the exchange thereafter. Both sides agreed to continue exploring synergies between the Investment Plan for Europe and the Belt and Road Initiative. The expert working group co-chaired by NDRC and the Commission and including the EIB and the Silk Road Fund, and other Chinese sovereign banks will report on progress at the next HED. The HED also welcomed the progress of the EU-China Connectivity Platform, since the Memorandum of Understanding was signed in the margins of last year's meeting. Both sides acknowledged the work done towards the identification of an initial list of pilot projects and towards setting up an Expert Group on financing and investment. This will identify different financing options and opportunities for cooperation relating to these pilot projects, as mandated by the Chairs' Meeting of the Connectivity Platform. The Expert Group was to meet before the end 2016 to discuss how to practically implement this commitment in areas such as public procurement and export credit.

All this sounds promising. Moving ahead however, will require time and effort-and willingness to compromise.[1] The challenge for the EU and China now is to identify and work on the nuts and bolts of their cooperation on BRI. Given their different working methods and cultures, European and Chinese policymakers, bankers and business leaders will not find it easy to work

---

[1] For a penetrating and well-balanced analysis of the opportunities and difficulties on the way to a sustainable EU-China relationship see John Farnell and Paul Urwin Crookes, *The Politics of EU-China Economic Relations: An Uneasy Relationship*, London, Palgrave, 2016.

together.[1] As always, the devil will be in the detail. Perceptions and expectations will have to be managed on both sides. Selecting projects will be difficult and time-consuming. And there will be no quick results. Since BRI involves so many countries and the scale of investment is so huge, involving a wide range of areas, the impact on the European Union is possibly huge and certainly multifaceted. Given this possible impact it does not come as surprise that the BRI initiative has raised a number of political and economic concerns on the part of the EU.

4. In conclusion: EU's major concerns about BRI

A first concern pertains to the question who will gain the ultimate leadership and control over the investment agenda and flows. Regardless of the shape of future China-EU cooperation, Beijing will likely continue to use both political and financial platforms such as the China-CEE fund or the NSRF-to secure further projects in the EU and its neighbourhood. Apart from the leverage such a setup entails for China, it also brings the issue of financial sustainability of China's loan-based approach to the forefront. The IPE is keen to attract private investment in infrastructure to avoid adding to already dangerously high levels of public debt in many European countries. However, it remains to be seen whether potential borrowers in Europe can ignore the prospects of using China's extremely favourable loans for major developmental projects expected to immensely benefit local economies.

Second, the operating mechanism remains unclear. EU officials seem to be particularly worried about whether Chinese-backed platforms and projects can reach high standards for governance as well as technical and environmental

---

[1] See Zhongqi Pan (ed.), *Conceptual Gaps in China-EU Relations. Global Governance, Human Rights and Strategic Partnerships*, London, Palgrave Macmillan, 2012 and Anna Michalski and Zhongqi Pan, *Unlikely Partners? China, the European Union and the Forging of a Strategic Partnership*, London, Palgrave, 2017.

requirements. The challenge is to produce a cooperative platform that satisfies both sides.

Third, concerns arise from more than just the thorny questions of how to cooperate in infrastructure development. In order for increased flows of goods and finances envisioned by the BRI to materialize, a set of broader support policies and incentives, such as the Bilateral Investment Treaty (BIT) currently being negotiated, must be in place. BIT will provide stimuli for economic growth to both the EU and China as it will open markets to investment in both directions. For China the main driver is security against a possible backlash against its investments in Europe. Beijing wants insurance, in the form of statutory investment protection by investor-state dispute settlement (ISDS). For the EU the most important point is to ensure the same level of access to China's market to European companies as Chinese companies enjoy in Europe. At the moment, European companies face restricted or prohibited access to many sectors and are denied opportunities to bid for public procurement projects. More broadly, the issue of equality within the relationship is a top concern for the EU. While Beijing hopes that European markets will be able to absorb some of its industrial overcapacity and ever-increasing amounts of Chinese goods, the EU appears more concerned about whether BRI will create more export opportunities for European products and services and facilitate more balanced trade between the two.

Finally, there is the concern that BRI may not be an equally beneficial deal even within proposed "trilateral" or third-party market arrangements. China and the EU increasingly compete in global markets. Chinese products now directly compete with European goods, and increasingly, high-tech industries and products. As an example, when Chinese companies "win" energy and transport infrastructure projects in the CEE region, this directly translates to a market loss for European companies that have so far dominated in these countries. Given China's willingness to offer attractive financing and implementation by Chinese enterprises, this trend seems to continue. To regulate the competition and ensure that business interests on both sides are satisfied will require coordination and compromise that might be beyond Brussels and Beijing.

A Study of Sino-Turkey Relationship under the Framework of the Belt and Road Initiative*

Tianqin Yan & Jian Shi

Abstract

Turkey straddles both Europe and Asia, and it bridges these two continents. After Chinese Central Government proposed the Belt and Road Initiative (hereafter referred to as BRI), Turkey begins to assume a more important strategic role and position. Turkey's special geographical location and membership of various international organization make Turkey an important hub of transportation, trade and energy; meanwhile it is also exposed to all kinds of challenges and risks. In recent years, the relationship between China and Turkey has been full of ups and downs. When the BRI which aims to revive the ancient Silk Road and facilitate Eurasian connectivity was proposed by China, Turkey was willing to support it, for Turkey's local development projects dovetail with this initiative, and both China and Turkey can benefit a lot from the enhanced cooperation. Under the framework of the belt and Road Initiative, the bilateral relationship between China and Turkey has been much improved, which is in the interest of the two peoples, but there still exist some challenges and obstacles, which should be resolved cautiously by the two sides.

* This paper is supported by the directional research project on a special region or a special country: Approaching the Changing Foreign Policy of Turkey under the Background of Building "the Belt and Road Initiative" (Number of the Project: 17GBQY104), funded by the Ministry of Education of China.

As a transcontinental country, Turkey plays a very important geological role connecting Asia and Europe. Turkey boasts a long history and an ancient civilization. Turkey's predecessor, the Ottoman Empire was the final point of the ancient Silk Road in China's Western Han Dynasty (206BC-AD25), thus Chinese people have been contacting with Turkish people over two thousand years. The 16th century witnessed some travelogues of both Chinese travelers to Ottoman Empire and Turkish travelers to China. It was reported that some Ottoman envoys came to Beijing and paid tribute to the Emperor of Ming Dynasty in 1524[①].

The ancient Silk Road started from China, went through Turkey and finally reached Europe. The ancient Silk Road helped Chinese people and Turkish people to forge historical cooperation and friendship. Both the two peoples had protected the ancient Silk Road for centuries.

As a member of the NATO and the candidate of the European Union, Turkey, a regional power in the Middle East has close relations with Western countries. Meanwhile, it has complicated ties with Central Asian countries in terms of ethnicity, religion and culture. Undoubtedly, Turkey's role in regional affairs as well as global affairs should not be underestimated. Turkey has a population of 80,800,000,[②] and it is a country with strategic importance. As a country straddling Europe and Asia, its engagement in the Belt and Road Initiative is essential for the successful implementation of the project. That is why it is of great significance for Chinese scholars to do indepth research about Turkey, especially, Sino-Turkey relations.

1. A Brief Review of Sino-Turkey Relations

The Republic of Turkey was founded in 1923, and in 1931, under

---

① https://en.wikipedia.org/wiki/China%E2%80%93Turkey_relations Accessed2018/6/20.
② http://www.invest.gov.tr/en-US/turkey/factsandfigures/Pages/TRSnapshot.aspx Accessed 2018/9/6.

the leadership of Mustafa Kemal Atatürk, Turkey established diplomatic relations with the Republic of China under the rule of Chiang Kai-shek. Before establishing diplomatic relations with the People's Republic of China, Turkey had maintained relations with Taiwan for a long time. During the Cold War period, Turkey sided with the Western Camp and had serious prejudice against "Red China". Turkey did not establish formal diplomatic relationship with China until 1971 when the bilateral relations between the U.S.A. and China had improved. In August 2018 China and Turkey celebrated the 47th anniversary of the establishment of their diplomatic relations. The bilateral relations between China and Turkey have steadily improved since 1971.

In November 2008, invited by Koksal Toptan, speaker of the Turkish Grand National Assembly, Jia Qinglin, Chairman of the National Committee of the Chinese People's Political Consultative Conference (CPPCC) and China's top political adivisor visited Turkey. He met then-Prime Minister Recep Tayyip Erdoğan and then-president Abdullah Gül in Ankara. Later, he went to Istanbul to attend a business forum entitled "Turkish-Chinese Economic and Commercial Opportunities Forum".[1] Jia's visit to Turkey enhanced the cooperation between China and Turkey.

About half a year later, Turkish President Abdullah Gül visited China. He was the first Turkish president who visited China in 14 years and he was also the first Turkish president who visited Xinjiang Uygur Autonomous Region in China. In Beijing, President Gül had talks with Chinese President Hu Jintao and attended a Turkey-China business forum. During his trip to China, he also visited Shenzhen and Xi'an, and Xi'an Northwest University awarded him a honorary doctorate. His visit greatly boosted the bilateral economic relations, for seven cooperation agreements on many fields including energy, finance and culture were signed between the two countries. [2]

---

[1]   http://www.chinadaily.com.cn/china/2008-11/27/content_7244165.htm Accessed 2018/8/5.

[2]   https://en.wikipedia.org/wiki/China%E2%80%93Turkey_relations Accessed 2018/8/5.

Unfortunately in 2009, the relations between China and Turkey deteriorated owing to Turkey's inappropriate response to Ürümqi riotsin July 2009. The two countries did not reconcilliate until then Chinese Premier Wen Jiabao visited Turkey in 2010. During the visit, leaders of the the two sides signed agreements to lift bilateral relations to the level of "strategic cooperation", and Turkey became China's strategic partner. In the same year, Chinese and Turkish air forces conducted joint military exercises at Konya air base in central Anatolia. This is unprecedented, which shows that the two countries have remarkably increased mutual trust.[1]

In 2012, as vice-president of China, Xi Jinping visited Turkey. He reaffirmed China's commitment to strengthen cooperation with Turkey in trade, investment and high-tech development.[2] What topped his agenda were large-scale projects in nuclear energy and infrastructure construction. Only three months later, Turkey's then Prime Minister Recep Tayyip Erdoğan reciprocated then vice president Xi Jinping's visit. In the same year, Turkey acquired the status as a "dialogue partner" of Shanghai Cooperation Organization (SCO).

Right after the unsuccessful coup d'etat happened on July 15, 2016, Chinese Vice Foreign Minister Zhang Ming went to Turkey to show China's support to the AKP (Justice and Development Party) government. In May 2017, when Turkish President Erdoğan came to China to attend the Belt and Road Initiative Forum in Beijing, a large delegation followed him. Following the forum, China and Turkey signed a series of agreements on reciprocal establishing cultural centers, international highway transportation and extradition of criminals.

Meanwhile, China and Turkey are trying to intensify their cooperation through many channels of dialogue. For instance, at the invitation of the ruling

---

[1] http://www.mei.edu/content/map/turkey-china-relations-strategic-cooperation-strategic-partnership Accessed 2018/7/8.

[2] http://paper.people.com.cn/rmrbhwb/html/2012-02/22/content_1010523.htm?div=-1 Accessed 2018/7/8.

AKP, the Communist Party of China (CPC) delegation led by Hu Changsheng visited Turkey in December 2017. The CPC delegation met separately with party representatives from AKP, the Vatan Party and the Republic People's Party.[1]

Owing to the joint efforts made by the governments as well as ordinary citizens, the bilateral relations between China and Turkey have been much improved, and the trade volume between the two countries is increasing day by day.

2. Enhanced Sino-Turkey Cooperation in Trade and Economy

China began to trade with Turkey in 1965. In 1974, the two countries signed a bilateral trade agreement. In 1982, a bilateral joint committee of economic, trade and technological cooperation was established. In 1990, an agreement on protection of reciprocal investment was signed by the two counties. In 1995, an agreement on avoidance of double taxation was signed by the two sides. Owing to Turkey's advantageous geographical location, Chinese investors can have access to markets in central Asia, the Middle East and the Mediterranean via Turkey.

As the 17th largest economy worldwide and the sixth largest in Europe, Turkey attracted enormous direct investment owing to its geographical convenience and preferential policies available for foreign investors. At present, the two countries are closely cooperating in many areas such as transportation, energy, aerospace industry, satellite projects and etc.

For instance, on December 19, 2012, China's Long March carrier rocket successfully sent Turkish earth observation satellite GK-2 into orbit from the launch pad at Jiuquan Satellite Launch Center in Gansu Province.

---

[1] http://www.mei.edu/content/map/turkey-china-relations-strategic-cooperation-strategic-partnership Accessed 2018/7/10.

Currently, a growing number of Chinese banks and companies such as Bank of China, Industrial and Commercial Bank of China, Huawei Technologies Co Ltd., Aviation Industry Corporation of China, China North Industries Corporation, China Tianchen Engineering Corporation Co. Ltd. (abbreviated as TCC), ET Solar, COSCO Shipping Lines Co., Ltd., China Wanda Group, CRRC Corporation Limited (CRRC), Northern Heavy Industries Group Co., Ltd., China Merchants Holdings Co. Ltd., COSCO Pacific Ltd., China Investment Corporation (CIC), etc. are investing and doing business in Turkey.

For instance, early in 2004, together with two Turkish companies, China Railway Construction Corporation and the China National Machinery Import and Export Corporation won the bid to build a part of Turkey's first high-speed railway linking Ankara and Istanbul, which is about 158 kilometers' long. It was completed in 2014.

In May 2015, the Industrial and Commercial Bank of China successfully bought 75.5% stake of Turkish Tekstibank.[1] In December 2016, Chinese smart phone giant ZTE bought 48.04% stake of Turkish Telekom Netaş with $101,280,539.[2] In the same month in 2016, Turkish banking watchdog the Banking Regulation and Supervision Agency (BDDK) granted to the Bank of China the operational rights in Turkey. The headquarter of the subsidiary of the Bank of China locates in Istanbul in Turkey.[3] China Development Bank granted a loan of $200 million to Turkish Eximbank in August 2018.[4]

It is reported that before the lira crises occurred in August 2018, Industrial and Commercial Bank of China had granted Turkey a $2.7 billion loan for Turkey's infrastructure projects and a $3.6 billion loan package for energy and transportation investment in Turkey.[5] In July 2018, the subsidiary of the Industrial and Commercial Bank of China signed agreements totaling $3.8

---

[1] http://www.xinhuanet.com/fortune/2015-05/27/c_127845681.htm. 2018/7/18.

[2] http://www.ctc.mofcom.gov.cn/article/doublestate/201711/396571.html. 2018/7/18.

[3] http://www.boc.cn/aboutboc/ab8/201605/t20160506_6855280.html.2018/7/18.

[4] http://www.sohu.com/a/165509971_267106.2018/7/18.

[5] http://www.globaltimes.cn/content/1116093.shtml Accessed2018/7/18.

billion with Turkey at a forum on the BRI, which was held in Turkey.[1] What is more, while being challenged by the crises, Turkey's President Erdoğan claimed that Turkey planned to use Turkey's lira and China's Yuan in bilateral trade to replace the US dollar.[2]

China also cooperates with Turkey in producing metros. Several years ago, China's CRRC Zhuzhou Electric Locomotive Research Institute Co., Ltd (CRRC Zhuzhou Institute) established a joint venture CRRC MNG Rail System Vehicle and Trade Co., Ltd. (CRRC MNG Company) together with Turkish MNG Group, and this joint venture began to produce metros for Ankara since 2014.[3]

After the Belt and Road Initiative Forum for International Cooperation in 2017, China and Turkey signed a series of cooperation contracts in large-scale project, security and defense, finance and cultural exchanges. One important agreement is on international transportation of travelers and cargo, according to which, transportation vehicles of the two countries can get into or pass each other's territories.[4] This agreement is essential for transportation connectivity of the BRI.

In April 2017, Chinese Nanjing Kisen International Engineering Co., Ltd. and CNBM International Engineering Co., Ltd. signed a 7500 t/d cement production contract with Turkish YALIM Group.[5] In order to further get integrated into the Eurasian market, the Power Construction Corporation of China (PowerChina), a leader in China's hydropower industry opened its Eurasia headquarters in Istanbul on May 23, 2017. The corporation has divided its worldwide market into six regions, and it has established six regional headquarters to manage 259 international branches.[6]

---

[1] http://africa.chinadaily.com.cn/a/201808/18/WS5b778482a310add14f386764.html Accessed 2018/7/18.

[2] https://www.jfdaily.com/news/detail?id=99947 Accessed 2018/7/19.

[3] http://www.ctc.mofcom.gov.cn/article/doublestate/201805/400491.html Accessed2018/7/19.

[4] http://www.ctc.mofcom.gov.cn/article/doublestate/201710/2536.html Accessed 2018/7/20.

[5] http://www.ctc.mofcom.gov.cn/article/doublestate/201710/2505.html Accessed 2018/7/20.

[6] http://en.powerchina.cn/2017-05/31/content_29556625.htm Accessed 2018/7/20.

In the same year, SINOPEC Shengli Oil field Company signed a geothermal power project which is worth $80 million in 2017,[1] and HT-SAAE Automotive Electronics Co. Established battery factories and assembly plants in Turkey. As one of the top machinery manufacturers, Xuzhou Construction Machinery Group Co., Ltd. (XCMG) set up a subsidiary in Ankara, capital of Turkey in 2018.

On December 29, 2017, China Nuctech Company Limited (Nuctech), an advanced security & inspection solution and service supplier signed a supply contract with IGA, according to which, Nuctech would provide 450 sets of different types of security systems to the new airport in Istanbul, covering all security check channels. The airport under construction is the biggest one in the world. When the whole project is completed, the passenger flow volume may reach 200 million in a year. The contract was signed by Yusu Akçayoğlu the CEO of IGA and Chen Zhiqiang the president of Nuctech. [2]

Recently, China's e-commerce giant Alibaba group has bought a stake of a fast-growing mobile e-commerce platform Trendyol, which focuses on online fashion retail. This e-commerce platform was founded in 2010, which is influential in both Middle East and North Africa.[3] But so far, the size of the deal is still undisclosed. In fact, China signed e-commerce cooperation agreements with Turkey in 2015.

Nowadays, Turkey is planning to build Edirne-Kars high-speed railway which runs between easternmost and westernmost cities of Turkey by cooperating with China. At present, the two countries are reaching a conclusion of the negotiation about the joint construction project. The project may cost $35 billion, and China will provide $30 billion in loans.[4]

---

[1] http://www.ctc.mofcom.gov.cn/article/doublestate/201710/2480.html Accessed 2018/8/22.

[2] http://www.nuctech.com/en/SitePages/SeNormalPage.aspx?d=406&nk=ABOUT&k=NEWS CENTER Accessed 2018/7/20.

[3] http://www.ctc.mofcom.gov.cn/ruarticle/bilateralinfo/bilateraleconomy/201808/403000.html Accessed 2018/8/22.

[4] https://yaleglobal.yale.edu/content/can-china-and-turkey-forge-new-silk-road Accessed 2018/8/22.

At present, China stands as Turkey's third largest trading partner, the second largest source of imports and the 15th largest market of exports. Trade volume between the two countries has increased from $238 million in 1990 to $27.7 billion in 2016. Owing to complicated factors, that figure in 2017 dropped to $26.35 billion. The accumulated direct investment of China increased from $509 million in 2015 to $809 million in January 2017 in Turkey.[1] In 2017, The value of Turkey's exports to China was $2.94 billion, accounting for 1.9% of its total value of exports. The value of Turkish imports from China was $23.41 billion, accounting for 10% of the value of its total imports, and this figure decreased by 2.8% compared to that of the previous year. Turkey's trade deficit with China remained to be $20.47 billion, decreasing by 11.4% compared to that of the previous year.[2]

China mainly exports electronics, textiles, mechanical equipment to Turkey, while Turkey mainly exports minerals such as marble, chrome, copper and chemical raw materials to China. Chinese Ministry of Commerce revealed that in 2016, Chinese FDI in Turkey reached $642.3 million. According to the statistic figure issued by Turkish Ministry of Economy, 786 Chinese companies registered in Turkey as of 2017.[3] According to the long-term goal set by Chinese and Turkish governments, the trade volume between the two countries should surpass $100 billion by 2020. [4]

Undoubtedly, Turkey provides China with an important market for foreign contracted projects. To a large degree, the increasing trade volume between the two countries should be attributed to the BRI, which is drawing the two countries closer.

---

[1]   http://www.globaltimes.cn/content/1048523.shtml Accessed 2018/7/20.

[2]   http://www.askci.com/news/finance/20180227/154246118697_2.shtml Accessed 2018/7/20.

[3]   http://www.mei.edu/content/map/turkey-china-relations-strategic-cooperation-strategic-partnership Accessed 2018/8/3.

[4]   http://world.huanqiu.com/hot/2015-05/6529987.html Accessed2018/8/3.

3. Improved Sino-Turkey Relations under the Framework of the Belt and Road Initiative

The BRI was put forward by President Xi Jinping in September 2013 when he visited Kazakhstan. So far, 69 countries have participated in this project, and Turkey plays an essential role in the implementation of the this initiative, which refers to " the Silk Road Economic Belt that links China with Europe through Central and Western Asia by inland routes, and the 21st Century Maritime Silk Road connecting China with Southeast Asia, Africa and Europe by sea. The network spreads through over 60 countries and regions, with a total population of 4.4 billion".[1] Turkey is very supportive to the BRI. In 2015, Turkey became a member of the Asian Infrastructure Investment Bank (AIIB), and Turkey invested $2,609 million in the bank. [2] Undoubtedly, Turkey's support to this initiative is of great significance to China. The visits by President Xi Jinping to Turkey and President Recep Tayyip Erdoğan to China in recent years have drawn the bonds between Turkey and China much closer than ever before.

In 2015, when President Xi Jinping attended G20 Leaders Summit in Turkey, he signed a memorandum of understanding with Turkey's President Erdoğan, which provides a framework of cooperation between China and Turkey for jointly implementing the BRI. In 2016, during the G20 Hangzhou Summit, President Xi and President Erdoğan signed another memorandum of understanding on bilateral cooperation under the framework of BRI. Several consultations have been held between the departments of transportation of the two countries so as to implement the consensus reached by President Xi and President Erdoğan.

As a matter of fact, several years ago, Turkey wished to revive the ancient Silk Road. Some projects undertaken or initiated by Turkey can well dovetail the BRI. For example, the Middle Corridor initiative proposed by Turkey is

---

① http://www.globaltimes.cn/content/1046728.shtml Accessed 2018/8/4.
② http://world.huanqiu.com/hot/2016-01/8410716.html Accessed 2018/8/9.

able to connect China with Europe via Kazakhstan, Turkmenistan, Caspian Sea, Caucasus region and Turkey .[1] By cooperating with Azerbaijan and Georgia, Turkey completed a joint railway project which connects Baku-Tbilisi-Kars in 2017. This railway project is the most important part of the Middle Corridor project which enables a train from Beijing to reach London within two weeks. Apparently, this provides the overall Middle Corridor project with a very important link. At a summit of BRI held in May 2017, Turkey's Middle Corridor Plan was regarded as part of the BRI. The "Middle Corridor" initiative led by Turkey is essential to the BRI.

In addition, in 2013, Turkey opened the Marmara Tunnel under the Bosporus Strait, which helps Asia to connect with Europe by rail under the sea. At present, many China Railway Expresses from Beijing and Xi'an run to London via Turkey. In 2016, Yavuz Sultan Selim bridge, the third cross-over suspension bridge over the Bosporus was constructed, which contributes a lot to the connectivity of the BRI.

It should be mentioned that the Caravanserai Project promoted by Turkey, which aims to enhance cooperation among customs authorities of the Middle Corridor countries will be very beneficial to the BRI. Countries along the new silk road should work together to standardize the paperwork to shorten the time of rail transportation and accelerate customs clearance. If Turkey can convince other countries along the Belt and Road Initiative such as Iran, Kazakhstan, Kyrgyzstan, Tajikistan, Turkmenistan and Uzbekistan to simplify customs and border crossings, the trade volume between Turkey and China will increase remarkably, which can not only help Turkey to reduce its trade deficit with China but also help some landlocked provinces such as Xingjiang to accelerate their economic development.

Undoubtedly, the BRI will greatly bencfit from such projects supported by Turkey. Turkey is an essential actor of the BRI, so it is willing to support and participate in it.

---

[1] http://www.globaltimes.cn/content/1117753.shtml Accessed2018/8/28.

Chinese President Xi Jinping and Turkish President Recep Tayyip Erdoğan met on the sidelines of the 10th BRICS summit in Johannesburg, South Africa, on 26 July, 2018. Both of them agreed to make joint efforts to construct the Belt and Road Initiative, to carry out people-to-people and cultural exchanges, to deepen cooperation in trade and economy, infrastructure construction, investment, security and counter-terrorism and etc. [1]

In August 2018, owing to many complicated factors, Turkish lira devalued remarkably, which triggered a series of crises in Turkey. After the crises, Chinese Foreign Minister Wang Yi held phone talks with Turkey's Foreign Minister Mevlut Cavusoglu to express China supports the Turkish government's efforts to safeguard its economic stability. China's positive response makes it possible for the two sides to strengthen strategic communication and deepen cooperation under the framework of the BRI. [2]

In fact, people-to-people exchanges are increasing between China and Turkey. For instance, 2012 was claimed to be the " Cultural Year of China in Turkey". To enhance people-to-people exchanges, both China and Turkey eased visa restriction. From April 16, 2015, Chinese citizens with ordinary passports could apply online for electronic visas to Turkey, which greatly simplified the procedure of visa application.

2018 is announced as the "Year of Tourism of Turkeyin China". Actually, as Turkey boasts a long history and ancient civilization, it has a lot of historical relics. Owing to the favorable opportunity brought about by the special promotion campaign, an increasing number of Chinese tourists are traveling to Turkey. In April 2018, Turkish Minister of Tourism predicated that the number of Chinese tourists to Turkey was likely to exceed 400,000 in this year.[3] As a matter of fact, in 2017, about 247,277 Chinese tourists traveled in Turkey, and

---

① http://www.globaltimes.cn/content/1112648.shtml Accessed2018/8/20.
② http://www.globaltimes.cn/content/1116209.shtml. 2018/8/20.
③ http://en.people.cn/n3/2018/0820/c90000-9492469.html. 2018/8/20.

the figure has increased by 47.57% compared with that in 2016.[①]

After holding the opening ceremony in Beijing on April 17, the 2018 Turkey Tourism Year kicked off in Shanghai on April 20. A large-scale Turkish legendary dance show Troy was performed by Turkish dance group Fire of Anatolia at Dancing Theatre of Jing'an district of Shanghai. The Minister of Culture and Tourism of Turkey Numan Kurtulmus watched the performance. To help Chinese people know more about Turkey and attract more tourists from China in Turkey Tourism Year, Turkey will hold 60 cultural activities which can help Chinese people to know more about Turkey's tourist resources, dance, music, film, painting and etc. [②] Most of the artistic activities will be held in Shanghai. There is no doubt that the promotion campaign launched by Turkey did take some effect. In the first half year of 2018, the number of Chinese tourists who went to Turkey has increased by about 100% year-on-year.[③] At present, there are direct flights that connect Istanbul with Shanghai, Beijing, Guangzhou and Hong Kong everyday. Probably, in the future, the frequency of flights will be increased, and more cities in China will have such direct flights. Chongqing does not have direct flights to Istanbul, but in 2017, Chongqing became Istanbul's sister city.

To promote mutual understanding and enhance cultural exchanges between China and Turkey, China has established four Confucius Institutes in Turkey, locating at Middle East Technical University, Okan University, Bogazici University and Yeditepe University. The first one was established at Middle East Technical University in 2008, co-hosted by Xiamen University. The last one was established at the Yeditepe University in Istanbul, co-hosted by Nankai University. At present, several Turkish universities including Ankara University have set up Chinese departments. Thanks to the promotion efforts made by Confucius Institutes in Turkey, Turkish Ministry of Education gave

①   http://www.globaltimes.cn/content/1099452.shtml. 2018/8/20.
②   http://www.globaltimes.cn/content/1099452.shtml. 2018/8/25.
③   http://usa.chinadaily.com.cn/a/201808/04/WS5b64f612a3100d951b8c893c.html. 2018/8/25.

permission to Turkish middle schools to open optional Chinese courses. Now Turkey is allowed to build similar institutes to teach Turkish language and publicize Turkish culture in China. Such institutes or cultural centers are likely to be built in Beijing, Shanghai and other big cities.

Mutual understanding can hardly achieved without the efforts made by mass media in both China and Turkey. Once, in Turkey there was a Chinese TV show which was entitled as *Sisters of Flower* shot in Istanbul, and many Chinese famous people were invited to participate in the show. Undoubtedly, this TV show helped Turkish public to understand some aspects of Chinese culture and increase their interest in China.[①] What is more, Chinese people should have more chances to watch Turkish movies, and vice versa, for movies can be regarded as a kind of very important medium of cultural communication. Besides, more literary works of these two countries should be translated, by reading translated literary works, the two peoples will surely know more about each other and enhance mutual understanding.

Apparently, the cooperation between China and Turkey under the framework of BRI has boosted the bilateral relations to a higher level, but there still exist some challenges and obstacles which hinder the further development of the bilateral relations.

4. Potential Problems and Opportunities

As members of the G20, both China and Turkey take similar positions in many international issues. For instance, both China and Turkey are against terrorism and separatism, and both sides support Iran Nuclear Agreement. What is more, both sides are against America's trade protectionism. When China proposed the BRI, both countries are aware of each other's importance, and the bilateral relations have been much improved. Nevertheless, owing to various

① http://www.globaltimes.cn/content/1061634.shtml Accessed 2018/8/25.

complicated reasons, peoples of Turkey and China still do not know much about each other, and they even still have some misunderstandings with each other.

Many Chinese people still do not trust Turkey, and they think China should be vigilant against Turkey because during the last 50 years Turkey has caused many troubles for China. For instance, in the Korean War, Turkey sent a Turkish Brigade with 5,000 soldiers to fight along with America. The Turkish Brigade fought against the 38th Group Army of the Chinese People's Liberation Army in the Battle of Wawon in November 1950 and against the Chinese 50th Army in the Battle of Kumyanjang-Ni in January 1951.[①]

In 2000, Turkey refused to give permission to China to drag the aircraft carrier Varyag through the Bosphorus Straits. Only one and half year later, the aircraft was allowed to pass through the straits after complicated negotiations. In September 2013, China did not win the bid for the construction of the Sinop nuclear plant. In fact, Turkey gave the tender to the Japanese-French consortium at the last moment. In November 2015, just before President Xi Jinping went to attend the G20 Antalya Leader's Summit, Turkey canceled its order to buy China's HQ-9 missile. Undoubtedly, the timing of the cancellation was humiliating and embarrassing for Chinese people. That is why many Chinese people are tired of Turkey's tricks with China.

To some degree, the BRI may help Turkey to offset its economic reliance on Europe and deepen the cooperation and mutual trust between Turkey and China. The initiative has great potential to shape Eurasia's future, which will greatly contribute to the common prosperity of the countries along the New Silk Road. Nevertheless, Turkey's ambiguous attitude towards separatists from Xinjiang province may pose some obstacles to the bilateral relations.

China is glad to see that Turkish leaders have reiterated that Turkey would firmly oppose terrorist forces such as the East Turkistan Islamic Movement which has been designated as a terrorist organization. When Turkish foreign

---

① https://en.wikipedia.org/wiki/China%E2%80%93Turkey_relations Accessed2018/9/2.

minister Mevlüt Çavuşoğlu met his Chinese counterpart Wang Yi in Beijing on August 3, 2017, he promised to eradicate anti-Chinese militants and forbid separatist activities targeting or opposing China.[1]

After the unsuccessful coup d'etat happened in July 2016 in Turkey, the relations between China and Turkey have been much improved, and the joint efforts made by the two sides have yielded positive results. But some other obstacles still lie ahead. For instance, with regards to the bilateral trade, the volume is still far from being promising. Turkey is unhappy with the deficit. Owing to various complicated factors, it is unlikely that the trade volume between the two countries can reach $100 billion envisaged for 2020.

Since the failed military coup happened in July 2016, the relations between Turkey and the West have been full of strifes. Turkish President Erdoğan indicated for several times that Turkey might give up its quest for EU accession and strive for full membership of Shanghai Cooperation Organization. Some people may think the tension between Turkey and the West may lead to Turkey's fundamental shift in its strategic orientation toward the East. Nevertheless, Turkey's efforts to boost its relations with China does not mean Turkey will shift its strategic importance from the West to East. Actually, it seems that Turkey still has not formulated a clear policy towards China. Turkey's policy towards China may lie "somewhere between seeking to diversify its relations with the major powers and making a sharp break from the past by shifting its strategic orientation from the West to the East".[2]

To further improve the bilateral relations between China and Turkey, both sides should make joint efforts to enhance people-to-people and cultural exchanges. For instance, Chinese government should take more effective measures to attract more Turkish students to study in China. To enhance mutual

---

① http://www.mei.edu/content/map/turkey-china-relations-strategic-cooperation-strategic-partnership Accessed 2018/9/2.

② http://www.mei.edu/content/map/turkey-china-relations-strategic-cooperation-strategic-partnership Accessed2018/9/5.

understanding and trust, the mass media of both countries should play more active roles and shoulder more responsibilities.

What is more, China can boost communication and deepen cooperation with Turkey within the framework of multilateral mechanisms such as the United nations and the G20 or through the "BRICS Plus" model and engagement in Shanghai Cooperation Organization (for Turkey has been an SCO dialogue partner).

In one word, facing the deteriorating relations with the West, especially its NATO ally the U.S.A., Turkey is willing to enhance its relationship with China under the framework of BRI. At present, the joint efforts made by the two countries have yielded positive results, but in order to achieve more consolidated cooperation and closer relationship, more active efforts should be made by both sides.

Preparing for the Challenges:
To Promote the Dialogue between the Youth of China and EU

Jian Shi* Dan Yi* Zhuyu Li** Qi Mei Chen Zhang***

Abstract

This paper is based on the report from the results of the Jean Monnet Project "European Integration: Realities and Challenges-the Perspectives from Chinese Youth", that we had implemented. The objective of the project is to understand the status of the Chinese college students' knowledge about the EU and the European Integration. We hope that we could better understand how Chinese college students understand the EU, the European Integration and the China-EU relations through the survey of their basic knowledge about EU and European integration. Based on the first-hand information we had collected from the survey, this report, in one way or another, answers the following questions: How the Chinese college students know EU and the European Integration? Are they concerned about the EU and its development? What channels the Chinese students have in their learning and understanding about the EU and the European Integration? Are there ANY significant statistical differences among those Chinese college students from different

---

* Centre for European Studies, Sichuan University, China. Authors would like to appreciate the comments and suggestions for the earlier draft of the paper from Dr. H. Hennig-Schmidt, University of Bonn, Germany. This paper is supported by the project 18AGJ008 from the National office of the Philosophy and Social Science.
** Corresponding Author
*** International Office, Sichuan University

cities or different types of the universities? We believe: if we are not clear even about these basic questions related to the youth at the root, and then we would only limit our discussion of the China-EU Strategic Partnerships between the governments and scholars, the discussion and the perspective of the developments of China-EU Relations would not be a full-sighted, especially concerning the future and further development. Data in this report are based on those from the 23 universities over China, total valid samples are 5446.

1. Introduction

From the List of the outcomes of the 19th China-EU Summit on June 2, 2017: The leaders of both sides applauded the positive achievements of the summit, and commended the fruitful progress of China-EU relations in politics, economy, culture, people-to-people dialogue and other fields. Following the principles of mutual respect, equality, mutual trust and mutual benefit, the two sides will continue to make a full use of the 70 or so China-EU dialogue and cooperation mechanisms, including the Summit, the High-Level Strategic Dialogue, the High-Level Economic and Trade Dialogue and the High-Level People-to-People Dialogue, to enhance the partnerships for peace, growth, reform and civilization, and to further expand bilateral, regional and global cooperation.[1]

For China and the EU, the political will and policy actions of both sides are the fundamental driving power for promoting cooperation and development. From the perspective of specific cooperative behaviors, however, both the economic &trade areas and the cultural exchanges all require the two sides to continuously explore and understand each other,

---

[1]   http://english.gov.cn/premier/news/2017/06/04/content_281475676073214.htm (Accessed at February 26, 2018).

expand and deepen the cognition of the participants for each other. The so-called "high-level people-to-people exchange dialogue" requires not only the participating institutions such as the governments, the sectors of culture and education to establish mutual understanding and trust, but also requires the extensive public awareness, whether within the EU or in Chinese universities. For both sides, the logical extension of the official discourse of "equality and mutual trust" will inevitably involve the mutual congnition and understanding between the two peoples.Therefore, it is of great significance for both policy-makers and researchers to recognize the importance of the mutual understanding. This article will give some results from the data analysis of the survey of the EU's cognitive questionnaire research project which we had done at 23 universities in 2016-2017 in China, these 23 universities are distributed over China, and we had totally collected 5446 college students' valid data.

The Cognitive process is an individual cognitive activity, acquiring and processing information heavily influenced by the collective contexts and the information sources. No matter in China or in EU member states, college students' communities tend to be one of the most important groups for researchers to examine so as to weigh public opinion. On the basis of what have been done already in 2014 in Europe[1]—questionnaire surveys of European college students' cognition of China in 5 universities in Spain, Belgium and the Netherlands, and the results show: Most European college students are willing to make friends with Chinese people, and they are optimistic about the development of China-EU relations. However, there are statistical significant differences in the cognition of China and China-EU relations between the students in each of these universities. In the insufficient information or maybe

---

[1] Jian Shi, Dan Yi, Zhuyu Li (2015) "The Differences of Recognition in China-EU Dialogue: A Survey and Analysis of the China-EU Relation Recognition among the Students from Four European Universities", *Journal of Sichuan University*, 2015, No. 6: 77-85. (Chinese with English abstract)

some errors there under the background of information transmission, media reports tend to be unable to avoid a biased idea, for the European students cognition of China and China-EU relations could be obviously blocked. We should also have a good understanding of the situation of the Chinese college students' cognition of the EU, especially how they perceive the EU. In order to enhance the communication and dialogue between the two sides.

The understanding and judgment of the major international issues between China and Europe Union should start from the basis of mutual cognition of the peoples of both sides. Full and in-depth field research can enhance this mutual understanding and help strengthen the dialogue between China and the EU, so as to avoid miscalculation and arbitrary decision-making.

This paper has particularly carried out cognitive surveys of the Chinese college students' understanding of and their attitude towards EU and China-EU relations. Via questionnaire surveys and interviews, we are able to collect the first-hand research material to conduct empirical investigation, research and comparative analysis. The results we achieve could be used to summarize and analyze the Chinese youth's understanding/recognition of European Union, and these results could be crucial to the decision makers both in China and EU in various promotion and concerned work. From the previous survey we have done in Europe, there are a few questions we need to make clearer in the Chinese youth:

1/. First, how the Chinese college students know EU and the European Integration? Are they concerning about and caring for the EU and its development?

2/. Second, through what channels the Chinese students get to know and understand the EU and the European Integration?

3/. Third, are there significant statistical differences among those Chinese college students from different cities or different types of the universities?

2. Description of the Survey

Based on the survey by CASS 2007, H. Zhou[1] published the paper, "The Chinese Perception of the EU-A Preliminary Analysis of the Survey on the Chinese Perception of the EU and the Sino-EU Relations", and in Chapter 5 "How Chinese college students view the EU and China-EU relations?", they gave such results of the Chinese college students in 2007: most students come from Beijing, Shanghai, Wuhan, Guangzhou and Xi'an, valid samples are 1302 (including some students coming from European Studies Major[2]), compare the other target groups (government officials, business men, scholars and citizens), the college students have the lowest cognition of the EU, only 33.5%, even lower than the common citizens' awareness of the EU 34.1%, the government officials 52.5%, the scholars 69.1%.[3] This finding might mean that the group of the college students are not concerned about the EU, since they have 67.3% coginition of USA. Such cognitive outcomes are clearly incompatible with the development of China-EU relations. In recent years, China-EU relations have been developing rapidly, and both sides are committed to enhancing mutual cooperation. So is there any change in the status quo of the Chinese college students' perception of the EU?

This research paper is based on what we have done from 23 universities in China in 2016-2017, from the south to the north, from the bigger cities to the relatively small ones, and from some Chinese top universities to some local ones. The outcomes would hopefully answer the 3 questions mentioned

[1] Hong Zhou etc (2008) "The Chinese Perception of the EU-A Preliminary Analysis of the Survey on the Chinese Perception of the EU and the Sino-EU Relations", <Chinese Journal of European Studies>, Vol. 2:1-49, 2008. (Chinese with English abstract)

[2] Our survey in 2017 are randomly, not specially including the students on European Studies.

[3] Hong Zhou etc (2008) "The Chinese Perception of the EU-A Preliminary Analysis of the Survey on the Chinese Perception of the EU and the Sino-EU Relations", <Chinese Journal of European Studies>, Vol. 2: 37, Table 5-1-1.

above. The most important objective of this project for us is to promote the understanding of European Union or European Integration among the Chinese people, especially the Chinese Youth, since they are the future of the world and the future of the China-EU relation development.

The basic hypotheses in the paper are:

I.   In the EU Jean Monnet Programme covered area, the Chinese college students know EU and European Integration better.

II. There are differences among the Chinese college students from different cities and different levels of their school in their understanding about the EU and European Integration.

Methodologyof our research would have the debates of the questionnaire design, information campaigns after the survey, data collection and analysis, some interviews combined with questionnaire survey. The information campaigns would be an opportunity for us to communicate with the involved Chinese youth personally, and discuss with them in different social, educational, cultural and geographical contexts. Our survey in different universities had been done with all the participants making anonymous answer and joining the survey freely, same as that we didin Europe.

To compare and answer the 3rd question we mentioned in the first section, there are three tiers of cities in the chosen target group: the biggest, the medium and the small; there are also three tiers of institutions: the top national ones, the middle provincial institutions and the small regional ones. The regional distributions of our survey are different with 2007, the survey in 2016-2017 involves those universities/colleges located in the small and medium-sized cities, as well as different types of universities. This new way can better observe cognitive situation of the Chinese college students.

Collected data come from the following universities in the different areas of China:

Southwest(10): Sichuan University (SCU, Chengdu); Guizhou University (GZU, Guiyang); Sichuan International Studies University

(SCISU[①], Chongqing); Southwest Jiaotong University (SWJTU, Chengdu); Southwest University of Finance and Economics (SUFE, Chengdu); Southwest University for Nationalities (SWUN, Chengdu); Southwest Medical University (SWMU, Luzhoucity, Sichuan); Sichuan University of Science and Engineering (SUSE, Zigong, Sichuan); Sichuan University of Arts and Science (SUAS, Dazhou, Sichuan); Chengdu University of Technology(CUT, Chengdu)

Central& North (8): Renmin University (RUC, Beijing); China University of Politic Sciences and Law (CUPL, Beijing); Capital University of Economics and Business (CUEB, Beijing); Nankai University (NKU, Tianjin); Hebei University (HBU, Baoding); Shanxi University (SXU, Taiyuan); Hunan University (HU, Changsha); Hunan Normal University (HNU, Changsha);

East (5): Nanjing University(NJU, Nanjing); Shanghai International Studies University (SISU, Shanghai); Shanghai Jiaotong University (SHJU, Shanghai); Fudan University (FUDAN, Shanghai); East China Normal University (ECNU, Shanghai)

The types of the universities include the Ministry of Education, the province and the local, covering the comprehensive, the engineering, the medical and also the specialized universities, such as political science &law, economic and trade.

Periods of Survey:

March 1-June 1, 2016 (before UK voted for its exiting the EU); and the September 1-March 1,

2017. Although we considered to divide the two periods of thequestionnaires, that is before June 23,

2016 and after, to explore if there is any significant difference for samples coming after the referendum/Brexit. But after we analyzed the data

---

① SCISU original is SISU, the same as Shanghai International Studies University (SISU) in the East, so we use SCISU in the paper to show the difference of the location.

of the twouniversities from Beijing (CUPL, CUEB), those came in the end of October, 2016, we have found that there is no difference at all, and also due to the balance, we decide not to divide these data in two parts.

As we mentioned above, the survey done in the 23 universities had all the participants make anonymous answer and join the survey freely. The members of the project run the most of the 23 universities to collect the questionnaires, meanwhile also give lectures after the data collections. EXCEL and SPSS are used for the data input and data analysis by the research group members of the project.

3. Results for the Chinese College Students' knowing EU

Due to the large number of the research questionnaires, we will mainly focus on the three questions related to the EU and China-EU relations in the first section to give our relevant research results. First we should figure out whether or not the students are willing to make friends with the Europeans. The answer for the special question: **"I am willing to make friends with Europeans"**(single choice) to show the positive answer (Very strong +strong) is 92.5%, negative (not and strongly not) is only 0.6%, uncertain rate is 6.9%. This shows that the most Chinese youth would like to make friends with the Europeans. In 2013 and 2014, the similar question "**I am willing to make friends with Chinese**" from our surveys in European college students in 5 universities in 5 different cities in Europe was averagely 80%, quite lower than that of the Chinese students.

3.1. To answer the first question: how the Chinese college students get to know the EU and European Integration? Are they concerned about the EU and its development?

In case to understand the basic knowledge about the EU, we list the following 5 questions related to the **EU,** each one only allows asingle choice, the Three-item scale are [Yes, No, Uncertain]

Table 1. the Answer Rate of the Basic knowledge of the EU (single choice, % of participants)

		Yes	No	Uncertain
1	The European Union (EU) is the largest organization of regional integration in the world and has 28 member states in total	49.1	11.0	39.9
2	The EU's top three institutions are: European Parliament, Council of the European Union and European Commission	50.2	10.4	39.4
3	The European Community is the predecessor of the European Union, and its founding countries are France, Germany, Italy, the Netherlands, Belgium and Luxembourg	52.1	13.8	34.1
4	The EU's Motto is Unity in Diversity	58.1	9.6	32.3
5	In 2015 the EU is the largest trading partner of China and China is the second largest trading partner of the EU	31.5	26.8	41.8

We have seen that there is not so cheerful for the answers, only around half of the participants (N=5446) know some basic information about the EU. Then, if we further ask, "Are you concerned about the EU's development?" The following Table 2 gives the results.

Table 2. Are you concerned about the EU's development? (single choice, % of participants)

Positive Very concerned +Concerned	Uncertain	Negative Unconcerned +Totally unconcerned
39.9	16.0	44.1

We can see only less than 40% concerned about the EU's development, this is lower than the negative opinion rate over 4%. We would like to ask if our students over 92% would like to make friends with the Europeans, how they would think about the EU, and why such lower percentage to concern about the EU, for sure the EU is not Europe[①].

To try to understand how the Chinese college students pick up China- EU relationship, the results from Table 3 may give us some hints.

---

① The whole survey including more questions focus on the Europe and the EU.

Table 3. Related the China-EU relationship (single, choice, % of participants)

NO	Items	Positive	Uncertain	Negative
1	There are no big conflicts of strategic interests between the EU and China, and this is the premise of friendly cooperation.	83.7	12.2	4.1
2	The EU and China should become a real substantially comprehensive strategic partnership.	67.8	25.7	6.5
3	The EU and China could strengthen unity and mutually support each other on addressing big international issues.	90.5	8.0	1.5
4	China and the EU should strengthen cooperation in the field of international politics so as to counterbalance the US.	67.6	22.9	9.5
5	China and the EU should enhance communication and improve mutual understanding, especially the People-to-People Dialogue.	92.8	5.9	1.3

* Originally there is a 5-item Scale: 1. Strongly agree; 2. Agree; 3. Not necessarily; 4. Disagree; 5. Strongly disagree. We put the 1+2 as POSTIVE, 4+5 as NEGATIVE.

Clearly, the Chinese college students make very positive answeres to look at the coopration of China and the EU, even only less 40% stduents concern about the development of the EU. The Chinese college students also have high expressions for strengthening dialogue and communication between China and the EU and their working closely on the international issues.

3.2. To try to answer the second question, what channels the Chinese students have to know and understand about the EU, the European Integration?

No matter what information those students get, and what their impressions about the EU or Europe, first we would like to make sure that most information they get not from their own experiences, because there is less than 5% of the students have the direct personal experiences in Europe. So their information about the EU and Europe only can go through the ways indirectly.

In 2007, through the survey by CASS (headed by Hong Zhou[1]), from 976

---

[1]   H. Zhou, etc (2008) "The Results of Survey on Chinese public perceptions of the EU and China-EU relations and a preliminary analysis", <Chinese Journal of European Studies>, Vol. (2008) 2: pp. 1-52, p.7, Figure 2-1-1 .

Chinese city residents in 5 big cities (Beijing, Shanghai, Wuhan, Guangzhou, Xi'an), they mainly get the information about the EU through: "Television (83.2%); Newspaper (52.3%); Internet (50.2%)".[1]This means Chinese city residents'generally understanding/cognition of the EU has been mainly guided by the mass media, specially from TV news channel. The situation now somehow is quite different from the European college students in our survey of 2014, the main channels for the European students to know China are "Internet (61.9%); Newspaper (60.4%); Television (54.2%)"[2]. So, we will see what the main channels for the Chinese college students to know the EU and European Integration. The following Table gives the results from our survey in 2016-2017.

Table 4. Through which channels you knew EU (multiple choices)

	Means	% of participants
1	TV and Broadcast	72.1
2	Internet	44.9
3	Social networking platforms (Micro-blogging, WeChat, etc)	39.1
4	Newspapers and magazines	37.9
5	Books	35.2
6	Movies	34.9
7	Class learning	32.7
8	TV, special programms	23.1
9	Talk with the Chinese friends	9.5
10	Talk with the European friends	4.4
11	Visit to and travelling in Europe	3.8
12	Other	1.7

---

[1] 2007 Survey in 5 cities from Chinese city residents, N=976.

[2] J. SHI, D. YI & ZY LI(2015), "To adjust the strength and tactics of the China Internet External publicity", <European Studies Forum>, No. 18: 117119.

From Table 4, we can see the main channels for the Chinese college students nowadays are TV, Internet and the Social networking platform and the newspapers. It is not a surprise the Social Networking platforms coming to the third if we know that according to the data launched by the China Internet Network Information Center (CNNIC) on August 3, 2017[1], till June, 2017, "China's Internet population reached 751 million, with a penetration rate of 54.3%. The number of mobile Internet users is 724 million, with 96.3% of mobile Internet users". "Chinese netizens are still dominated by the people at the age-group of 10-39-years-old, accounting for 72.1% of the overall population: among them, the proportion of netizens aged 20 to 29 years old is the highest, reaching 29.7%." 99% of the college students who participated in our survey were under 28-years-old, and they are in the group that occupies quite a large percentage of mobile Internet users in China. From the further analysis, we also found that the cognitive channels of social networking platforms are changing as the research progresses from the spring of 2016 to the spring of 2017. Here's an intuitive picture to show this:

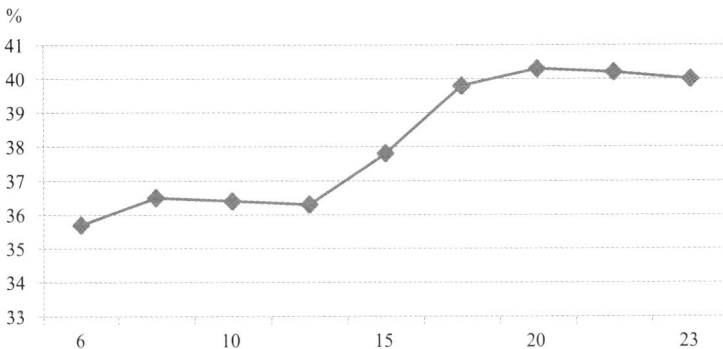

Figure 1. **"Social networking platforms" (The vertical axis)% to "The number of the universities participating in the survey" (The horizontal axis)**

From Figure 1, with increasing the number of the universities participating, the percentage of "Social networking platforms" is constantly changing. From

---

① http://www.cnnic.cn/hlwfzyj/hlwxzbg/hlwtjbg/201708/P020170803598956435591.pdf.

less than 36% the first six universities increasing to 20 universities, the rate increases to more than 40%. At the end of all the 23 universities involved, the rate of "Social networking" fell to nearly 40%. Obviously, the various universities participating in the survey differed in the EU's cognitive channels, so that we could further see whether there were statistically significant differences in cognition in different universities. This is what we need to answer the third question we mentioned in the first section.

3.3. The third, are there significant statistical differences among those Chinese college students from different cities or different types of universities?

Before discussing this question, we need to say: due to the consistency of mass media in China, we removed the "consistency of external sources of information and information dissemination" that was taken into account in different parts of Europe for Chinese cognitive differences. At the time, it means the possible differences between different member states and languages. In the paper, we only consider "university differences/urban location differences". By statistical difference chi-square test, we know all the 23 universities participating the survey on the five basic questions of the EU have the significant statistical differences, because all those 5 questions in Table 1 have test values α less than 0.01.

Let's have a closer look at the universities in different major cities, such as Nanjing University (Nanjing, valid samplesare 295) and Nankai University (Tianjin, valid samples are 289) in Table 5:

Table 5. Nanjing University compared with Nankai University (K^2 -Test)

	Basic knowledge of the EU	α-value
1	The European Union (EU) is the largest organization of regional integration in the world and has 28 member states in total.	0.11
2	The EU's top three institutions are: European Parliament, Council of the European Union and European Commission.	0.006**
3	The European Community is the predecessor of the European Union, and its founding countries are France, Germany, Italy, the Netherlands, Belgium and Luxembourg.	0.21

Continued Table

	Basic knowledge of the EU	α-value
4	The EU's Motto is Unity in Diversity	0.002 **
5	In 2015 the EU is the largest trading partner of China and China is the second largest trading partner of the EU.	0.35

Note: Level of the significant statistical differences: *α< 0.05, **α<0.01; ***α<0.001

We have found that there are statistically significant differences in the answers to Question 2 and Question 4. We know Nanjing University and NankaiUniversityare in big cities, students from Nanjing University come from the School of Social Science, and the students from Nankai University come from the School of Mathematics, both disciplines are not directly related to the European studies.

Why there is the difference? One factor to consider might be: Nanjing University has no any EU Jean Monnet project that is specially for promoting European Integration, while Nankai University has several Jean Monnet projects, that will bring at least some relevant courses or related activities at the campus.Similarly, we can do a comparative study of multiple latitudes. For different types of universities, such as normal universities and engineering universities, we chose Shanghai Jiaotong University (engineering, Shanghai) to compare with East China Normal University (normal, Shanghai). The same as the above, we use the statistical Chi-square Test to compare the two universities with the answers of the five questions in Table 5 on the Basic knowledge of the EU. The results show: there is only a statistical significant difference in the answer to the Third item, it then means, there is the statistical significant difference on the answer about the six founding members of the EU. It is very interesting to know that the Chinese students from the different types of universities have such a difference, it shows that the beginning of the European Integration is not well known to the Chinese students. The same test will be used to compare the Shanghai International Studies University with Hunan Normal University at Changsha, Hunan province, we get the following table:

Table 6. Shanghai International University Compared withHunan Normal University (K^2 -Test)

	Basic knowledge about the EU	α-value
1	The European Union (EU) is the largest organization of regional integration in the world and has 28 member states in total.	0.032*
2	The EU's top three institutions are: European Parliament, Council of the European Union and European Commission.	0.089
3	The European Community is the predecessor of the European Union, and its founding countries are France, Germany, Italy, the Netherlands, Belgium and Luxembourg.	0.002**
4	The EU's Motto is Unity in Diversity	0.088
5	In 2015 the EU is the largest trading partner of China and China is the second largest trading partner of the EU.	0.057

Note: Level of the significant statistical differences: *α< 0.05, **α<0.01; ***α<0.001

Now, through the survey we can understandthe Third item, there are significant statistical differences among those Chinese college students from different cities or different types of the universities. Through further analysis we can see that universities with Jean Monnet Programme know the EU and the European Integration better, or even those universities which have carried on the EU/European Studies Centre Programme (ESCP) in 2005-2007 know the EU and the European Integration better than those with none of them (Jean Monnet Programme, ESCP). That is to say, with the promotion or without the promotion of the EU and the European Integration among the youth is different. We may say this is the difference in dialogues, or at least the promotion events can play certain role in the cognition of the college students in China about the EU and the European Integration.

4. Conclusion

Based on the collected data (through the samplıng survey of the questionnaire and interview interaction), we will be able to summarize and achieve a better picture of the Chinese college students' understanding of the EU and the European Integration. Comparing studies have been based on the sampling from different types of universities and different cities in China. This will further help us to understand the status of the Chinese youth's cognition of the European Union, and the results can be taken into account in the policy-making for the decision makers, also for reference in the work of the strategic people-to-people dialogue between China and the EU.

The implementation of the China-EU diplomatic strategy and the realization of mutually beneficial cooperation depend on mutual understanding between the two sides in addition to their political will. If there is no real and deep mutual understanding between the two peoples, the four partnerships of 'peace, growth, reform and civilization' in China and the EU will not be able to build a solid foundation for the public support. The people to people dialogue, one of the 3 pillars of China-EU diplomatic support, must also be built on the platform of mutual understanding and mutual trust. Further, for the young people, in China and in Europe, especially the students from universities are the future and centre of the politics, economy, trade and cultural exchange between both sides. How they know each other and have cognitionof each other will decidethe future of China-EU relations.

From our survey we can understand that the internet and the social networking platform play an increasingly important information dissemination and penetration functions both in Chinese and the European college students, these can affects their perception of the world anytime and anywhere, they also affects their mutual understanding and judgment. In the use of traditional mass media for macro information transmission (at the same time), how to make use of the Internet, especially the real-time interactive social networking platform, to form the effective communication of the college students from China and Europe, to provide real and attractive information on both sides and to promote mutual understanding are the questions and tasks in front of us that we can not ignore, and even it is a very urgent issue for us now.

Acknowledgments

The paper is supported by projects *562031-EPP-1-2015-1-CN-EPPJMO-PROJECT*, and *574575-EPP-1-2016-1-CN-EPPJMO-CoE* that both co-financed by the European Union and Sichuan University. It is also supported by National Social Sciencee Fund 18AGJ008.

References

Project: The EU through the eyes of Asia, 2007, 2008 http://www.asef.org/pubs/asef-publications/1892-the-eu-through-the-eyes-of-asia.

1. Matthieu Burnay, Joelle Hivonnet, and Kolja Raube, "'Soft Diplomacy" and People-to-People Dialogue between the EU and the PRC'". *European Foreign Affairs Review* 19, Special Issue (2014): 35-56.

2. Kenneth Chan, "Images, visibility and the prospects of soft powerof the EU in Asia: the case of China", *Asia Eur J* (2010) 8:133-147, DOI 10.1007/s10308-010-0259-6.

3. Hanns W Maull, "The politics of the EU: China's relationship with Europe", *Asian Journal of Comparative Politics,* 2017, Vol. 2(1) 55-69.

4. Lai Suetyi, Shi Zhiqin,"How China views the EU in global energy governance: A norm exporter, a partner or an outsider?" *Comparative European Politics* 2017 , 15 (1): 1-19.

5. Li Zhang, "EU perceptions in Northeast Asia: a cross-nationalcomparative study of press coverageand citizens' opinion", *Asia European Journal*, 2010, 8:161-175.

6. Wang Shichen, "China's People-to-people Diplomacy and Its Importance to China-EU Relations: A Historical Institutionalism Perspective", *JCIR:* 2016, VOL. 4, No. 1: 1-19.

7. Zhu Liqun, "Chinese perceptions of the EUand the China-Europerelationship", Chapter 8 in *China-Europe Relations-Perceptions, policies and prospects*. Edited by David Shambaugh, EberhardSandschneider and Zhou Hong, Routledge 2008, p. 148-173.

PART II

SUSTAINABILITY AND OPPORTUNITIES FOR EU-CHINA RELATIONS

EU-China Cluster Collaboration Initiative-The Role of Clusters in Economic Development

Boguslawa Drelich-Skulska and Anna H. Jankowiak

Abstract

China and the European Union are the home regions of many important and very well-developed clusters in various fields of activities. The mutual cooperation between the Chinese and European clusters has been growing in the recent years, and for that reason, in the document China-EU 2020 Strategic Agenda for Cooperation, clusters are being mentioned as a part of sustainable development in the field of science, technology and innovation. China- EU 2020 Strategic Agenda for Cooperation provides a list of key initiatives, which should be undertaken in the short period of time. In the document, both parties agreed to "Establish a China-EU cluster cooperation initiative to strengthen collaboration in the fields of strategic interest such as sustainable growth and urbanization". The aim of this chapter is to present the role of clusters and cluster policy for the sustainable development in China and the EU, and the elements of cluster collaboration initiative that was established as a part of 2020 Strategic Agenda.

Introduction

The mutual relations between China and the European Union have been exerting a profound impact on the form of the worldwide trade, commodity, capital and investment flows for many years. Good relations between both of the parties are particularly important in the global economy, in which China is taking up a leading position in many aspects of the world's market, while the European Union accounts for a considerable percentage of production and world consumption. Initiated in 1975, the mutual relations grew stronger at the beginning of the 21st century as a result of admitting China as a member of the World Trade Organisation in 2001. Repeated meetings between the European Union leaders and the Chinese authorities have resulted in development of subsequent documents that provided the framework for further collaboration. China-EU 2020 Strategic Agenda for Cooperation agreed on during the 16th EU-China Summit held in November 2013 has been the most comprehensive document so far. China-EU 2020 Strategic Agenda for Cooperation is a comprehensive document setting out China and the EU's shared aims to promote cooperation in the areas of peace and security, prosperity, sustainable development and people-to-people exchanges, to take forward the China-EU Comprehensive Strategic Partnership over the coming years. This document was a new opening in bilateral relations between China and the EU, making them more institutional and covering a far greater number of strategic areas than before. The document clearly defined the initiatives that should be undertaken or developed in the following four areas (EU-China, 2013, pp. 3-16): **I. PEACE AND SECURITY, II. PROSPERITY** (trade and investment, industry and information, agriculture, transport and infrastructure), **III. SUSTAINABLE DEVELOPMENT** (science, technology and innovation, space and aerospace, energy, urbanization, climate change and environmental protection, ocean, regional policy, social progress, public policy, cooperation on global development), **IV. PEOPLE-TO-PEOPLE EXCHANGES** (culture, education and youth, facilitation of people-to-people exchanges).

In accordance with the presented document, the mutual cooperation is necessary not only in the area of economic or commercial relations, but also, the initiatives undertaken are supposed to ensure peace and security, and a broadly defined prosperity. The strategy includes a description of the tasks within the economic area, which need to be undertaken not only by the governments of

China and the EU member-states, but also tasks that are focused on cultural cooperation and education, which means are directly related to the societies of parties to the contract. A key element of the strategy-essential from the perspective of achieving the objective of this chapter, is the part concerning the sustainable development and, in particular, the level of innovation and clusters. In the Strategy, "both sides agree that innovation has an important contribution to make to achieve sustainable development, and that effective protection of Intellectual Property Rights is crucial to support the effective development and deployment of innovative solutions and emerging industries" (EU-China, 2013, p.9). The main assumptions about how to cooperate in order to create innovation were included in point 1 of the section on sustainable development, entitled "Science, technology and innovation". The three key initiatives include (EU-China, 2013, p.9):

1. Reinforcing cooperation on science, technology and innovation, involving industry, universities and research institutes, so as to tackle common challenges; complement mutual strengths and deliver win-win results in the areas of human resources, skills, technology, research infrastructure, financing of innovation, exploitation of research findings, entrepreneurship and framework conditions for innovation within the framework of the China-EU Agreement for Scientific and Technological Cooperation. Employ the China-EU Steering Committee and the China-EU Innovation Cooperation Dialogue to this end.

2. Establishing a China-EU cluster cooperation initiative to strengthen collaboration in fields of strategic interest such as sustainable growth and urbanisation.

3. Joint research and innovation initiatives will be further explored, in particular in the areas of food, agriculture and biotechnology, sustainable urbanisation, aviation, water, health and ICT, by developing joint funding programmes and promoting enhanced mutual participation of Chinese and EU researchers and innovators into respective programmes.

In the presented document, the clusters are treated as both an element/

instrument in the process of increasing innovation level and the prime mover stimulating the economic development, which will be presented later in this chapter.

1. Sustainable development and the role of clusters

Sustainable development (SD) is one of the most important challenges faced by today's world. It is perceived as a key trend in the global ecological policy and socio-economic development (Fiedor, 2013, p.10-11). Starting from the United Nations Conference on the Human Environment in Stockholm, in 1972, the scope of problems included within the concept of sustainable development has gradually extended.

In 1970s, the main area of considerations on sustainable development was almost exclusively the issue of the dwindling natural resources, resulting from the progressive economic and demographic growth, and the resultant pollution. This approach was presented in the report "The Limits to Growth" presented in 1972 by the researchers and managers from the Club of Rome (Donella et. all, 1972).

The next decade brought a widely used definition of this concept, a very general and content rich, which was published in "Our Common Future" report, also known as the Brundtland Report, developed by the UN World Commission on Environment and Development in 1987. According to this report, sustainable development is defined as development that seeks to meets the needs of the present generation without compromising the ability to meet their own needs by the future generations. It includes two key concepts (Our Common, 1987, p.37):

- the needs, in particular, the basic needs of the poor in the world,

- the limitations arising from the state of technology and social organisation on the ability of the environment to satisfy present and future needs.

It means that in the SD definition referred to above, the main emphasis has been placed on the intergenerational dimension of needs' satisfaction and on its sustainable character. Publication of the Brundtland Report not only contributed to dissemination of the very name sustainable development and to defining of this concept, but also, most of all, to attaching an international importance to this breakthrough vision of development. The Report defined three areas, recognizing the need to integrate activities within them, as a condition necessary to improve the life quality of all people along with the rational use of the natural resources[1]. The priority areas mentioned at that time included the economic growth and equal sharing of benefits, conservation of natural resources and the environment, and economic development.

One of the fundamental international agreements on sustainable development was the Declaration of the United Nations Conference on Environment and Development, i.e. Agenda 21-a global action plan signed as a result of the United Nations Conference "Earth Summit", in Rio de Janeiro, in 1992, and the Earth Charter, i.e. the Rio Declaration. Agenda 21 is a document that defines a comprehensive action plan for the 21st century to be implemented by both international organizations, in particular, the United Nations, and by the governments of the individual countries and various social groups. This programme indicated how to balance the economic and social development with due respect to the environment. On the other hand, the Rio Declaration included 27 principles of the sustainable development policy, which individual countries, respecting the needs of the future generations, should take into account in social, economic, scientific areas and in legislation. Both of the above documents equated the environmental factors with the socio-economic development.

The next UN Summit, which took place on 20-22 June 2012 in Rio de Janeiro (Rio+20), was held to establish new sustainable development goals. It resulted in adopting a declaration, in which the participants undertook to

---

[1]   http://www.earthsummitwatch.org (accessed: 30.01.2018].

establish new assumptions for the sustainable development policy to 2015. A declaration entitled "The Future We Want" was adopted at Rio+20. The content of the declaration, divided into six major sections, expressed the willingness to renew commitments to SD and to promote the idea of sustainable future on the economic, social and environmental plane[①]. Unfortunately, a careful analysis of the Rio+20 final document shows that declarations and representations predominate over specific solutions.

An analysis of the international instruments can lead to a conclusion that the idea of sustainable development is a strategy of simultaneously recognizing and solving the contemporary economic, social and environmental problems (Zrównoważony…, 2011, pp.13-17). The equality of the three components has been also acknowledged in the long-term vision of development, in the strategic documents of the European Union (COM/2001/264), which reads: in the long term, economic growth, social cohesion and environmental protection must go hand in hand. Therefore, the economic growth must support social progress and respect the need to protect the environment.

Currently, the sustainable development is a concept referred to in a variety of legal acts, political documents and development strategies at all management levels of the economy from local to global ones. Activities promoting the sustainable development ideas are becoming increasingly undertaken at the level of the central administration, but also at the level of local governments and public institutions. It should be noted however, that the concept is complex and interdisciplinary in nature, which ensues from the ecological dimension being included in the anthropocentric system of values equally with other dimensions, such as economic, social, political, and spatial dimensions, which in turn requires a holistic approach. In view of the above, not just one universally accepted model of sustainable development exists, but many

---

① More on the topic: K. Czech, *Szczyt Ziemi Rio +20-jaka przyszłość zrównoważonego rozwoju?* https://www.ue.katowice.pl/fileadmin/_migrated/content_uploads/3_K.Czech_ Szyt_ziemi_rio__20....pdf (accessed: 30.01.2018).

models. They are determined by the conditions changing over time and space.

Nonetheless, as is noted by many researchers of this phenomenon, due to the interdisciplinary nature, a positive element of cognition is hidden. The ongoing dialogue is a stimulant to seek a consensus, but is also a source of a clash between various approaches in the scientific community. Moreover, it allows to integrate the different interests of actors in the socio-economic life.

As Kruk notes "in the regional perspective, the sustainable development will concern not only balancing the relations of society-economy-environment at the mezoeconomic level, but also the components that make up each of these dimensions" (Kruk, 2011, p.218). The issues connected with conducting activity at the regional level are also becoming increasingly important, including the ability to control the directions of entrepreneurship development at the regional level. Such chances are created by the cluster initiatives. This mainly applies to environmental protection, rational use of natural resources, satisfaction of social needs, creating appropriate conditions for functioning of the labour market, preservation of cultural heritage, providing opportunities to public participation in the decision-making process and in actions aimed at development of the regions. And also, dissemination of knowledge and creation of conditions for the development of the knowledge-based economy (Kruk, 2011, p.226).

One of the main objectives of stimulating the cluster initiatives by the governments and local governments should be implementing the principle of sustainable development. In this context, it is about integrating the strategic objectives of the companies within the cluster with the environmental and social objectives. Therefore, development of the regions through cluster initiatives will foster integration of the objectives adopted at the level of the country's economic policy with the objectives of the regions and companies gathered within the initiatives. The idea of sustainable development should create a framework for the principles of using the environmental resources, the quality of the products, and the impact exerted by companies operating within the cluster on society (Kazimierski, Kazimierska, 2015, pp.21-46).

2. Clusters as a source of innovation, knowledge transfer and growth

The concept of the clusters is widely described in the literature; but no single definition exists, the scope of which would cover all the aspects of clusters' functioning. The base definition developed by Porter is constantly being extended by new elements, which ensues from the continuous evolution of clusters in the global economy. One should not strive to create a single definition of these entities, but to get to know the diverse aspects of their functioning and the impact on different groups of stakeholders.

According to Porter, clusters are "geographic concentrations of interconnected companies and institutions in a particular field, linked by commonalities and complementarities". Clusters include: linked industries and other entities (suppliers), distribution channels and customers (demand), related institutions (research organization, universities, training entities, etc.) (Porter, 2001, p. 246). A key aspect of this definition is the geographical proximity of the cluster actors and the simultaneous cooperation and competition of the associated entities. Please note however, that a growing number of businesses is not dependent on the geographical location of their seat and operates independently from the proximity of their business partners. By applying modern technologies, companies operate on the Web or become global, which can result in a new understanding of cooperation within the clusters.

Rosenfeld defines a cluster as "a spatially limited critical mass (that is sufficient to attract specialized services, resources, and suppliers) of companies that have some systemic relationships to one another based on complementarities or similarities." (Rosenfeld, 2002, p.10). Rosenfeld also notes that the geographical proximity is essential for knowledge exchange between cluster participants, "Informal learning, acquiring know-how, and trust building require the face-to-face contact that occurs through social, professional or trade, and business situations.", however, external relations with entities not belonging to the cluster can result in the inflow of new knowledge and innovation from the outside (Rosenfeld, 2002, p.19). According to Crouch and Farrell "the more general concept of cluster suggests something looser: a tendency for firms in similar types of business to locate close together, though without having a particularly important presence in an area." (Crouch et al., 2001, p.163). Therefore, following Jankowiak, it can be stated that "a cluster is a spatial concentration of entities associated by means of a network of interdependences of various character, which achieve synergy through cooperation, contributing to creation of know-how, growth of innovation and competitiveness of the economic entities and regions" (Jankowiak, 2014, p.28).

Clusters are mainly considered in the context of creating know-how and innovation, exerting impact on the level of competitiveness and innovation of an economic entity and the region and in the context of their importance for the economic development of the country, in which they operate. Many authors emphasize the importance of knowledge transfer between the cluster actors. According to Pohl "A cluster is characterized on the one hand by the value of spatially concentrated knowledge sharing, on the other hand by a spatially specialized division of labor"(Pohl, 2015, p.18). The knowledge in the clusters is the source of innovation, which is based on interactions with the associated entities and entities from the outside. Clusters help to increase the level of innovation by providing links between the previously dispersed scientists and researchers by means of connecting proper researchers with the relevant industry, which results in interaction of science with the market. Further, clusters combine different competences of the entrepreneurs themselves and enable to include the local businesses in the networks of TNCs and their global supply chains. It is due to the high-performance clusters that the human capital, its skills and the capital are combined in one network to make an innovative environment, in which you can create a previously hidden knowledge. Development through creation of knowledge is a factor developing competitiveness of the regions (Choe, Roberts, 2011, p.64).

From the perspective of the goal of this chapter, the analysis will also cover the third of the three planes of clusters' operation, which is their importance for the economic development. Anbumozhi, Thangavelu, and Visvanathan identify the key benefits of industrial clusters and those are as follows (Anbumozhi, Thangavelu, and Visvanathan, 2013, p.10):

– Promotion of national and regional economic development, as industrial clusters strengthen the capacity to generate employment and local wealth;

– Poverty alleviation, as industrial clusters may empower specific oppressed groups in society, leading to a more equitable distribution of income;

– Transition to a market economy by reinforcing the influence of the private sector and promotion of privatization;

– Promotion of good governance, as industrial clusters encourage broad participation from the private sector, knowledge institutes, and local communities in the economic, political, and social activities of a country;

– Promotion of a more flexible, innovative, and competitive economic structure, as industrial clusters can easily adapt and adjust to market changes.

At present, the clusters are becoming increasingly connected with sustainable development, which results in changes being made in the definitions of the clusters. The literature presents the definitions departing from the traditional, business understanding of clusters, and highlights their activities towards the society. Anbumozhi, Thangavelu, and Visvanathan concluded that "Industrial clusters lend themselves to sustainable development—directly through economic development, incomes, and well-being generated for the working people; and indirectly, through their wider impact on the local economy and environmental conservation." (Anbumozhi, Thangavelu, and Visvanathan, 2013, p.2). The importance of clusters in sustainable development can be manifested in the following (Knauseder, pp. 9-11):

– Clusters strengthen regional identity and thus encourage the participation of stakeholders in the process of sustainable regional development.

– Clusters promote specific collaborations and networks, in which common sustainability goals can be achieved more easily.

– Clusters foster knowledge creation, knowledge spillovers and joint learning and thus promote sustainable innovations in a "learning region".

– Clusters facilitate the sustainable upgrading of local SMEs.

3. Cluster policy as a tool for economic growth

Clusters can grow based on two basic methods. The first one is bottom-up, in which the networking initiative comes from the stakeholders that are usually companies or entities creating knowledge (such as universities or specialized laboratories). The second method is top-down, in which the clusters are initiated by a local or national authority responsible for cluster policy in the country. Today, the cluster policy, also known as the cluster-based policy, is a focal point of the local and regional policy pursued by governments in countries around the world, as it has been noticed that the innovative clusters of enterprises participate in creation of economic development and clusters have been considered the driving force of economy. According to the definition, the cluster-based policy is a collection of instruments and measures used by the authorities at different levels in order to increase the competitiveness of the economy through the development of new or stimulating development of already existing clusters, mainly at the regional level. This policy is based on the assumption that the main driving force is the market, it is based on cooperation and collaboration of various actors, is strategic in nature and allows to create a new value (Drelich-Skulska, Jankowiak, 2014a, p.65).

The entities of the policy are obliged to organize services in the cluster environment, for example through collecting and sorting information and economic data for the clusters that will be useful for the associated entities and creating an information system for the enterprises about the possible, additional ways of financing the activity. Further, the purpose of the policy is to create investment incentives by building the cluster brand, investing in high technologies and supporting IT centres in the cluster. Another aspect of the cluster-based policy is to build and strengthen the networking in the clusters and invest in the human capital. Table 1 shows good and bad practices noted in the modern cluster policy.

Table 1. Do's and Don'ts of modern cluster policy

Don'ts	Do's
Support individual specialised firms	Support new activities, in particular those being undertaken by groups or networks of related industries
Create clusters from scratch (i.e. implementing 'wishful thinking' of policy-makers)	Facilitate the growth of clusters by building upon existing strengths (i.e. implementing evidence-based policy by building upon a comparative analysis of regional strengths and 'entrepreneurial discovery')
Fund large numbers of widely varied clusters	Fund strategic cluster initiatives that focus on promoting the strengths, linkages and emerging competences and which are in line with the aims of national/regional smart specialization strategies
Follow growth trends without reflection	Capitalise upon regional competences to diversify into new activity areas and to develop emerging industries
Follow a narrow sectoral cluster approach	Follow a systemic cluster approach focusing on related industries by capturing cross-sectoral linkages
Develop and implement cluster policy in isolation from other policy areas	Adopt an inclusive and participatory cluster approach (i.e. involving businesses, investors, academics and policy-makers, and making links with related policy themes such as R&D, innovation, entrepreneurship, access to finance, SME internationalisation etc.)
Support cluster initiatives that are only inward looking	Support cluster initiatives that have an international perspective on the positioning of the cluster in international value chains
Focus exclusively on strengthening regional Partnerships	Build regional partnerships as a basis for joining European Strategic Cluster Partnerships

Source: K. Izsak, C. Ketels, G. Meier zu Köcker, T. Lämmer-Gamp, (2016) *Smart Guide to Cluster Policy*, European Commission's Directorate-General for Internal Market, Industry, Entrepreneurship and SMEs, Belgium, p. 23.

In the recent years, the public authorities in most of the national economies in the world have recognized the importance of the effective cluster policy that might influence the economic development of the country. Therefore, many different policies began to be implemented in order to create favourable conditions for the emergence of cluster initiatives and creation of new groups, as well as for ensuring further development of the already existing clusters. There is no single model of cluster policy, every country adapts it to its own needs, and to the political, economic and social environment. Cluster support programmes are created in the United States and Europe, but also in Asia, which indicates that the cluster policy is a key element of the economic policy.

The interactions between the actors affecting the process of formulation and implementation of the policy are leading to a considerable diversity of the final solutions, even if the same initial idea stands behind each of them. Cluster policy in the world is the perfect example here. Not only the approach to cluster support is heterogeneous, but also the concept of cluster use as a tool in a widely understood socio-economic policy. It is that complicated nature of policy formulation described earlier, which results in such differentiation. For that reason, *inter alia*, in some economies, especially highly-developed ones (e.g. in Japan), the cluster policy is intertwined with the innovative policy; and in countries at a different stage of development, usually in the catching-up or developing countries (e.g. in India), it appears in the context of the development policy. Each country has a complex and multilevel environment rich in interest groups, which results in a specific policy-mix that is a set of policy assumptions, objectives and political instruments dependent on the local possibilities and restrictions.

4. Clusters and cluster policy in China

Asian countries, including China, are increasingly becoming a place, in which clusters are created as a result of both bottom-up initiatives, and with strong support of public institutions. The Asian region is attractive for placement of direct foreign investments, which establishes many new businesses. The entities transfer their experience in cluster creation from other locations, and the local business benefits from it. The Asian countries have a strong industrial tradition so the clusters are formed, as it were, naturally, as a consequence of concentration of specialized industry in a particular area. In the studied region there are many small and medium-sized enterprises, which are involved in the international trade and only due to creation of a cluster they are able to exert a greater impact on the market. It is also worth noting that the local authorities carry out an effective cluster policy, which supports the cluster initiatives and makes economic entities aware of the potential benefits offered by this form of cooperation (Drelich-Skulska, Jankowiak, 2014b, p.81).

The cluster policy in China is undoubtedly a part of the innovation policy in this country, though both of them do not have a clear institutional character. According to Arvanitis and Haixiong "a complex of activities and policies taken together can be considered instruments of innovation policy and these can be grouped into five categories: creation of science and technology development parks and high-technology (high-tech) zones; support to specific enterprises with high potential for technological development; 'marketization' of research centres; creation and support of industrial clusters; and creation of innovation centres" (Arvanitis, Haixiong, 2009, p.50).

Cluster policy in China is not as explicit as it is in other countries in the world, e.g. in Japan, where it is conducted in a systematic way and has different stages over the years. In the strategy formulated by the National Development and Reform Commission "Opinion on facilitating the development of industrial clusters" from the year 2007, the Chinese central government has recognized clusters contribution to the industrial development and assurance of the economic development of the country. The document also includes specific actions, which are the basis of cluster policy. Among the activities listed: to strengthen the planning and guidance, to encourage better utilization of resources, to nurture leading enterprises and enhance specialization, to encourage innovation, to promote sustainable development, to encourage brand building of enterprises and their products, to develop producer services and to ensure coordinated relocation of manufactures (Li&Fung, 2010, pp.13-14). Therefore, the cluster policy in China is a resultant of the innovation policy and industrial policy, and it is carried out both centrally and at the level of the individual provinces. The majority of the industrial clusters in China was established on the initiative of public undertakings, whose development takes place with the support of national authorities. The purpose of the provided support is "to avoid overcrowding of the industrial sector, harsh competition, and degeneration of the entrepreneurial spirit" (Arvanitis, Haixiong, 2009, p.52). The beginnings of clusters' creation and regional concentration of industry in China should be traced back to establishment of special economic zones (SEZs). SEZs started to be created in 1979, when 3 special zones were established in Guangdong as an element of the Open-Door Policy. Within ten years, 19 special zones were established, and the original objective-doubling of the per capita gross domestic products-was achieved. In 1989, the Chinese authorities proceeded on to introduction of the "one village, one product"[1] plan, which assumed selection of a specialized city and helping in its further development. Specialization means that at least 30% of the production and employment must be concentrated in one sector of industry (the so-called specialized sector). Once the city is selected, a package of preferential programmes is created in order to concentrate even a greater number of economic entities connected with the production of a particular good in the selected location (to a limited extent also similar and complementary products or components). Ultimately, the cities, officially recognized as specialized, are eligible to receive funds for creation of innovation centres, supporting development of new technologies and supporting development of relations between cluster participants. Examples of such cities, which also comply with the Porter's cluster definition, are Socks City, Sweater City, Kid's Clothing City, Footwear Capital, etc. "One village, one product" can be interpreted as a regional development policy and local industrial promotion (Jankowiak, 2017, p.76).

---

[1]   "One village, one product" was originally created by the Governor of Oita Prefecture, Japan in 1979; other names of this concept in China are: "one town, one product", "one city, one product", "one district, one product", "one hamlet, one product".

China's manufacturing landscape is characterized by a large number of industrial clusters. According to Medina, it is possible to identify five types of clusters in China, and they are as follows (Medina, 2010 , pp.21-24):

1. Self-growth clusters-this type of clusters was developed in 1980s. They were established by small, family companies, which based their business model on an intensive use of manpower. These clusters produce low-tech goods, and the entry barriers to the cluster are not significant. An example can be production of fireworks in the provinces of Jiangxi and Hunan and metal processing in the city of Zhongshan.

2. Export-oriented clusters-creation of this kind of clusters was the consequence of foreign investors' placement in selected regions, in which they had access to cheap labour and raw materials. These clusters were established mainly in the Pearl River Delta region, in cities, such as Shenzhen, Zhuhai, Zhongshan, Shunde, Nanhai and Dongguan. The export-oriented clusters dominate in such industries as electronics and electrical products, textiles and clothing, footwear, plastics, financial services and logistics.

3. High technology clusters-are mainly located in the area of Beijing, which is the place of operation of many companies producing high-tech goods and of the research centers. Due to inflow of technology with the foreign investors, the capital city of China has become a kind of technological centre of the country.

4. Resource-driven clusters-the existence of this type of clusters is strongly linked with availability of raw materials in certain regions of the country. The main areas of operation of these clusters are forestry, mining or quarrying. The existence of the resource-driven clusters results in further specialization of other industries in China and creation of new production clusters, for example furniture production as development of the wood industry or jewellery as a consequence of metal mining. Those clusters can be found mainly in the provinces of Hunan and Jiangsu.

5. Market-driven clusters-mainly the clusters of wholesale distributors operating in support of other clusters. These ratings can be found in a pure form or in a mixture of the above points.

The most comprehensive program of the Chinese central authorities is the TORCH Programme initiated in 1988. It aims to promote innovation and high-tech industrialisation. The program successfully contributes to development of innovative clusters in China. In accordance with the objectives formulated by the Chinese authorities in the 13th Five-Year Plan for Economic and Social Development of the People's Republic of China from 2016 to 2020, the policy of developing the Chinese clusters will be dynamically implemented. It was assumed that 19 world-class city clusters will be created in China by the end of implementing the current economic plan, in: Beijing-Tianjin-Hebei region; Yangtze River Delta; Pearl River Delta; Shandong Peninsula; Taiwan Straits; Central Plains region; middle reaches of the Yangtze River; Chengdu-Chongqing region; Guanzhong Plains region; Beibu Bay; central Shanxi; Hohhot-Baotou-Ordos-Yulin region; Central Guizhou; central Yunnan; Lanzhou-Xining region; Ningxia section of the Yellow River; northern foothills of the Tianshan Mountains; Lhasa and Kashi. Creation and development of clusters in China will be carried out with the support of the national authorities, which was noted in the development plan to 2020. "We will establish sound mechanisms for coordinating the development of city clusters and promote coordination in industrial division of labor, infrastructure, ecological conservation, and environmental improvement between cities in different regions in order to achieve the integration and efficient development of city clusters" (13th Five-Year, 2016, p.94). Industrial clusters play a significant role in the economy of China and are key drivers for employment, economic growth, and development, and that is the reason for their important role in the bilateral cooperation with the European Union.

5. Clusters and cluster policy in the European Union

The European Union pays a lot of attention to clusters, particularly in the context of creating innovation and industrial development of various regions. The activities taken at the EU level are mainly addressed to small and medium-sized enterprises considered to be the beneficiaries of the regional clusters' existence. The purpose of the initiatives undertaken is "to promote the development of more world-class clusters in Europe, notably with a view to fostering competitiveness and entrepreneurship in emerging industries and facilitating SMEs' access to clusters and internationalisation activities through clusters" (Izsak, Markianidou, Leon, et al., 2015, p.1). The support for the development of clusters in the European Union has been included in the Europe 2020 strategy, which provides for assisting the member states in enhancement of the the smart specialization and cluster initiatives for the rejuvenation of Europe's industry. In the Europe 2020 strategy, under the flagship initiative: "An industrial policy for the globalisation era", the Commission undertook "to improve the business environment, especially for SMEs, including through reducing the transaction costs of doing business in Europe, the promotion of clusters and improving affordable access to finance" (Europe 2020, p.15). Further, under the flagship initiative: "Innovation Union" the member states were given the task of strengthening collaboration between universities, research community and business, which is a practical fulfilment of the conditions set out in the definition of clusters' activity.

There are a number of policies, programmes and activities at the EU level, which support clusters in the emerging industries. Two projects can be mentioned as an example "European Creative Districts" funded as pilot actions by the European Parliament from 2013 to 2015, six projects for "Clusters and Entrepreneurship in support of Emerging Industries" funded by the Competitiveness and Innovation Framework Programme from 2014 to 2016 or the Horizon 2020 action for "Cluster facilitated projects for new industrial value chains" that have started in 2015 with a budget of 24.9 million EUR from the Innovation in SMEs work programme. The European Union also provides tools for studying clusters and the effectiveness of the national cluster policy. The European Cluster Observatory is an example that provides information, mapping tools and analysis of EU clusters and cluster policy with a particular focus on emerging industries. To promote international cluster cooperation EU created the European Cluster Collaboration Platform (ECCP) that facilitates cluster cooperation within the EU and helps clusters access international markets. The European Commission also organizes a series of events aimed at mutual adjustment of existing clusters and help in establishing cooperation between the European clusters (International Cluster Matchmaking Events) and training for managers (European Foundation for Cluster Excellence).

The above-presented numerous initiatives and activities undertaken by the European Commission support the operation of the clusters in the member states, providing institutional and financial support, on the one hand, and, on the other hand, the tools necessary to measure the effectiveness of the activities taken by the national authorities. Despite many EU regulations, so far the member states have failed to develop a single, coherent cluster policy for all the countries. This can ensue from a great diversity of the European Union countries. The European clusters are at different development levels, and the national authorities spend different financial resources to support the clusters. Some of the European countries boast a long-term tradition of supporting clusters, while others, only start to develop their policy. In 2015, the European Cluster Observatory identified 16 actively working national cluster programmes in 15 EU countries, while in the other ones, there are some support programmes, but not in the form of an institutional aid.

Irrespective of the actions that form an element of the cluster policy in the individual Member States, the European clusters are developing dynamically. Economic activities that are located in clusters account for about 39 % of European jobs and 55 % of European wages (Izsak, Ketels, Meier zu Köcker, Lämmer-Gamp, 2016, p.16). At present, the European Union has as much as 3043 strong regional clusters which account for 46% of all traded industries employment (Ketels, Protsiv, 2016, p.12). According to the data presented in the European Cluster Panorama 2016 (Ketels, Protsiv, 2016, p.i):

- 3 000 strong clusters across Europe account for more than 54 million jobs and 45% of all traded industries' wages (23% of the overall economy),

- wages in strong clusters are close to 3% higher than in industries not located in such regional hotspots, and the wage gap towards both other traded industries and the overall economy is growing,

- 103 leading clusters are in the top 20% of European peers across all four performance dimensions measured (size, specialisation, productivity, and dynamism),

- all parts of Europe have clusters; 55% of all European regions have between 30% and 60% of traded industries employment in strong clusters,

- strong clusters have shown resilience through the crisis; their share in total traded industry employment and wages has from 2008 to 2014 increased slightly to 45% (jobs) and 51% (wages),

- the industrial cluster landscape is constantly evolving as a result of changes in market conditions, technologies, and competition; about one fifth (20%) of all clusters significantly changed in their market position (strong, medium, weak) between 2008 and 2014.

The development of the European clusters is a dynamic process that can be a model for other regions. The European clusters are mainly formed on the initiative of the companies specializing in a specific production or services, while their operation is widely supported by diverse tools of the cluster policy and dedicated units of the European Union that provide advice and funding.

6. China-EU cluster collaboration initiative

Based on the considerations in this chapter, it may be concluded that the objectives of the cluster policy in China and in the European Union coincide, and the understanding of clusters and their importance for the sustainable development is the same. Another common feature is the institutional structure of the policy, as it is carried out at the level of the central authority in China and the European Commission in the European Union, and at the level of the individual Chinese provinces and the European countries. The endeavours of both centres to create innovative and competitive economies and create knowledge by the clusters is a common ground for agreement, and also allows to identify points of contact in the mutual relations.

In accordance with the provisions of China-EU 2020 Strategic Agenda for Cooperation, the parties of the agreement shall endeavour to develop the bilateral relations in the context of the inter-cluster cooperation. For that purpose a range of actions is undertaken to stimulate the cooperation between the Chinese and European clusters. Table 2 presents selected initiatives activating collaboration between clusters from 2016 to 2017.

Table 2. Cluster collaboration events between China and EU organized in 2016-2017

Date	Name	Target	Type
5 July, 2016	West China Business Delegation to Europe 2016	SME	Matchmaking
8 July, 2016	The Dragon-Starplus Eu-Chinese Brokerage Event	Cluster managers, Investors, SME	Matchmaking
16 November, 2016	Chinese opportunities: business Tour to Shenzhen, China 16th-21st November 2016 for the ICT and greentech sectors	Cluster managers, Investors, SME	Matchmaking, Workshop
23 November, 2016	Explore green business opportunities in China	SME	Matchmaking
20 March, 2017	Clean Technologies business mission to CHINA	SME	Matchmaking
4 April, 2017	International IPRs SME Helpdesks Stakeholders Meeting	Cluster managers, Large audience, SME	Conference, Matchmaking
14 June, 2017	Business Seminar: Opportunities in Asia for SMEs	Cluster managers, SME	Matchmaking, Seminar
4 December, 2017	Healthcare & Medical Technologies Business Mission, Shanghai	Cluster managers, Cluster Policy Makers, Investors, Large audience, Project coordinators, SME	Seminar, Workshop

Source: European Cluster Collaboration Platform, China, https://www.clustercollaboration.eu/international-cooperation/china#int-coo-news-pane (date of access January 2018).

The most widely implemented initiatives are cluster matchmaking missions, many editions of which have already been held both in China and in the European Union. Matchmaking tour to Portugal and China coordinated by the European Research and Innovation Center of Excellence in China (ERICENA) may be an example. ERICENA is an example of institutionalized cooperation between the European Union and China. It is a project established in January 2017 by the European Commission as part of Horizon 2020, assuming provision of comprehensive and diversified services to support and facilitate relations with China in the area of research, innovation and business. The first tour took place in January 2017, and the second in October 2017. During the stay in China, the informative sessions were conducted in Beijing, Chengdu and Qingdao, and were attended by more than 1.5 thousand people from companies, state or regional governments, clusters, business associations, EU-China Cooperation experts, universities and R&D institutions. During the sessions, more than 50 most competitive clusters in China were presented. The meetings and matchmaking sessions of this type are held on a regular basis. Some of them are dedicated to a specific industry (e.g. Food Safety Technologies & Services in May 2017, in China) or are universal and not limited to one branch of industry. The meetings create an excellent opportunity to meet the foreign partners, acquire knowledge about the operation of clusters from your business environment and about functioning inside the cluster. According to Zhihong (Executive Deputy Director General of the Torch High Technology Development Centre) "The objective of our visit is to learn from EU experience how to better organise cluster initiatives and create better links with international partners, particularly for those firms active in the fields of emerging industries, creative industries, clean tech and renewable energy" (SME Internationalization). Another example of events supposed to bring closer the cluster entities from China and the EU can be NATUREEF-Sino-Europe Agro Innovation Business Mission to China organized in June 2017, or Urban EU-China Event Cluster organized in Brussels, in October 2017.

China is one of the key partner countries in the European initiative The

European Strategic Cluster Partnerships-Going International (ESCP-4i). It was created at the beginning of 2016 by the European Commission, DG Growth and the Executive Agency for SMEs of the European Commission. The ESCP-4i "are transnational cluster partnerships that develop and implement a joint internationalisation strategy and support SME internationalisation towards third countries beyond Europe"(ESCP-4i in brief). The purpose of this initiative is "to intensify cluster and business network collaboration across European countries and also across sectoral boundaries and to support the establishment of European Strategic Cluster Partnerships to lead international cluster cooperation in fields of strategic interest towards third countries beyond Europe and notably in support of the development of emerging industries" (Cluster Go International). In this programme, one may apply for grants up to EUR 200 thousand, which are designed to support the cooperation between clusters and business organizations. In the first edition, 25 clusters were selected from among 140 associated clusters (from 23 member countries). 15 clusters received funding for activities related to action "Clusters Go International", while 10 others were put on the reserve list receiving non-financial support. From among 25 clusters participating in the programme, as many as 12 of them indicated China as a target market for their operations and mutual collaboration. Chinese market-oriented clusters gather almost 7 thousand small and medium-size companies and represent various sectors of the EU economy, starting from the transport and logistics, through environmental services, up to the high-tech sectors, such as electronics, IT and telecommunication. Such a choice ranks China in the second place (after the United States) among the most popular directions of cooperation within the ESCPs-4i project.

Another example of the Chinese-European cooperation is the European Network of Research and Innovation of Centres and Hubs (ENRICH). This unit was established as part of a Horizon 2020 strategy in October 2017 and is seated in Beijing and Chengdu. ENRICH is a global network of centres and hubs that promotes the internationalisation of European science, technology and innovation. The main task of this unit is to assist the European organisations and companies entering the Chinese market. The first meeting organized by ENRICH in China in October 2017 was attended by representatives of 20 EU countries.

The main purpose of the Dragon-Star Plus programme from 2015 to 2018 is to support the bilateral contacts and cooperation. In particular, the Dragon-Star Plus programme is responsible for:

• Support the European and Chinese research communities to establish collaborations under Horizon 2020 and beyond.

• Provide a cooperation platform and tools to policy makers, aiming ultimately to support and enhance the bilateral cooperation, through the concept of mutual benefit.

• Provide an ERA-NET style platform to funding agencies for exchanging best practices and planning joint activities in the field.

The programme assumes that it will have a positive effect on policy drafting and implementation, on-going research collaboration, reciprocity, member and associated states cooperation (funding agencies), addressing societal challenges, innovation, social- economy and technology. It should be noted that even though the development of clusters and cluster cooperation is not a direct purpose of the program, its objectives and activities can be given as an example of cooperation between EU and China in the studied area. In the framework of Dragon-Star Plus, the EU-China Think Thank Workshop was organised for example in November 2017, during which an interesting and up-to-date topic was discussed directly related to the Chinese clusters that is "The Future of Manufacturing. Industry 4.0 Meets Made in China 2025".

Summary

Sustainable development is one of the most important challenges faced by today's world. It is perceived as a key trend of the socio-economic development. The concept of sustainable development has been referred to in a variety of legal acts, political documents and development strategies at all management levels of the economy from local to global ones. Activities promoting the sustainable development ideas are becoming increasingly undertaken at the level of the central administration, but also at the level of local governments and public institutions. Its concept is complex and interdisciplinary in nature, which ensues from the ecological dimension being included in the anthropocentric system of values equally with other dimensions, such as economic, social, political, and spatial dimensions. One of the main objectives of stimulating the cluster initiatives by the governments and local governments should be implementing the principle of sustainable development. In this context, it is about integrating the strategic objectives of the companies within the cluster with the environmental and social objectives, which enhances the level of innovation and competition of the national economies.

China-EU 2020 Strategic Agenda for Cooperation is a comprehensive plan setting out the directions of collaboration between the major players of the global economy. The mutual cooperation aims to achieve sustainable development also by means of creating strong relations between the Chinese and European clusters. The cross-border cooperation is the basis of the cluster development strategy both in China and in the European Union. It seems that it is a huge challenge for both parties of the agreement, because not only the clusters themselves, but also the cluster policies forming them, are at different stages of development and have different activity profiles. The ambitious goal set in the Strategic Agenda should be accompanied by an in-depth analysis of problems, such as barriers and risks limiting the collaboration between the Chinese and European clusters, or the potential benefits from collaboration. Among such barriers, lack of mutual trust between the business partners should be indicated first of all, along with lack of financing for activities aiming to establish cooperation, conflict of interests and competition on the market, geographical distance, as well as problems with communication emerging due to the cultural and linguistic differences. Undeniably, the greatest challenge is mutual recognition of the models for functioning of clusters and units associated in them (which ensue from different systems of conducting business in China and the European Union) and identification and promotion of potential profits brought by the collaboration. Among the benefits, exchange of knowledge and know-how can be indicated, along with exchange of experiences and good practices, as well as joint business project and economic activity on partner's markets.

In the summary of activities carried out by the European Commission in cooperation with the authorities of China, it should be noted that the collaboration between the Chinese and European clusters is not at an advanced stage at present, although obviously, different initiatives are undertaken to stimulate the creation of the cluster partnership. So far, the group that has been the largest beneficiary of bilateral cooperation are the economic entities to whom a larger part of the initiatives is directed. The weakest point is the scientific cooperation and cooperation in the area of R&D, which could, in fact, provide a stable platform for further development of the bilateral relations.

Since China- EU 2020 Strategic Agenda for Cooperation has entered into force, no common institution has been established to comprehensively implement the objectives set in the document aimed at cooperation between the clusters. Both the European and the Chinese authorities recognize the need for collaboration, but their activities are dispersed. Various programmes, which provide the economic entities and cluster management units with information, assistance and funding are growing in number, but such a support is not institutional, it rather has a one-time character and often accidental.

References

13th Five-Year Plan for Economic and Social Development of the People's Republic of China (2016-2020); *en.ndrc.gov.cn/newsrelease/201612/ P020161207645765233498.pdf.*

Venkatachalam Anbumozhi, Shandre Mugan Thangavelu and Chettiyappan Visvanathan, *Eco-industrial clusters: A prototype training manual*. Tokyo: Asian Development Bank Institute, 2013.

Rigas Arvanitis and Qiu Haixiong, "Research for policy development: Industrial clusters in South China". in: Michael Graham and Jean Woo (eds.), *Fuelling Economic Growth: The Role of Public-Private Sector Research in Development*, International Development Research Centre, Ottawa, 2009.

KyeongAe Choe and Brian Roberts, *Competitive Cities in the 21st Century: Cluster-Based Local Economic Development*, Asian Development Bank, Manila, 2011.

Cluster Go International, (2016), COS-CLUSINT-2016-03-01, https://ec.europa.eu/easme/en/cos-clusint-2016-03-01-cluster-go-international.

Colin Crouch, Patrick Le Galés, Carlo Trigilia and Helmut Voelzkow, *Local Production System in Europe: Rise or Demise?* Oxford: Oxford University Press, 2001.

Katarzyna Czech, "*Szczyt Ziemi Rio +20-jaka przyszłość zrównoważonego rozwoju?"* Report, 2013.ttps://www.ue.katowice.pl/fileadmin/_migrated/content_uploads/3_K.Czech_Szyt_ziemi_rio__20....pdf (accessed: 30.01.2018)

Dragon Star Plus, http://www.dragon-star.eu/dragon-star-plus/.

Bogusława Drelich-Skulska, Anna H. Jankowiak, "Polityka innowacyjna versus polityka klastrowa jako źródło przewagi konkurencyjnej we współczesnej gospodarce światowej*". in: Bogusława Drelich-Skulska, Anna H. Jankowiak, Szymon Mazure (eds.), *Klastry jako nośnik innowacyjności przedsiębiorstw i regionów. Czy doświadczenia azjatyckie można wykorzystać w warunkach gospodarki polskiej*?, Publishing House of Wroclaw University of Economics, Wroclaw, 2014a.

Bogusława Drelich-Skulska, Anna H. Jankowiak, "Zrównoważone modele polityki klastrowej w wybranych krajach azjatyckich i w Polsce"*, in: Bogusława Drelich-Skulska, Anna H. Jankowiak, Szymon Mazure (eds.), *Klastry jako nośnik innowacyjności przedsiębiorstw i regionów. Czy doświadczenia azjatyckie można wykorzystać w warunkach gospodarki* *polskiej?*, Publishing House of Wroclaw University of Economics, Wroclaw (2014b).

ESCP-4i in brief, https://www.clustercollaboration.eu/eu-cluster-partnerships.

EU-China 2020 Strategic Agenda for Cooperation (2013), http://eeas.europa.eu/archives/docs/china/docs/eu-china_2020_strategic_agenda_en.pdf.

Europe 2020, A European strategy for smart, sustainable and inclusive growth, (2010), Brussels, 3.3.2010 COM(2010) 2020, https://www.eea.europa.eu/policy-documents/com-2010-2020-europe-2020.

European Cluster Collaboration Platform, China, https://www.clustercollaboration.eu/international-cooperation/china#int-coo-news-pane.

Boguslaw Fiedor, "Normatywny charakter koncepcji trwałego rozwoju a potrzeba poszukiwania jej podstaw mikroekonomicznych", *Handel wewnętrzny*, 2013, Vol.I:7-20.

Kincsö Izsak, Christian Ketels, Gerd Meier zu Köcker and Thomas Lämmer-Gamp, *Smart Guide to Cluster Policy*, European Commission's Directorate-General for Internal Market, Industry, Entrepreneurship and SMEs, 2016, Belgium.

Kincsö Izsak, Paresa Markianidou, Lorena Rivera Leon, Kastalie Bougas, Thomas Teichler, Helmut Kergel, Thomas Köhler, Gerd Meier zu Köcker, and Kai Pflanz, "European Cluster Trends*"*, *European Cluster Observatory Report*, 2015.

Anna H. Jankowiak, "Klastry jako nośnik innowacyjności-ujęcie teoretyczne*"*, in: Bogusława Drelich-Skulska, Anna H. Jankowiak, Szymon Mazurek (eds.), *Klastry jako nośnik innowacyjności przedsiębiorstw i regionów. Czy doświadczenia azjatyckie można wykorzystać w warunkach gospodarki polskiej?*, Publishing House of Wroclaw University of Economics, Wroclaw, 2014.

Anna H. Jankowiak, "Cluster-based development: A Chinese cluster policy*"*. in: Bogusława Drelich-Skulska, Anna H. Jankowiak (eds.) *The Development Challenges of Asia-Pacific Countries*, 2017, Research Papers no.

486, Publishing House of Wroclaw University of Economics, Wroclaw.

Ron Johnston, *Clusters: A Review. Mapping Australia's Science and Innovation System Taskforce*, Department of Education, Science and Training, Australian Center for Innovation Limited, March 2003.

Jan Kazimierski, Sylwana Kazimierska, "Klastry jako potencjał rozwoju regionu", *Logistyka*, 2015, No.3.

Christian H.M. Ketels, Sergiy Protsiv, "European Cluster Panorama 2016", Center for Strategy and Competitiveness Stockholm School of Economics, *European Cluster Observatory*, 2016.

Julia Knauseder, "Business clusters as drivers of sustainable regional development?", *Report,* 2009, University of Vienna. https://emnet.univie.ac.at/uploads/media/Knauseder_01.pdf.

Honorata Kruk, "Zrównoważony rozwój regionów-ujęcie teoretyczne", (w:) Kryk B., (ed.), *Trendy i wyzwania zrównoważonego rozwoju,* Zapol, Szczecin, 2011.

Li&Fung Research Center, Industrial Clusters Series, Issues 6, June, 2010.

Donella H. Meadows, Dennis l. Meadows, Jorgen Randers , William W. Behrens III, *The Limits to Growth*, A Potomac Association Book, 1972. http://collections.dartmouth.edu/teitexts/meadows/diplomatic/meadows_ltg diplomatic.html (accessed: 24.01.2018).

Francisco López Medina, "Cluster policies in two emerging economies: Mexico and China", *Korea Review of International Studies*, 2010, vol. 13, no. 2.

Our Common Future. Report of the World Commission on Environment and Development (1987), https://stat.gov.pl/zrownowazony-rozwoj/akty-prawne-i-dokumenty-strategiczne/ (accessed:24.01.2018).

Alina Pohl, "Eco-Clusters as Driving Force for Greening Regional Economic Policy", *Policy Paper*, 2015, no 27.

Michael E.Porter, *Porter o konkurencji,* PWE, 2001, Warszawa.

Stuart Rosenfeld, *Just Clusters: E Economic Development Strategies that Reach More People and Places,* Carrboro, NC: Regional Technology Strategies, Inc., 2002.

SME Internationalisation Through Clusters between EU and China to Gain Momentum, EU Project Innovation Centre (Chengdu), http://www.eupic. org.cn/article/detail.html?id=448.

Zrównoważony rozwój-idea, definicje, mierniki, (w:) M. Stanny, A. Czarnecki, *Zrównoważony rozwój obszarów wiejskich Zielonych Płuc Polski. Próba analizy empirycznej,* Instytut Rozwoju Wsi i Rolnictwa Polskiej Akademii Nauk, Warszawa, 2011. http://admin.www.irwirpan.waw.pl/dir_ upload/site/files/Monika/ksiazka2011/r01.pdf.

The perspectives on interregional cluster cooperation under BRI Frame

Arkadiusz M. Kowalski

Abstract

The objective of the chapter is to present the role of clusters in the Belt and Road Initiative (BRI), and to analyze corresponding opportunities of developing interregional economic cooperation. This relates to the observation that clusters gradually extend beyond the scope of a given location, entering business relations with actors based in other locations. The rationale for this research is connected to one of the key objectives of the Belt and Road Initiative, which is to boost international and interregional co-operation within Eurasia, by e.g. strengthening transport linkages. As the investments under BRI will become platforms for clustering of industries, the key elements of the new Silk Road will be not only emerging logistic and transport clusters, but also international networks of local cluster structures integrated across the whole value chains in different areas. This finding is very important for China, which experience dynamic process of clusters development, not limited to megacities, like Beijing and Shanghai, but also taking place in second-tier cities, such as Chongqing, Chengdu or Wuhan. The chapter also presents three of the most important locations on the New Silk Road in Poland: Warsaw, Łódź and Kutno. All of them constitute the local clusters of different types of actors and are the elements of the network developed under BRI frame. As Poland is not the final destination in BRI, but rather remains a gateway, through which China can get access to its largest trading partners in Western Europe, making use of central location in Europe may result in the development of transit and logistics clusters in this country, with strong advantages for economic development.

Introduction

The rationale for the paper relates to one of the key objectives of the Belt and Road Initiative, which is to boost international and interregional co-operation within Eurasia, by e.g. strengthening transport linkages. In terms of industrial co-operation, the investments under BRI will become platforms for clustering of industries. Hence, the pillar elements of the new Silk Road will be not only emerging clusters (mainly logistic and transport clusters), but also international networks of local cluster structures integrating industrial chains, so all involved countries and regions can build on their comparative advantages and entire industrial sectors can develop in concert. The objective of the paper is to present the role of clusters in the BRI, and analyse corresponding opportunities of developing interregional economic cooperation. This relates to the observation that clusters gradually extend beyond the scope of a given location, entering business relations with actors based in other locations. Special focus is put on the process of dynamic clusters development in China in recent years. It is not limited to megacities, like Beijing and Shanghai, but also takes place in second-tier cities, such as Chongqing, Chengdu or Wuhan, which have become important locations for high-technology clusters. From this perspective, special role of BRI in regional development of China is presented, as it aims to develop inland regions, with focus on the city clusters along the middle reaches of the Yangtze River, especially around Chengdu and Chongqing, which may become an important pivot for opening up the western region. The paper presents also three of the most important locations on the New Silk Road in Poland: Warsaw, Łódź and Kutno. All of them constitute the local clusters of different types of actors and are the elements of the network developed under BRI frame.

1. Defining clusters and their role in economic development

Clustering has become a very important topic, with clusters being seen as a key factor influencing entrepreneurship (Pascal 2005), innovativeness and regional development (Porter 1990, 1998, 2008). In modern world economy, economic activity, especially in high-tech sectors, tends to concentrate around metropolitan areas and specialized regional clusters (Sölvell 2008, p. 110). The classical definition states that clusters are "geographic concentrations of interconnected companies, suppliers, service providers, firms in related industries, and associated institutions (e.g. universities, standards agencies, and trade associations) in particular fields that compete but also cooperate" (Porter 1998, p. 197). From the above definition, we may derive two important characteristics of clusters (Kowalski, 2016):

- geographical concentration of companies and other actors in a specific sector, connected with the phenomenon of the regional specialization,

- "coopetition" between cluster actors, encompassing both competition and cooperation.

Several authors (e.g. Porter, 2008; Ketels, 2009) demonstrate a positive relationship between employment in strong clusters and economic performance, meaning that regions with a higher level of specialization in an industry are characterised by higher productivity in this industry. The elements that constitute clusters are: a specific territory, a specialization in one or more segments of a supply chain and a population of firms and institutions (Camuffo 2011, p. 815). From the other hand, Anderson et al. (2004, p. 1) identify seven building blocks of clusters:

1) geographic concentration;

2) the core and defining specialisation of clusters;

3) the actors, mainly companies and scientific units;

4) dynamics and linkages;

5) critical mass;

6) the cluster life cycle;

7) innovation,

while noting, however, that not all these elements must be present in the case of each specific cluster.

One of the difficulty in analysing clusters is the ambiguity of the cluster concept itself. According to some representatives of economic geography (Martin and Sunley 2003, p. 9), "Porter's cluster metaphor is highly generic in character, being sufficiently indeterminate to admit a very wide spectrum of industrial groupings and specialization". They point out following questions, to which the cluster theory does not give a precise answer:

- At what level of industrial aggregation should a cluster be defined, and what range of related or associated industries and activities should be included?
- How strong do the linkages between firms have to be?
- How economically specialized does a local concentration of firms have to be to constitute a cluster? (Martin and Sunley, 2003, p. 10).

The cluster concept gives little attention to the scale of geographical coverage of a group without determining whether clusters exist nationally, regionally or locally (Perry 2007). The difficulties in precisely addressing these challenges are reflected in Porter (1998, p. 204) recognition that cluster boundaries "rarely conform to standard industrial classification systems, which fail to capture many important actors in competition as well as linkages across industries. Because parts of a cluster often fall within different traditional industrial or service categories, significant clusters may be obscured or even go unrecognized". However, the ambiguity of the cluster concept makes it very flexible model that may be used in analyzing different types of spatial structures, including BRI investments.

2. Clusters as a new approach to international economic cooperation

In the traditional approach, research into clusters focused on their impact on competitiveness at the mesoeconomic level, which means it primarily concerned the development of a specific sector in a given regional economy. Hence, clusters used to be regarded as closed production systems, restricted to a particular location and capable of entering into external interactions only at the beginning and at the end of a production chain. Meanwhile, the growing internationalization of the economy-which leads to the removal of trade barriers, strengthens transport and communication systems, and promotes the introduction of uniform market regulations-contributes to more intense cooperation and a stepped-up international flow of resources, a process reflected in cluster operations.

Cluster initiatives increasingly extend beyond the scope of a given location, entering into interactions with actors based in other regions or even countries. According to J.H. Dunning (2002), the fact that cluster operations extend beyond their local areas calls for a revision of conventional models explaining the spatial concentration of economic activity, and the role of business clusters in the development of competitiveness. The evolution of clusters shows that they are becoming a factor contributing to the globalization of the economy. According to one of the definitions, globalization means an "increased network of interactions among a growing number of players, as a result of which the situation of individual entities is increasingly dependent on mega- rather than meso-trends" (Hausner, Kudłacz, Szlachta, 1998, p. 14). Globalization therefore means that in order to maintain their competitive capacity, clusters and the businesses they bring together are increasingly working out strategies for the internationalization of their operations, including by outsourcing or foreign direct investment (Rabellotti, Carabelli, Hirsch, 2009). To sum up, it is possible to state that clusters have entered a new stage of evolution in which, after the development of cooperation chiefly at the local level, the time has come to build trans-regional and cross-border cooperation networks (Kowalski, 2017). On the one hand, clusters have become a new way of thinking about competitiveness; on the other, they have become an important element of international economic cooperation, thus fitting into the research on BRI.

In practice, internationalization is not yet regarded as a priority by most cluster initiatives, but it is increasingly possible to see examples of active cooperation on the international arena. The internationalization of the cluster and its component companies and other types of entities may apply to the following types of activities:

1) production, when the profile of enterprises operating in a cluster needs to be expanded to include the range of complementary resources offered by their foreign partners,

2) trade, in particular in the case of small and medium-sized enterprises belonging to a cluster that have not developed ties abroad which would enable them to export manufactured goods on their own,

3) research (e.g. undertaking joint R&D or cooperation for the sake of technology transfer), which plays a particularly important role in the context of internationalization processes involving innovation (techno-globalism),

4) education and training when training programs, conferences, and study visits are organized to upgrade the qualifications of market players and to exchange knowledge and experience at the international level.

The modern global economy is characterized by a growing international fragmentation of production, as a result of which clusters are included in global value chains (GVC). In this context, M. Porter (2008, pp. 252-253) observed the so-called location paradox whereby, despite the progressive globalization, a sustainable competitive advantage of companies on international markets is often rooted in the local environment and various aspects of proximity. This research topic is part of the concept of globalization, based on the mutual penetration of global economy components and local economic and social structures that enter into networks of international links. This process also concerns clusters, which in many cases produce intermediates that are the basis for the functioning of global value chains.

The increasingly dense network of raw materials and intermediates flowing between various locations leads to fragmented production processes. According to research by B. Los, M.P. Timmer and G.J. Vries (2015), these processes are gradually losing their regional character and are becoming increasingly global in nature. At the same time, the creation of value chains across national boundaries contributes to a situation, in which clusters can promote greater internationalization of the local economy and represent an effective means of attracting foreign direct investment and of their integration with domestic entities, while taking into account the specific conditions prevailing in a given country (Kowalski, 2017). Cluster structures, by increasing the attractiveness of a region as an investment destination, not only contribute to a greater inflow of capital, but also help permanently bind investors to the local economy. A standout example of such a process is Ireland, where the inflow of foreign direct investment, in particular from USA, has contributed to the creation of clusters in sectors such as ICT, (bio)pharmaceuticals and international services (Kowalski, 2014). Likewise, Poland's best developed cluster, the Aviation Valley in the southeastern Podkarpackie province, has emerged with the significant involvement of foreign investors.

Transnational corporations are developing their chains by acquiring resources specific to a given region, including local knowledge (Bellandi, 2001). Such a strategy leads to a process known as multiple-embeddedness, whereby companies build permanent and in-depth relationships with many industry clusters (Zucchella, 2006). This is accompanied by a dispersion of cluster value chains into cooperative and competitive relationships between different industrial agglomerations that occupy either different or identical positions in a value chain (Nadvi, Halder, 2005). Such de-localization processes pose a threat to clusters because they may cause value to migrate to other regions. On the other hand, they can facilitate the inclusion of regional businesses into international networks, thus opening possibilities of expansion into international markets. According to J. Humphrey and H. Schmitz (2002, p. 1020), the following methods can be used to improve competitiveness and upgrade a cluster as part of a global value chain:

– process upgrading, based on increasing the efficiency of processes through the reorganization of a production system or the introduction of advanced technology,

– product upgrading, based on diversifying the product range and manufacturing high-value-added products,

– functional upgrading, based on adopting new functions or replacing the combination of already performed tasks with those that increase the level of specialization in activities,

– inter-sectoral upgrading, based on cluster companies undertaking new types of business activities and entering new value chains while using competences acquired through prior participation in other value chains.

G. Gereffi and J. Lee (2016, p. 30) and P. Knorringa and K. Nadvi (2016, p. 58) analyzed clusters and global value chains in terms of governance. Clusters have a horizontal management system that primarily concerns coordination of local cooperation between businesses and other organizations inside and outside the cluster structure. The management of global value chains is, in turn, based on a vertical system that combines customers and suppliers in different countries. While the co-existence of both systems in a given area may create conflict situations resulting from factors such as asymmetry, their proper coordination contributes to a beneficial synergy effect and industrial advancement. It also helps upgrade the regional economy, enabling it to improve its competitive position internationally. The entry of clusters into global value chains thus ensures a holistic view of business processes, in both top-down and bottom-up terms. At the same time, the overlapping of these two approaches is part of an analysis of multi-polar governance of global value chains (Ponte, Sturgeon, 2014).

3. Clusters in China as the Elements of the Silk Road Economic Belt

In recent years, industrial clusters have been emerging very rapidly in both number and scale in China, especially in better developed provincial economies of coastal China (Kang, 2007; Kiminami, Akira 2016; Knorringa, Khalid 2016,

Hu, Xie, Hu 2016; Wei, Zhou Greeven, Qu 2016; Zhu et al. 2018; Wang, Jian 2018; Kou 2018). Hence, this process was accompanied by intense increases in regional disparities in this country (Chen, Nijkamp, Tabuchi, van Dijk J. 2014). As the research of Herrerias and Ordóñez (2014) demonstrated, the growth rate of the stock of physical capital in eastern provinces is twice as high as in the western provinces during the post-reform period (after 1978), and one and a half times higher than in the central regions. However, although megacities, like Beijing and Shanghai, have long captured much of the spotlight as potential investment destinations, the real economic miracle of China occurs behind the scenes in second-tier cities, such as Chongqing, Wuhan, Ningbo and Dalian, which have become important locations for high-technology clusters (Wang, Lestari, Yang 2015). An important factor driving clusters development in China were foreign direct investments. The study conducted by Fri, Pehrsson, Søilen (2013) demonstrated that multinational corporations are investing in Chinese regions where related industries are clustered, both those that are vertically and horizontally integrated. On the basis of the analyses of Beijing, Hebei, Shanghai, Jiangsu, Chongqing and Sichuan clusters, these economists stated that the phases of cluster development in China are related to the level of innovation in a cluster, measured by the number of patents. Another study conducted by O'Connor and Gu (2014) showed the importance of creative industry clusters in China, helping to develop creative class (Florida 2014) and leading to a convergence of culture with advanced technology.

One of the objectives of Belt and Road Initiatives is to strengthen the global transport network, connecting China with other countries, boosting inter and intraregional cooperation. The focus is on taking the advantage of the existing bilateral and multilateral cooperation mechanisms to promote the development of regional cooperation, and on elimination of transport bottlenecks, the development of trans-border transport infrastructure and the creation of new international corridors and multimodal hubs (State Council 2015; Summers 2016). This will result in the emergence of important industrial clusters along developing traffic routes. Through industrial agglomeration and radiation effects, the construction industry, metallurgy, energy, finance, communications, logistics, tourism and the like will make up an integrated economic corridor (Yiwei, 2015).

The renewal of local space, such as regional clusters, megacities or free trade zones, allows to deepen and to diversify the network of firms' interactions. There is evidence that, with the ongoing urbanization and globalization, economic motives gain ground (Heiduk, McCaleb, 2015). The importance of cities and clusters in BRI was depicted in the concept of the Silk Road Cities Network, proposed by Ni, Kamiya, and Ding (2017). The authors presented the idea of the system of inter-city connections among cities along the New Silk Road. The main cities along the Silk Road serve as the nodes of the system, the land bridges as the centerline, high-speed rails as catalyst, air transport as accelerator, sea routes as engine. Through the flows of the production factors, goods and services, chains of cities will be clustered into a network complex. Hence, urban landscape of different areas involved in BRI will be mapped out along the main traffic routes as belts and clusters. The core content of the Silk Road Cities Network will be constituted with industrial systems, production factors, and commercial services. However, the development of Information and Communication Technologies (ICT) and digitization of economy, the geographical nature of Silk Road Cities Network may continually transform to a more mobile one.

The basis of the cluster approach in the organization of the transport sector along Belt and Road Initiative involves the promotion of cross-border cluster cooperation by intergovernmental institutions. Moreover, it would secure a balanced use of existing and potential capacity of the infrastructure of national transport systems, and the intensification of cooperation within international transport corridors of the region. Transport hub operators and companies in the logistic clusters in many countries are taking the BRI as the way to capitalize on emerging business opportunities (Van der Putten et al. 2016). Chhetri et al. (2017) postulate a cluster-led strategic policy framework that would formulate actions and strategies through which logistics networks can be strategically aligned, together with their functional integration with BRI-oriented global trading hubs and transport corridors. Along developing connectivity infrastructure, industrial clusters and services networks will emerge, forming an integrated economic belt, and establishing a link China and the EU. The construction of the intercontinental infrastructure will be the basis for further regional integration, giving rise to a huge Eurasian market (Fasslabend 2015).

The BRI vision document (State Council 2015) makes the recommendation to develop inland regions, with focus on the city clusters along the middle reaches of the Yangtze River, especially around Chengdu and Chongqing. It is mentioned that China should build Chongqing cluster into an important pivot for developing and opening up the western region, and make Chengdu, and other important cities, like Changsha, Hefei, Nanchang, Wuhan, and Zhengzhou leading areas of opening-up in the inland regions. Moreover, development of cross-border transport corridor connecting the eastern, central and western regions is recommended, together with deepening industrial cooperation with countries along the Belt and Road Initiative. This will result in accelerated advances of industrialization and urbanization in the central and western China. Hence, the urban system will undergo profound changes, as the population size and economy scale will expand, and new cities will be formed (Ni 2016). Along with the extension of the transportation network, the economic interactions and division of labor between the major cities will be expanded to the satellite cities, opening up the west and south regions (Ni, Kamiya, Ding 2017).

4. BRI and destinations in Poland

Poland, as the largest country in Central and Eastern Europe, is one of the key players in the context of the construction of the New Silk Road. Hence, the Belt and Road Initiative is a project with huge potential for Polish regional development. Among the most significant locations on the New Silk Road, there are: Warsaw, Łódź and Kutno. All of them constitute the local clusters of different types of actors and are important elements of the network developed along BRI transportation channels. Warsaw, with around 1,7 million inhabitants, is the largest Polish city. Analyzing income competitiveness, it has also the biggest GDP per capita (134 thousands PLN in 2015) among large cities (over 200,000 people). Its special status as a capital city plays a huge role in determining its role in Polish economy, as well as in BRI. The size of the metropolitan area, the proximity of offices, including central ones, and a well-developed transport and transport infrastructure make Warsaw an unattainable competitive leader in Poland and an important location on the map of New Silk Road connecting Asia and Europe. This is proved with the highest level of urban entrepreneurship in Poland, in the context of which Warsaw is in the highest position in terms of such indicators like the number of companies, and newly registered companies per 1000 inhabitants. One can, however, find some inaccuracies between statistical data and reality, because in the capital city, there are registered many enterprises, which transfer production to other regions of the country, but are statistically assigned to Warsaw. Chinese investment may play an important role in improving the infrastructure needed to enhance economic development of Poland, including Warsaw. An example are current talks between Polish government with Chinese partners to get them to finance the new Central Airport, which will be located between Warsaw and Łódź, and which will be a huge logistics center with train lines and cargo facilities. Now, regular train operates between Suzhou for Warsaw, with a journey time of around 14 days. It transports mainly electronic products, branded clothes and sophisticated instruments manufactured in Suzhou and Shanghai.

One of the most popular logistics train route for Chinese trade with Europe is the rail cargo service between Chengdu and Łódź, launched in 2013. With the location in central Poland and close to key motorways: A1 and A2, the terminal is one of the key logistic hubs in Europe. This also refers to developing communication infrastructure providing easy access to major business centers in the European Union. The advantage of this region is convenient transport connections to Warsaw, which takes only about 70-minute travel by train or car.

Łódź used to specialize in textile industry, whereas today it is transforming into a city of modern technologies and creative industries. Among major industries developed, there are: business process outsourcing (BPO), logistics, household appliance manufacturing, electronics, and B2B services. Many transnational corporations opened their branches and started production with the intention of further expansion. For example, well-known international companies, such as HP, Fujitsu, Dell, Gillette, Infosys, Philips, UPS, Samsung, have their subsidiaries in Łódź. What is important, the city has excellent science and higher education base, which offers a large number of graduates educated in the fields searched for by employers. Another advantage are competitive office rental costs in modern office buildings. Moreover, the Łódź Special Economic Zone offers fiscal incentives and consulting services for investors. It carries out numerous activities aimed at developing economic cooperation with China. For example, Łódź Special Economic Zone was a strategic partner of the third Poland-China Regional Forum held in Łódź on June 2015. Many B2B meetings between Chinese and Polish companies were organized, and Łódź is fast becoming a recognizable city in China. The logistics and warehousing centre (the so-called Super Hub) in Łódź Special Economic Zone may be seen as one of the most important European gates to China and the Chinese gates to Europe.

Another important location on the New Silk Road is Kutno, which constitutes one of the most important railway stations in Poland. It is located in Łódź Voivodeship and on the international railway line E20 Berlin-Moscow. In fact, it has developed a network of domestic and international rail connections as it lies at the intersection of north-south and east-west transport routes, which makes it a very convenient place for consolidation of European goods on the way to China. There is a modern and fully functional transshipment center, entirely equipped for container handlings operations that enables time and costs efficiency in intermodal operation at the Kutno terminal. It is important to stress that Łódź and Kutno terminals are supposed to complement rather than compete with each other. Łódź will remain the point of distribution and confectioning of goods sent from Europe and preparing them for further clearance to China, whereas Kutno is to be a place for completing trains from all over Europe, and then sending them to Asia.

Because of the favorable geographical location of Poland, the BRI project can bring significant economic benefits to this country. The country's investment attractiveness is also influenced by the large internal market. Among the factors that make Poland an important element of Belt and Road Initiative (BRI), there are (PAIIIZ):

- central geographical location in Europe,
- large, diverse and entrepreneurial population,
- well-educated and competitive labor force and qualified specialists,
- lower labor than in other European countries,
- massive inflow of European structural funds,
- geopolitical stability based on the EU membership,
- steadily improving conditions for running business.

It should be noted that China does not perceive Polish territory as the key destination in the New Silk Road. However, Poland remains an important country, through which Chinese companies can get access to their largest trading partners, primarily Germany, France and the United Kingdom. The central location of Poland in Europe means that it can become an important place of transit and a natural logistics and reloading center, which will also affect the investments, in particular in the modernization of transport infrastructure. The direct financial benefit for Poland, as well as for other countries on the New Silk Road route, will be payments for transit. In addition, the expansion of transport corridors between Asia and Europe may contribute to greater opening of eastern markets for Polish exports, in particular agri-food products. The development of terrestrial routes increases the security of Chinese deliveries, which may be important for the functioning of the economy. On the other hand, BRI may help Polish companies to internationalize their economic activity, not only through export, but also through foreign direct investments (FDI). In the context of international capital flows, Poland, together with other

Central and Eastern European (CEE) countries, were traditionally recipient economies. However, studies provided by e.g. Kowalski (2018) showed that in recent years, we observe relatively small, but dynamically growing outward foreign direct investments (OFDI) made by companies located in CEE. This pattern confirms that CEE economies, including Poland, are moving forward the stages of internationalization, which result in the growing value of OFDI, as explained by the Investment Development Path (IDP) hypothesis, first formulated by Dunning (1981).

Conclusions

Despite globalization process in the world economy, the role of proximity is not diminished, as economic activity, especially in high-tech sectors, tends to concentrate around metropolitan areas and specialized regional clusters. However, growing internationalization of the economy made clusters' activities increasingly extending beyond the scope of a given location. Companies from different clusters are entering interactions with partners based in other regions and countries, developing trans-regional and cross-border cooperation networks. That is why in the case of such intercontinental project, like BRI, clusters play a special role in connecting actors from different locations, boosting international cooperation. In particular, strengthening trans-border transport infrastructure and the creation of new international corridors and multimodal hubs will result in the emergence of important industrial clusters along developing traffic routes. For China, it will become an occasion to promote more balanced regional development by opening up the western region in the country, as the BRI vision document makes the recommendation to develop inland regions, with focus on the city clusters along the middle reaches of the Yangtze River, especially around Chengdu and Chongqing. It is worth to stress the importance of cities in BRI, as highlighted by the concept of the Silk Road Cities Network, presenting the idea of the system of cities clustered along the New Silk Road clustered into a network complex. This network will also include Polish cities, among which three important players in the BRI frame presented in this Paper are Warsaw, Łódź and Kutno. Apart from being part of the whole Eurasian network developed along New Silk Road, these cities form themselves local clusters engaging different types of actors, mostly (but not only) enterprises specialized in logistics and transportation. As Poland is not the final destination in BRI, but rather remains a gateway, through which China can get access to its largest trading partners in Western Europe, making use of central location in Europe may result in the development of transit and logistics clusters in this country, with strong advantages for economic development.

Acknowledgments

The paper was prepared in the framework of the research project No 2016/21/B/HS4/03025 financed by the National Science Center, Poland.

References

Thomas Anderson, Sylvia Schwaag Serger, Jens Sörvik and Emily Wise Hansson, *The Cluster Policies Whitebook*, Malmö: IKED, 2004.

Marco Bellandi, "Local Development and Embedded Large Firms", *Entrepreneurship & Regional Development*, 2001,13(3), pp. 189-210.

Arnaldo Camuffo, Roberto Grandinetti, "Italian industrial districts as cognitive systems: Are they still reproducible?" *Entrepreneurship & Regional Development*, 2011, 23(9-10), pp. 815-852.

Jiyong Chen, Wei Liu, Yibo Zhang and Yangyi Sheng, "An empirical study on FDI international knowledge spillovers and regional economic development in China", *Frontiers of Economics in China*, 2010, Vol.5, No.3, pp. 489-508.

Prem Chhetri, Mathews Nkhoma, Konrad Peszynski, Anjali Chhetri and Paul Tae -Woo Lee, "Global logistics city concept: a cluster-led strategy under the Belt and Road Initiative", *Maritime Policy & Management*, Vol. 45, No3:1-17, 2017.

John H. Dunning, "Explaining the International Direct Investment Position of Countries: Towards a Dynamic or Developmental Approach", *Weltwirtschaftliches Archiv*, 1981, 117 (1), pp. 30-64.

John H. Dunning, "Regions, globalization and the knowledge-based economy: the issues stated", in: John H., Dunning (ed.), *Regions, Globalization and the Knowledge-based Economy*, Oxford: Oxford University Press, 2002, pp. 7-41.

Werner Fasslabend, "The Silk Road: a political marketing concept for world dominance", *European View*, 2015, 14(2), pp. 293-302, 2015.

Richard Florida, *The Rise of the Creative Class-Revisited: Revised and Expanded*, New York: Basic books, 2014.

William Fri, Tobias Pehrsson, Klaus Søilen, How Phases of Cluster Development are Associated with Innovation-the Case of China, *International Journal Of Innovation Science*, 5(1), pp. 31-44, 2013.

Gary Gereffi, Joonkoo Lee, "Economic and Social Upgrading in Global Value Chains and Industrial Clusters: Why Governance Matters", *Journal of Business Ethics*, 133(1), pp. 25-38, 2013.

Jerzy Hausner, Kudłacz T., Szlachta J. , *Identyfikacja nowych problemów rozwoju regionalnego Polski*, Warszawa: Wydawnictwo Naukowe PWN, 1998.

Guenter Heiduk, Agnieszka McCaleb, "What motivates China's cities to establish partner agreements with cities in Asia", Research Papers of the Wroclaw University of Economics, No 413, pp. 52-61, 2015.

Maria Jesus Herrerias, Javier Ordóñez, "Stochastic Regional Convergence in China: The Role of Regional Clusters in a Nonlinear Perspective (1952-2007)", *Pacific Economic Review*, Vol.19. pp. 153-169, 2014.

Xiao-ran Hu, Chengyang Xie, H.H. Hu, "Relationship Between the

Maturity of Industrial Clusters and Financial Support", In: *Proceedings of the 6th International Asia Conference on Industrial Engineering and Management Innovation*, Atlantis Press, pp. 77-85, 2016.

John Humphrey, Hubert Schmitz, "How Does Insertion in Global Value Chains Affect Upgrading in Industrial Clusters?", *Regional Studies*, 36, pp. 1017-1027, 2002.

Yi Kang, "Made in China: coastal industrial clusters and regional growth", I*ssues in Political Economy*, Vol.16, 2007.

Christian H.M. Ketels, "Clusters, cluster policy, and Swedish competitiveness in the global economy", *Expert report* No. 30 to Sweden's Globalisation Council, PRINT Edita, Västerås: Harvard Business School and Stockholm School of Economics, 2009.

Lily Kiminami, Akira Kiminam, *Agricultural Industry Clusters in China*, Springer Japan, 2016.

Peter Knorringa, Khalid Nadvi, "Rising power clusters and the challenges of local and global standards", *Journal of Business Ethics*, 133(1), pp. 55-72, 2016.

Kou KOU, "Effects of the Chinese Innovation System on Regional Innovation Performance", *Technology and Investment*, Vol. 9, pp. 36-51, 2018.

Arkadiusz M. Kowalski, "International Competitiveness of Countries with Dynamic Innovation Systems. Case study: Ireland", in: Marzenna Anna Weresa (ed.), *Innovation, Human Capital and Trade Competitiveness. How are They Connected and Why Do They Matter?*, Washington, D.C.: Springer, pp. 204-228, 2014.

Arkadiusz M. Kowalski, "Territorial location of ICT cluster initiatives and ICT-related sectors in Poland", in: Hansjog Drewello, Marisa Helfer, Madjid Bouzar (eds), *Clusters as a Driving Power of the European Economy*, Baden-Baden: Nomos, pp. 49-66, 2016.

Arkadiusz M. Kowalski, "The Internationalization of Polish Business Clusters", in: Marzenna Anna Weresa (ed.), *Poland: Competitiveness Report 2017. Internationalization and Poland's Competitive Position*, Warsaw: Warsaw

School of Economics-Publishing, pp. 245-258, 2017.

Arkadiusz M. Kowalski, "Benefits of Broadening the Analysis of International Competitiveness: The Case of CEE Countries", AIB Insights, 18(1), pp. 7-11, 2018.

Bart Los, Marcel P.Timmer, Gaaitzen J. de Vries, "How global are global value chains? A new approach to measure international fragmentation", *Journal of Regional Science*, 55(1), 66-92, 2015.

Ronald Martin, Peter Sunley, "Deconstructing clusters: chaotic concept or policy panacea*?*", *Journal of Economic Geography*, 3(1), pp. 5-35, 2003.

Khalid Nadvi, Gerhard Halder, "Local clusters in global value chains: exploring dynamic linkages between Germany and Pakistan", *Entrepreneurship & Regional Development*, 17(5), pp. 339-364, 2005.

Pengfei Ni, *China urban competitiveness report no. 14-New engine: Multi-center city network system*, Beijing: Social Science Literature Press, 2016.

Pengfei Ni, Marco Kamiya, Ruxi Ding, *Cities Network Along the Silk Road*, Springer, Singapore, 2017.

Pengfei Ni, Liu Kai, Peter J.Taylor, "The Urban Connectivity in China: A measurement based on the interlocking network model", *Economic and Social System Comparison*, Vol. 6, pp. 96-103, 2011.

Justin O'Connor, Xin Gu, "Creative industry clusters in Shanghai: a success story?", *International Journal of Cultural Policy*, 20(1), pp. 1-20, 2014.

PAIIIZ S.A., *Investment climate in Poland guide for Chinese enterprises*, https://www.paih.gov.pl/files/?id_plik=25607 [accessed: 28 Februeary 2018].

Vincent J. Pascal, "Clusters and Entrepreneurial Intensity: The Influence of Economic Clusters on Entrepreneurial Activity", *Journal of Research in Marketing and Entrepreneurship*, 7(1), pp. 5-27, 2005.

Martin Perry, "Business environments and cluster attractiveness to managers", *Entrepreneurship & Regional Development*, 19(1), pp. 1-24, 2007.

Stefano Ponte, Timothy J Sturgeon, "Explaining governance in global value chains: A modular theory-building effort", *Review of International Political Economy*, 21(1), pp. 195-223, 2014.

Michael E. Porter, *The competitive advantage of nations*, New York: Free Press, 1990.

Michael E. Porter, "Clusters and the new economics of competition," *Harvard Business Review*, 76(6), pp. 77-90, 1998.

Michael E. Porter, *On Compettition. Updated and Expanded Edition*, Boston: A Harvard Business Review Book, 2008.

Robetta Rabellotti, Anna Carabelli and Giovanna Hirsch, "Industrial districts on the move: where are they going?", *European Planning Studies*, 17(1), pp. 19-41, 2009.

Örjan Sölvell, *Clusters Balancing Evolutionary and Constructive Forces*, Ivory Tower Publishing, Sztokholm, 2008.

State Council, *Vision and Actions on Jointly Building Silk Road Economic Belt and Twenty-First Century Maritime Silk Road.* Xinhuanet, 2015. [online] 28 March. Available at: http://news.xinhuanet.com/english/china/2015-03/28/ c_134105858.htm [Accessed 12.02.2018 November 2016].

Tim Summers, China's 'New Silk Roads': sub-national regions and networks of global political economy, *Third World Quarterly*, 37(9), pp. 1628-1643, 2016.

Frans-Paul van der Putten, John Seaman, Mikko Huotari, Alice Ekman, Miguel Otero-Iglesias, (Eds.) , *Europe and China's new silk roads*, ETNC Report, 2016.

Kung-Jeng Wang, Yuliani Dwi Lestari, Tsau-Tang Yang, "Location determinants of market expansion in China's second-tier cities: a case study of the biotechnology industry", *Journal of Business & Industrial Marketing*, 30(2), pp.139-152, 2015.

Xiujie Wang, Liu Jian, "A Research on Upgrading and Development Strategy of China Automobile Industry Cluster", in: Check Teck Foo (Ed), *Diversity of Managerial Ideology*, Springer, Singapore, pp. 179-187, 2018.

Jiang Wei, Minfei Zhou, Mark Greeven and Hongyan Qu, "Economic governance, dual networks and innovative learning in five Chinese industrial clusters", *Asia Pacific Journal of Management* 33, No. 4, pp. 1037-1074, 2016,

Yiwei Wang, "'China's 'New Silk Road': A Case Study in EU-China Relations", in: Alessia Amighini and Axel Berkofsky (eds), *Xi's Policy Gambles: The Bumpy Road Ahead*, pp. 103-115, 2015.

Xiwei Zhu, Ye Liu, Ming He, Deming Lu and Yiyun Wu, Entrepreneurship and industrial clusters: evidence from China Industrial Census, *Small Business Economics*, pp. 1-22, 2018.

Antonella Zucchella, "Local cluster dynamics: trajectories of mature industrial districts between decline and multiple embeddedness", *Journal of Institutional Economics*, 2(1), pp. 21-44, 2006.

Competitiveness of Poland's exports to China: Comparison with other Visegrad countries*

Elzbieta Kawecka-Wyrzykowska and Łukasz Ambroziak

Abstract

Statistical data show that Visegrad countries (V4 which include the Czech Republic, Hungary, Poland and Slovakia) record high deficits in trade with China, albeit the situation of individual countries is different.

The objective of this paper is to assess the competitive position of Polish exports to China against the background of the other V4 countries, and to identify whether these countries use their comparative advantages. The conclusions address the issue of ways of improving the situation of the trade balances. They reveal that in the period analysed (2007-2016), the vast majority of exports (classified by HS Chapters) of all V4 countries to China possessed revealed comparative advantages. The situation of Poland was, however, the weakest in this regard. It was reflected by the calculation of two standard indices of trade competitiveness of countries were calculated, it is: revealed comparative advantages index (RCA) and trade coverage of import by export index (TC) as well as changes in the commodity pattern of V4 exports.

---

* In this article the statutory research of Elżbieta Kawecka-Wyrzykowska was used which was entitled: 'Competitiveness of Polish goods on Chinese market from the perspective of selected competitors in the period 2010-2016: conclusions for the export increase', Collegium of World Economy, Warsaw School of Economics, No. KGS/S18/10/18.

Several actions were suggested to reduce Poland's deficit in trade with China, including promotion of a broader use of BRI Initiative, higher institutional and organizational support on the part of public bodies, higher direct investment of Polish companies in China, increased export of products already competitive on Chinese market.

Data on trade relations comes from COMTRADE basis, organized by HS Sections. Data covered the period 2007 (a year before the recent deep crisis) 2016 (recent available data).

Introduction

Statistical data show that Visegrad countries (V4 which include the Czech Republic, Hungary, Poland and Slovakia) record high deficits in trade with China, albeit the situation of individual countries is different. The natural way to correct this situation would be to intensify exports.

The objective of this paper is to assess the competitive position of Polish exports to China against the background of the other V4 countries, and to identify whether these countries use their comparative advantages. The conclusions will address the issue of ways of improving the situation of the trade balances. The role of BRI Initiative will be taken into account.

1. Methodology of the analysis

Two indicators of the competitive position in trade were employed, namely trade coverage index (TC) and Dalassa's revealed comparative advantages index-RCA (Balassa 1965), see Box 1.

TC index determines the extent to which expenses on imported goods are covered by the revenue from their exports. It is used to study the relationship between the exports and the imports at the level of entire trade, sector or product. The TC index higher than 100% means that the exports value exceeds the imports value, thus the given country has the relative competitive advantage over its partners.

The RCA index compares the share of a given product in a country's total exports with the share of country's total exports in total world exports (Balassa 1965). Thus, the RCA ratio reflects the level of a country's export specialization in a given product as compared to the world (regional) average. The value of RCA ratio varies between zero and infinitive. When RCA>1, a country has a revealed comparative advantage compared to reference countries (the share of the given commodity group in the exports of a country is higher than the respective share in the world/regional exports). Otherwise, when the index is lower than 1 (the share of the given commodity group in the exports of the country in question is lower than the share of this product group in the world/ regional export) - the analysed country does not have revealed comparative advantages in the exports to a specific market.

Box 1. Indices used in calculations

Trade coverage (TC) index was calculated according to the following formula:

$$TC_{ij}=\frac{X_{ij}}{Y_{ij}}\cdot 100,$$

where:

TC_{ij} – trade coverage index in trade in the ith product group of the jth country with the world,

X_{ij} – exports of the ith product group (here: total exports or exports by HS section) of the jth country to China,

M_{ij} – imports of the ith product group (here: total imports or imports by HS section) of the jth country from China.

Revealed comparative advantages (RCA) indices were calculated according to the formula (Balassa 1965):

$$RCA_{ij} = \frac{X_{ij}}{\sum\limits_{i=1}^{N} X_{ij}} : \frac{X_{iw}}{\sum\limits_{i=1}^{N} X_{iw}}$$

where:

RCA_{ij} – revealed comparative advantage indexin the jth country export of the ith product group to China,

X_{ij} – exports of the ith product group (here: exports by HS section) of the jth country to China,

X_{iw} – world exports of the ith product group to China,

N – number of product groups (here: total exports).

Source: Based on Balassa,1965.

The results of the comparison of both indices for Poland and its competitors will allow for conclusions as regards the present areas of specialization of their exports and possible future changes.

Data on trade relations comes from COMTRADE basis. Data is organized by HS Sections and covers the period from 2007 (a year before the recent deep crisis) to 2016 (recent available data).

2. Characteristic elements of foreign trade of V4 countries with China

Graph 1, illustrating foreign trade of the V-4 countries with China, allows for several observations.

A striking difference between Poland and other V4 countries can be observed as regards those countries' value of trade with China. Poland, being much bigger country (in terms of the number of population and total exports) than the other V4 countries, exported to China in 2016 almost the same value as the Czech Republic, by 50% more than Slovakia and slightly less than

Hungary! This situation took place despite much better transportation location of Poland (due to the access to the Baltic sea, closer distance to huge harbours in Hamburg and Rotterdam and direct, close access to the railway from Poland to Chengdu!).

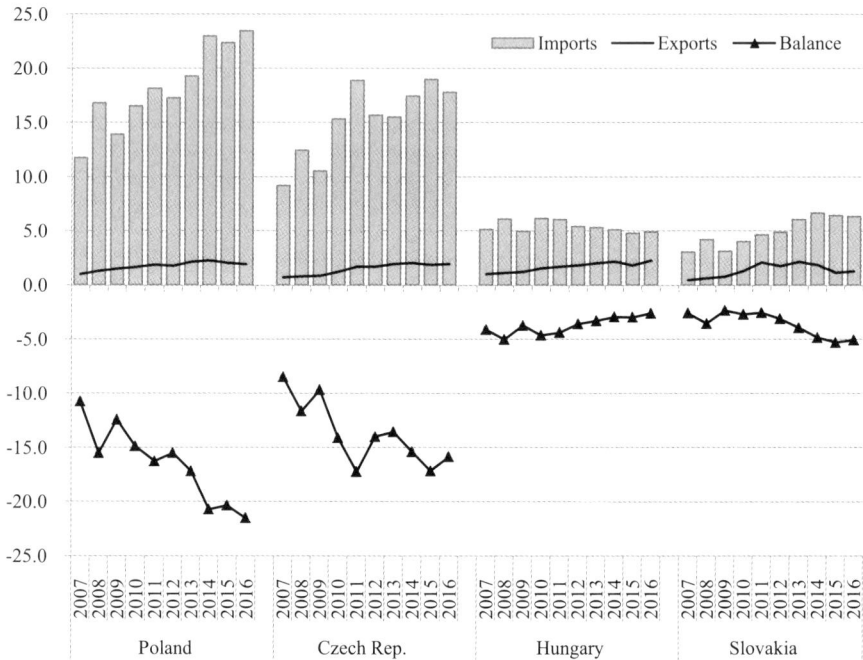

Graph 1. Foreign trade of V-4 countries with China (in billion USD)
Source: Own calculations based on COMTRADE basis.

All V4 countries registered deficit in trade with China in the period analyzed. The highest it was (in absolute and relative terms) in Poland. The level of TC ratio was here the lowest in recent years and has been decreasing recently (8% in 2016 and 13% in 2011, Graph 2). In the Czech Republic the situation was not much better (TC at 11% in 2016). These indicators reveal huge scale of unbalanced trade with China in both countries (it is low coverage of imports by exports). The situation was relatively the best in Hungary, where the TC index doubled in the years

2007-2016 (from 20% to 46%) and appeared to be the highest in the group of V4 countries. In turn in Slovakia-the high TC ratio in 2011 (45%), decreased substantially in the next years (to 18% in 2015 and 20% in 2016). Thus, Hungary possesses relatively the best position as regards trade deficit with China as it can mitigate this deficit easier than any other V4 countries. The worst situation in this regard is in Poland.

The situation in all countries was worsened by a fact that the reduction of the TC ratio was usually accompanied in recent three years by the reduction of the value of both, exports and imports in V4 countries (or very low increase of turnover), while at the same time the decline of exports was higher than the decline of imports (COMTRADE data).

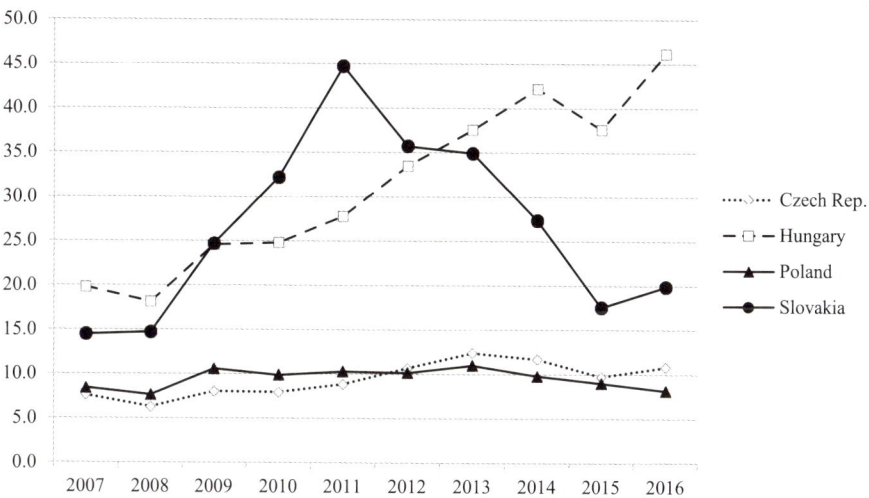

Graph 2. Trade coverage (TC) indices of V4 countries in trade with China
Source: As in graph 1.

3. Commodity pattern of V4 exports to China

Tables 1-4 reveal relatively high commodity concentration of exports of V4 to China. They show the commodity pattern of 10 top product groups in exports (by 4-digit HS headings) which allows for more detailed approach than the approach by HS Sections.[①]

The pattern of commodity concentration in exports of individual V4 countries was different. An important part of Poland's exports (25% in 2016) was consisted in raw materials and low processed industrial products; mostly copper and copper alloys(20%), while the remaining 5% was created by furniture and parts thereof. Goods which could be considered as highly processed ones (accessories of motors, turbo-jets, electrical transformers, automatic data processing machines, parts for electrical circuits) - amounted only to around 15% of total exports.

Czech exports and the whole trade were more similar to Poland, but with more industrial products in Czech exports. Accessories of the motor vehicles (HS 8708) were the most important single HS chapter in exports with the share at 10%. Other more processed goods included taps, cocks, valves, electrical apparatus for switching, microscopes, motor cars etc. - accounting all together for about 26% of total exports.

Slovak and Hungarian exports were dominated by highly processed products: one single HS heading (8703): cars and parts amounted respectively to 65% and 31% of their exports! If we add other highly processed goods, their share increased to around 82% and 60%, respectively, in the case of both countries.

---

① In terms of HS Sections the commodity concentration of exports was much stronger as the classification group was broader (2-digit level) and included a bigger number of products. In Slovak exports to China in 2016, 75% was made by one group: transport equipment, in the Czech Republic-machinery and equipment accounted for 53% of total exports; in Hungary-the share of the same group was 38% and of the second largest group (transport equipment) was 35%; in Poland-the biggest export group in recent years were base metals and articles thereof (mainly copper) - around 40%.

Table 1. 10 top products in Poland's exports to China in 2016

HS code	Code description	Value, in million USD	Share, %	Cumulative share, %
7403	*Refined copper and copper alloys*	*378.7*	*19.8*	*19.8*
9403	*Other furniture and parts thereof*	*85.8*	*4.5*	*24.3*
8708	Parts and accessories of motor vehicles	79.0	4.1	28.4
8411	Turbo-jets, turbo-propellers and other gas turbine	63.0	3.3	31.7
4002	*Synthetic rubber and factice derive from oils*	*55.2*	*2.9*	*34.6*
9401	*Seats*	*54.7*	*2.9*	*37.5*
8517	Telephone sets	39.3	2.1	39.6
8539	Electric filament or discharge lamp	36.9	1.9	41.5
8504	Electrical transformers, static converters and inductors	33.1	1.7	43.2
8544	Insulated wire, cable and other electric conductors	32.6	1.7	44.9

Remark: in italic we marked product groups which have not been identified as highly processed products.
Source: own calculations based on COMTRADE data.

Table 2. 10 top products in Czech exports to China in 2016

HS code	Code description	Value, in million USD	Share, %	Cumulative share, %
8708	Parts and accessories of the motor vehicles	183.9	9.6	9.6
8413	Pumps for liquids	123.6	6.4	16.0
8481	Taps, cocks, valves and similar appliances	82.3	4.3	20.3
8536	Electrical apparatus for switching or protecting electrical circuits	72.7	3.8	24.1
9012	Microscopes other than optical	71.5	3.7	27.8
8517	Telephone sets	64.0	3.3	31.1
9503	*Tricycles, scooters, pedal cars and similar wheeled toys*	*62.4*	*3.2*	*34.3*
4702	*Chemical wood pulp*	*58.1*	*3.0*	*37.3*
8544	Insulated wire, cable and other electric conductors	41.4	2.2	39.5
8538	Parts for electrical apparatus	39.5	2.1	41.6

Remark: as in Table 1.
Source: as in Table 1.

Table 3. 10 top products in Hungarian exports to China in 2016

HS code	Code description	Value, in million USD	Share, %	Cumulative share, %
8703	Motor cars and other motor vehicles	691.8	30.8	30.8
8407	Spark-ignition engines for motor vehicles	195.9	8.7	39.5
8471	Automatic data processing machines	82.5	3.7	43.2
3004	Medicaments	77.4	3.4	46.6
8537	Boards, panels, consoles, desks, etc.	72.3	3.2	49.8
8483	Transmission shafts and cranks	62.2	2.8	52.6
8607	Parts of railway or tramway locomotives	60.0	2.7	55.3
9032	Automatic regulating or controlling instruments and apparatus	56.6	2.5	57.8
8411	Turbo-jets, turbo-propellers and other gas turbine	45.9	2.0	59.8
0203	*Meat of swine, fresh, chilled or frozen*	*42.0*	*1.9*	*61.7*

Remark: as in Table 1.
Source: as in Table 1.

Table 4. 10 top products in Slovak exports to China

HS code	Code description	Value, in million USD	Share, %	Cumulative share, %
8703	Motor cars and other motor vehicles	822.0	65.1	65.1
8708	Parts and accessories of motor vehicles	114.7	9.1	74.2
8409	Parts of engines for motor vehicles	29.4	2.3	76.5
8414	Air or vacuum pumps, air or other gas compressors	24.5	1.9	78.4
4011	*New pneumatic tyres, of rubber*	*22.7*	*1.8*	*80.2*
9403	*Other furniture and parts thereof*	*17.2*	*1.4*	*81.6*
8542	Electronic integrated circuits	14.2	1.1	82.7
8477	Machinery for working rubber or plastics	14.1	1.1	83.8
8483	Transmission shafts and cranks	13.1	1.0	84.8
8544	Insulated wire, cable and other electric conductors	10.0	0.8	85.6

Remark: as in Table 1.
Source: as in Table 1.

To sum up, the least advantageous commodity pattern of exports (from the point of view of profitability of exporters and prospects for continuation of specialization in the next years) was observed in Poland.

Let's add that the above analysis of trade pattern-presented in the standard way, it is in the so called gross terms-does not inform properly about the actual value and commodity pattern of bilateral trade, as well as of trade balance. The reason is that it does not reflect the strong relations between Polish producers with producers in other countries within the so called global value chains (GVC) which operate in the framework of transnational corporations, in particular in German corporations. Germany, being the biggest trade partner of China in the EU, sells on the Chinese market a lot of products containing Polish parts and accessories. The standard trade statistics, published by countries and by international organizations, do not take account of this type of trade flows. The more precise information is offered by the statistics presented in terms of value added but requires quite a lot of time and skills to make respective calculations. It can be also obtained from the WIOD basis but always-with a few years delay (Ambroziak 2017).

4. RCA indices

In this chapter we compare the RCA indices of V4 countries in order to assess their comparative advantages (Table 5).

The biggest number of HS Sections which registered increase of RCA ratio in the years 2007-2016 was noted in Polish and Hungarian trade (15 Sections). The smallest number was in Slovakia-only 9 Sections and in the Czech Rep. the respective figure reached 14 Sections.

At the same time, in Poland there were only 2 HS Sections with the same level of RCA indices at the beginning and at the end of the analyzed period. In Hungary we identified also 2 Sections of the same category, in Slovakia-5 Sections and in the Czech Republic-none Section. Decreased level of RCA

Table 5. RCA indices in exports to China

	HS Section	Czech Rep.					Hungary					Poland					Slovakia				
		2007	2009	2010	2014	2016	2007	2009	2010	2014	2016	2007	2009	2010	2014	2016	2007	2009	2010	2014	2016
I	Animal products	0.28	0.05	0.09	0.14	0.15	0.54	0.23	0.24	1.50	5.53	3.36	2.02	2.76	8.31	6.71	0.00	0.00	0.00	0.04	0.03
II	Vegetable products	0.45	0.88	0.77	0.96	1.01	0.10	0.16	0.26	0.28	0.02	0.52	0.32	0.40	0.34	0.72	0.00	0.00	0.00	0.00	0.00
III	Fats and oils	0.17	0.00	0.00	0.00	0.07	0.00	0.00	0.00	0.03	0.54	0.02	0.06	0.17	0.91	0.39	0.00	0.00	0.00	0.00	0.00
IV	Prepared foodstuffs	0.17	0.23	0.26	0.33	0.58	0.03	0.08	0.22	0.32	0.36	0.31	0.21	0.40	5.14	1.52	0.00	0.01	0.00	0.06	0.08
V	Mineral products	0.25	0.23	0.43	0.03	0.28	0.06	0.10	0.12	0.04	0.22	2.74	1.98	1.27	2.98	2.73	0.00	0.01	0.00	0.01	0.02
VI	Chemical products	0.71	0.99	0.69	0.43	0.61	0.48	0.33	0.23	0.72	1.15	6.09	3.39	3.31	0.73	1.19	0.09	0.06	0.10	0.03	0.05
VII	Plastics	1.90	2.64	1.75	1.71	1.55	0.74	0.83	1.13	0.82	0.76	0.88	1.82	1.53	1.94	2.38	0.29	0.92	0.45	0.33	0.88
VIII	Leather products	0.58	0.26	0.67	1.04	0.61	0.15	0.15	0.20	0.20	0.10	0.04	0.21	0.19	0.17	0.16	0.01	0.00	0.01	0.01	0.04
IX	Wood and articles of wood	0.30	0.50	0.52	0.74	0.56	0.04	0.05	0.06	0.19	0.21	0.21	0.20	0.38	0.89	1.77	0.03	0.04	0.07	0.13	0.54
X	Pulp of wood and paper	0.81	0.92	1.23	5.64	3.45	0.44	0.16	0.06	0.11	0.24	1.83	0.82	0.77	0.50	0.93	0.00	0.04	0.04	0.03	0.13
XI	Textiles and textile articles	0.05	0.03	0.04	0.07	0.07	0.02	0.01	0.01	0.02	0.03	0.05	0.03	0.03	0.06	0.10	0.15	0.04	0.04	0.03	0.05
XII	Footwear	0.00	0.00	0.01	0.01	0.02	0.00	0.00	0.00	0.00	0.00	0.00	0.00	0.00	0.01	0.07	0.61	0.50	0.30	0.25	0.20
XIII	Ceramic products	4.35	1.61	0.94	0.64	0.64	0.09	0.06	0.07	0.45	0.50	0.59	1.08	0.70	0.90	1.08	0.16	0.11	0.12	0.15	0.09
XIV	Precious metals	0.21	0.05	0.08	0.01	0.01	0.00	0.00	0.01	0.01	0.02	0.03	0.04	0.05	0.04	0.03	0.00	0.00	0.00	0.00	0.00
XV	Base metals and articles thereof	0.63	2.42	2.37	0.86	0.70	0.24	0.28	0.43	0.77	0.49	4.14	6.65	6.45	5.06	3.72	0.35	0.22	0.13	0.18	0.24
XVI	Machinery and equipment	1.40	1.10	1.05	1.06	1.03	1.82	1.75	1.53	1.05	0.75	0.56	0.53	0.44	0.49	0.61	0.52	0.38	0.35	0.36	0.33
XVII	Transport equipment	2.98	3.39	3.72	3.64	4.15	2.59	2.26	2.88	8.03	11.95	1.09	1.95	2.51	1.33	1.73	31.07	31.58	27.66	27.81	25.12
XVIII	Precision instruments	1.12	1.62	1.59	1.91	2.59	0.56	1.11	2.23	2.55	2.46	0.32	0.69	0.56	0.59	0.80	0.08	0.15	0.20	0.15	0.27
XIX	Arms and ammunition	0.00	0.00	0.01	0.02	0.39	0.00	0.00	0.00	0.00	0.00	0.00	0.10	0.00	0.00	0.00	0.00	0.00	0.00	0.00	0.00
XX	Miscellaneous manufactured articles	0.16	0.32	0.41	0.90	0.85	0.02	0.05	0.05	0.32	0.28	0.31	0.32	0.51	0.97	1.11	0.15	0.12	0.12	0.30	0.25
XXI	Works of art	0.01	0.25	0.36	0.21	0.30	0.00	0.20	0.54	0.41	0.22	0.00	0.01	2.89	3.67	0.18	0.00	0.00	0.00	0.00	0.00

indices was observed only in 4 Sections in Poland, in 4 Sections in Hungary, in 7 Sections in Slovakia and in 7 Sections in the Czech Republic.

The strongest competitive position-as measured by RCA indices-was recorded in 2016 in all V4 countries in Slovakia in transport equipment: 25! in 2016. In 2007 and 2011 the index in this sector was even higher and amounted to 31(!) but the downward trend did not affect much exports as the share of this product group accounted for slightly less than 1% in 2016. The next sector with strong competitive position was transport equipment in Hungary (RCA index equal 12 in 2016). The other sectors in V4 countries were characterized by indices lower than 7 in 2016; among them were animal products in Poland (RCA index at 6.7 in 2016), animal products in Hungary (5.5); base metals and products thereof in Poland-mostly copper (3.7); transport equipment and pulp of wood and paper in the Czech Rep. (4.2 and 3.5 respectively). The level of other RCA indices was below 3. There were, however, a few such situations. Altogether: in Slovakia-only one (!) HS Section recorded in 2016 the RCA indices higher than the threshold 1 considered as the reflection of competitiveness of a given group of products. In the Czech Republic the index above 1 was calculated for 6 HS Sections, among them two Sections occupying the strongest positions in the country's exports (machinery and transport equipment with 52% and 12% shares, respectively). In Hungary only in 4 HS Sections the RCA index was above 1, including, however, transport equipment, one of the biggest export groups (35% in 2016). We should probably add to this group also machinery which registered in all previous years, except 2015-2016, indices well above 1. Poland had the longest list of HS Sections with the RCA index higher than 1 (10) which contained very important Polish exports (e.g. base metals and articles thereof). At the same time, however, the other equally important Section in the whole period in Polish exports, namely machinery and equipment-did not register comparative advantage in terms of RCA index.

Also, in some other cases one might identify relatively big exports with very low RCA indices (e.g. very low and decreasing RCA values for top exports in Slovakia).. In general, the number of HS Sections with high RCA indices did not correspond with the share of products subject to those RCA indices in total exports. What counts more for final conclusions, however, is the share of competitive products (with high RCA indices) in total exports and this approach is adopted in point 6.

5. Trade coverage ratios by HS Sections*

In the Czech Republic, the trade deficit characterized in the period analyzed all HS Sections, except for works of art and pulp of wood in recent few years (Table 6). Both groups played however a very small role in exports (0% and 4%). In the case of the biggest export products (machinery and equipment-52% of exports), the TC index was very low and amounted to 7.5%. For the other more important HS Sections, reaching from 12% to 6% of exports (transport equipment; precision instruments; miscellaneous manufactured articles; plastics) the TC indices varied between 29% and 53%. In general, in 16 Sections the level of TC ratios was below 50%.

In the case of Hungary, the exceptionally high surplus of exports over imports was observed for animal products which accounted however, for only 3% of total exports. The other HS Sections with TC above 100% were: transport equipment; works of art, mineral products; fats and oils; prepared foodstuffs; precision instruments. The first out of those Sections registered very high index in the whole period (470% in 2016) and was the second largest group in exports in 2016 (35%). Precision instruments-the third biggest export group (8%) - was also characterized by positive TC indices during the most of the period 2007-2014. In general, only in 11 Sections the TC indices were below 50% in 2016.

The most characteristic element of the ratio of exports to imports in Slovakia was an impressive level of this ratio for transport equipment

---

* The analysis is based on own calculations, not presented here, because of lack of space.

Table 6. TC indices in trade with China (in %)

HS Section	Czech Rep.					Hungary					Poland					Slovakia				
	2007	2009	2010	2014	2016	2007	2009	2010	2014	2016	2007	2009	2010	2014	2016	2007	2009	2010	2014	2016
Tot.	7.6	8.0	7.9	11.7	10.8	19.8	24.5	24.8	42.2	46.1	8.4	10.6	9.9	9.8	8.2	14.5	24.7	32.2	27.4	19.9
I Animal products	5.1	1.3	3.1	4.2	5.5	149.7	162.4	117.3	509.5	2450.1	11.9	8.1	12.3	60.1	50.6	0.0	0.1	0.0	3.9	3.2
II Vegetable products	5.9	15.3	15.2	28.8	37.8	5.9	13.0	24.3	30.7	3.4	4.4	4.4	4.9	4.4	9.6	0.0	0.0	0.1	0.0	0.0
III Fats and oils	43.8	0.0	0.0	0.0	18.0	0.0	0.0	0.0	91.3	405.4	1.9	3.7	7.9	15.5	8.2	0.0	0.0	0.0	0.0	0.0
IV Prepared foodstuffs	2.5	4.7	6.9	12.0	23.4	4.8	25.1	76.9	90.8	161.5	3.9	5.3	6.1	99.4	38.2	0.1	0.5	0.5	12.3	9.8
V Mineral products	28.7	27.2	61.7	6.6	56.7	131.5	265.0	280.9	23.0	420.3	88.7	64.3	41.4	88.2	64.7	0.0	1.0	0.0	1.3	2.6
VI Chemical products	10.9	23.0	18.8	12.8	20.2	34.4	32.4	27.4	71.1	86.3	70.3	62.2	59.2	10.8	16.3	4.0	4.5	10.5	1.8	4.4
VII Plastics	23.1	38.1	32.6	35.6	29.3	21.4	44.4	68.3	56.8	48.1	7.3	24.0	18.9	22.6	22.8	6.1	26.4	20.6	17.7	38.6
VIII Leather products	5.8	2.8	9.2	16.4	8.7	17.0	19.4	34.9	40.8	10.1	0.4	2.4	1.9	1.7	1.4	0.2	0.1	0.8	0.2	1.1
IX Wood and articles of wood	5.1	9.7	13.1	32.5	25.7	4.6	8.8	14.8	58.4	77.7	2.7	2.8	4.9	13.0	25.9	1.4	2.2	6.0	14.3	50.8
X Pulp of wood and paper	12.9	12.6	19.4	153.7	122.1	30.1	26.6	9.2	24.8	51.3	21.7	15.3	13.1	7.6	14.4	0.0	2.5	3.1	3.7	11.0
XI Textiles and textile articles	0.8	0.4	0.7	1.6	1.4	2.6	2.3	3.2	5.8	7.3	0.5	0.3	0.2	0.5	0.7	3.8	1.1	1.5	1.2	1.5
XII Footwear	0.0	0.0	0.1	0.1	0.3	1.2	0.0	0.0	0.0	0.1	0.0	0.0	0.0	0.0	0.4	11.5	15.5	8.1	3.2	2.4
XIII Ceramic products	46.9	22.9	14.5	20.0	22.4	2.7	3.5	4.1	32.0	38.0	2.8	8.8	5.5	8.8	9.9	3.5	2.3	3.7	6.2	4.3
XIV Precious metals	6.0	1.8	2.8	1.0	0.4	0.9	0.8	2.2	6.4	11.7	0.6	0.8	1.0	1.6	0.7	0.0	0.0	0.0	0.0	0.1
XV Base metals and articles thereof	6.4	31.2	39.1	18.0	13.1	19.2	18.6	34.6	68.7	38.3	27.7	76.6	71.2	55.1	33.4	6.6	7.2	6.3	8.6	7.3
XVI Machinery and equipment	7.0	5.8	5.3	8.5	7.5	18.8	22.6	20.6	26.9	22.5	4.4	4.9	3.8	4.6	4.6	4.9	7.3	8.4	7.3	5.2
XVII Transport equipment	44.7	57.4	94.6	87.6	86.4	245.1	327.7	502.8	803.1	715.4	7.9	24.8	37.0	16.1	18.9	623.1	830.9	1518.2	1486.6	685.1
XVIII Precision instruments	16.6	24.6	31.3	50.7	53.3	64.3	155.1	263.0	188.2	148.9	4.8	12.7	8.5	7.6	7.3	3.8	9.1	10.7	4.8	1.7
XIX Arms and ammunition	0.0	0.0	0.1	0.2	2.9	0.0	0.0	0.0	0.0	0.0	0.5	0.0	0.0	0.0	0.0	0.0	0.0	0.0	0.0	0.0
XX Miscellaneous manufactured articles	2.2	5.0	6.7	14.4	13.7	1.4	8.3	8.8	36.1	34.5	3.1	4.5	6.0	7.3	7.5	3.6	2.6	4.7	10.9	7.7
XXI Works of art	1.7	34.6	63.3	21.5	158.4	0.4	208.1	195.7	71.2	668.5	0.1	0.5	241.2	373.0	42.2	0.0	0.5	2.3	0.0	0.0

(fluctuating around 1500% in individual years) - 685% in 2016. For all other HS Sections the same index was however extremely low-less than 20%, except for two product groups with higher rates (wood and article of wood; plastics).

In Poland the situation looked in 2016 the worst in terms of TC indices as compared to the other V4 countries: a/ in no single HS Section exports were higher than imports; b/ in all Sections but two, the level of TC index was well below 50%. The situation was particularly bad in the Section machinery and equipment (TC equal 4.6), the biggest group in Poland's exports to China.

6. Main conclusions from the statistical analysis

In the period analysed (2007-2016), the vast majority of exports (classified by HS Chapters) of all V4 countries to China possessed revealed comparative advantages. The situation of Poland was, however, the weakest in this regard. The share of products with RCA index above 1 in Polish exports to China amounted in 2016 only to 63.9%. In Hungary the similar index was the highest-85%!, followed closely by the Czech Republic-82.5%. In Slovakia it reached 74%.

Also in terms of TC indices, Poland performed the worst among V4 countries. In no single HS Section the country registered the index above 100%. What is more troublesome is that the trade coverage ratio in 2016 was almost exactly of the same level as in 2007. This situation suggests that Poland has the biggest problem to reduce the deficit in trade with China. In Slovakia the share of products with higher exports than imports was the biggest and amounted to 74% in 2016! (it covered only one HS Section transport equipment). It was not one year phenomenon as the TC index much above 100% was registered for this Section during the whole analyzed period, albeit in recent two years the index decreased by above half (to 685%). The situation was quite good also in Hungary-with TC index above 100% covering around 47% of country's exports (mostly machinery and equipment and chemical products). What is more important, the total deficit has been decreasing year by year. In the Czech Republic, the positive trade balance characterized less than 4% of products exported.

The relatively worst situation of Poland-in terms of basic competitiveness indices and possibilities to reduce the trade deficit-has been confirmed by the commodity pattern of ten top products in exports of V4 countries. An important part of Polish exports has been absorbed by copper and copper alloys, it is a raw material and unprocessed articles thereof. Such exports are much dependent on world price fluctuations (despite volume increase of exports in 2015, the value of copper and copper exports decreased in this year as compared to the previous year, due to the decrease of prices).[1]

Even more important is that such exports are not very advantageous in terms of the type of specialization (low value added to each unit of a product). No other V4 country has exports so much concentrated on unprocessed and semi-processed products.

7. Prospects of the development of Polish exports to China in the nearest future[2]

In the short run it will be difficult to reduce substantially the high deficit in Poland's trade with China. As already mentioned, Poland is exporting to

---

[1] The respective data for copper and copper products in Polish exports to China in 2014-2015 was as follows:

	price, USD/kg	value, USD mn	Thous. tons
2011	6,80	703,5	103,5
2015	5,38	662,7	123,3
2016	4,78	378,7	79,3

[2] Although we concentrate here on chances of increasing exports from Poland, the majority of opinions are probably true for all V4 countries, especially those which take into account changes in the demand on the Chinese market.

this partner mostly low processed products, which are much less profitable as compared with high processed goods. Products dominating in Polish exports to China are also sensitive to frequent price fluctuations on world markets.

There are, however, some circumstances which offer the possibility to speed up the rate of exports and improve its commodity pattern in the medium term.

Good prospects for exports seem to exist in the case of processed food products. In recent several years this sector has been increasing its share in Polish exports (e.g. the share of prepared foodstuffs increased from 0.3% to 1.5% of total exports in 2007-2016 and most of this change took place in recent 3 years only). The selling of these products in China is not easy because of complex certification procedures. Still, Poland has been already known on the Chinese market for high quality of food. For example, Poland was in 2017 the only supplier from the EU who was allowed to sell poultry in China (Bułkowska 2018). Another example of chances used by Polish exporters was Polish fruit-growers who managed to introduce to the Chinese market Polish apples after the embargo imposed in 2014 by Russia on many Polish food products. The first train with Polish apples reached Chengdu in December 2016 (Bułkowska 2018).

Food products are one group of promising goods on the Chinese market and reflect changes going on in the demand pattern of better off Chinese consumers who look for new products. The other relatively new phenomenon is fast development of Chinese market for luxury goods (e.g. jewellery, luxury watches, perfume, cars), Drelich-Skulska et al., 2012, p. 32-33. This trend is related to very fast increase of the average wealth of Chinese people in recent years (especially before the crisis of 2007-2009), and in particular even faster growth of the most wealthy people (millionaires and multimillionaires). Poland does not have a tradition of producing many luxury brand products, in international reach particular. In some areas Polish producers are, however, able to compete with best foreign brands (e.g. in the area of jewellery, some cosmetics). Apart from brand products it is also a question of a proper selling strategy. Research has shown that a good strategy with regard to Chinese customers is to convince them that the goods offered them belong to the luxury goods as Chinese society is sensitive to the price level (Drelich-Skulska et al., 2012, p. 32-33). Such a strategy requires, of course, not only high quality of a product offered and a high price of this product but also a proper package, high standard of sales service etc. Chinese customers are ready to pay quite high price for a product but only when they are convinced that they will get something exceptional for their money. One example is American vitamins for children which are sold on the Chinese market at much higher price than in the USA: at USD 55 as compared to USD 12 in USA (Doing Business, 2012, p. 15).

Among the perspective product groups experts mention also: all types of cosmetics, cloth and accessories, furniture and house equipment, ecological construction materials and technologies (windows), medical equipment; alcoholic beverages, in that beer (Skulska et al., p. 32).

Fast development of the construction sector-in line with impressive GDP growth rates of the country and following urbanization-contributed substantially to the demand for furniture and other elements of household equipment (refrigerators, TV sets etc.) as well as for construction materials and accessories. It is also a chance for Polish furniture producers who have become world leaders due to high quality of products offered.

There are products, in which Polish producers have already gained some experience and position on Chinese market: for example, windows exported by Polish producer FAKRO, several brands of beer exported by Van Pur-the largest independent Polish brewing company, offering beers and non-alcoholic malt beverages [1] In both cases the scale of exports is, unfortunately, small as compared to total Polish exports and comparing to the huge size of the Chinese market. This is a good moment to stress, what Chinese experts mention often in discussions, that an important barrier for Polish exports is not sufficient amount of homogeneous products (of similar quality, size etc. in case of food) which are being offered for exports at a given point of time. In other words, Polish

---

[1] http://www.vanpur.com/?plus18=1.

exporters, usually medium-sized companies, have a problem to supply a bigger amount of products required by their Chinese partners.

The other important elements of rapid changes in the pattern of demand on the huge Chinese market are as follows:[1]

— development of the middle class of the society-in terms of the number of people involved, the level of their incomes and regions they live (it is not only in big cities but also in Central China) which results in higher demand for more sophisticated, more differentiated (foreign), and of better quality products;

— in general, from the point of view of Polish exporters an important issue is that the demand for foreign products has been developing in China faster than for domestically produced goods as products originating abroad are considered to be more prestigious.

A factor affecting exports is a big role played by e-commerce: China is nowadays the biggest market of Internet retail sale in the world. China's share in this type of trade exceeds 40%. The value of e-commerce reached in China in 2016 around USD 1 billion. It's been estimated that in 2015, 81% of Chinese consumers were customers of Internet platforms.[2] Thus, the main challenge for the Polish suppliers is to prepare an attractive export offer and to effectively acquire the potential clients. The competition is high, like on a traditional market, but the cost of access to the market is lower as compared to the traditional cross-border trade. Functioning of the "silk road" offers the possibility of quick delivery of goods requested by customers.

Sometimes the remedy to increase exports is relatively easy to be introduced. It's simply the bigger scale of exports as in the case of some products, the main barrier is insufficient amount of products requested by the partner (especially in the case of agricultural products).

A positive aspect of mutual cooperation is that China is exporting to Poland not only big quantities of goods but also investing in production in

---

① http://www.gochina.gov.pl/.
② http://www.gochina.gov.pl/.

Poland. The first big example was the purchase of steelworks Stalowa Wola by Liu Gong. Even more visible is the Chinese capital in Polish electronic sector production of TV sets and LCD screens (TLC company in Żyrardów, Digital View in Koszalin), in electro-machinery sector (Nuctech in Kobyłka near Warszawa) and in IT branch (ZTE, Huawei). These examples show that-similarly to activities in other countries-Chinese companies are departing from the trade exclusively in goods and moving towards investment as well. In the last areas they are concentrating in the areas of modern technologies (Góralczyk 2012, p. 28-29; Kaliszuk 2016).

Polish companies are also trying to invest in China. In 2011 more than 200 companies with Polish capital were registered in China, in the majority of small trade companies. Among the biggest Polish investors on this market there are: Selena, Kopex, Bioton, Rafako, PMP Poland, Fasing, GK Gwarant. At the same time, around 500 companies with Chinese capital were registered in Poland, in most cases (430) small companies employing not more than 9 persons.[①]

The additional element that should be taken into account while assessing chances of Polish exports to China is undoubtedly the export offer of our closest partners from V4 who are at the same time important competitors, taking into account such factors as similar level of economic development of V4, medium level of their innovativeness, close geographical location, relatively high FDI engagement (although at different levels in terms of per capita level), etc. From this point of view it's striking (in negative terms) that Polish exports contain relatively low share of products within HS Section 87, it is vehicles other than railway or tramway rolling-stock, and parts and accessories thereof. This Chapter includes first of all various cars and their parts and reflects involvement of western corporations (FDI) in car industry (or rather in the whole transport equipment sectors) in V4 (see Box 2). Polish products are, however, sold to China indirectly-through foreign (mostly German) companies operating in Poland which purchase accessories and parts and export them to Germany

---

① In 2011 slightly more than 200 companies with Polish capital were registered in China.

and branches in other countries to produce final goods exported to the next customers, including China (within the above mentioned global value chains).

Box 2. FDI in the transport equipment sector in V4 countries

The most foreign direct investment in the transport equipment sector was attracted by the Czech Republic. At the end of 2014 the stock of inward FDI in the transport equipment industry in this country exceeded EUR 10.6 billion. It accounted for nearly one-third of FDI in Czech manufacturing. The second largest recipient of foreign capital was the transport equipment industry in Poland (EUR 9.1 billion at the end of 2014). But FDI in this sector played a lesser role than in the Czech Republic (nearly 18%). At the end of 2014 in Hungary and Slovakia the stock of inward FDI in the transport equipment industry was below EUR 4 billion. In Slovakia the industry discussed accounted for as much as 24% of foreign capital invested in manufacturing. In Hungary, the respective share was about 15%; see more: Ambroziak (2016).

Poland is not using much the chances offered by the BRI. There are no precise statistics on cargo delivered by train to China but some estimates show that only slightly more than 3% of Polish exports in 2016 were delivered via this route (and only 0.7% in 2015, EUROSTAT-Comext). Broader use of this transportation mode by Polish exporters could result in faster deliveries of goods and contribute to reduction of the cost of this way of transportation in the future.

To this end, a campaign should be worked out and implemented on a broad scale in Poland to promote BRI among Polish businessmen. Also, a better program of promotion of cooperation of both countries is implemented when government's institutions is necessary. In Poland, what is of crucial importance is a proper information about specific elements of market access to China (e.g. language, certificates). Equally important is a necessity of easier access to financial instruments, indispensable in contemporary trade (credits, guarantees, etc.).

The "greenfield" activities should be supported by public administration of both partners. In recent years, a number of visits have been paid by top politicians of both countries, but so far all that has not resulted in visible additional exports.[1]

Summary and conclusions

The value of Poland's exports to- and imports from China doubled in the period analyzed (in USD billions: from 1 to 1.9 in exports and from 11.8 to 23.4 in imports) but the trend of changes was not smooth. Fluctuations of trade, in particular of exports, resulted mostly from cyclical changes of world prices of base metals (mostly copper) and articles thereof, as these products accounted for a very important part of total exports (the highest value was 48% in 2011 and the lowest one-26% in 2016).

The relatively high growth of trade has been recorded, however, from a low starting level at the beginning of the 21th century and China is still not an important outlet for Polish products (its share is less than 1%). At the same time, Poland occupies a very distant place on the list of foreign suppliers to China (close to the 60th place in 2016).

As a result of this unproportionate turnover, Polish deficit in trade with China is huge (USD 21.5 bn in 2016) and has been increasing in recent years. The analysis has revealed that its reduction through export acceleration will not be easy in the nearest future because of several factors:

– the starting position is very disadvantageous: the coverage rate of exports over imports is extremely low;

---

[1] https://www.money.pl/gospodarka/wiadomosci/artykul/jedwabny-szlak-chiny-polska-brama-do-ue,103,0,2318439.html.

– in a number of important products Polish exports do not possess revealed comparative advantage;

– exports are dominated by raw materials and semi-processed products which do not guarantee high revenue growth because their prices fluctuate much and demand for them is not growing fast.

Still, several factors were identified in this study that create new chances for Polish exporters offering their goods on the Chinese market. Among them there were:

– increase of the export offer of those Polish products which are already supplied to Chinese consumers and are in line with the changing demand of Chinese consumers (processed food, windows, cosmetics, furniture);

– promotion of a broader use of BRI Initiative;

– higher institutional and organizational support on the part of public bodies, both in Poland and in China;

– more intensive involvement of Polish companies in production and services in China (through FDI) which allows to be closer to customers and react faster in the case of demand changes.

References

Łukasz Ambroziak, "FDI and Intra-industry Trade in the Automotive Industry in the New EU Member States", *International Journal of Management and Economics*, 52(1), pp. 23-42, 2016.

Łukasz Ambroziak, "Decomposition of Poland's Bilateral Trade Imbalances by Value Added Content", *Entrepreneurial Business and Economics Review*, 5(2), pp. 51-69, 2017.

Bela Balassa, Trade Liberalization and Revealed Comparative Advantage, *Manchester School of Economic and Social Studies*, Vol 33, pp.99-123, 1965.

Małgorzata Bułkowska, "Chiny-strategiczny partner Polski w handlu z krajami spoza UE", *Przemysł Spożywczy*, No. 1, 2018.

"Doing Business in China, 2012 Country Commercial Guide for U.S. Companies", (2012), U.S. & Foreign Commercial Service and U.S. Department of State, p.15, cited from: Drelich-Skulska B., Bobowski S, Jankowiak A.H., Skulski P., (2012), "Nisze rynkowe dla polskich produktów w Chinach", Ekspertyza przygotowana na zlecenie Ministerstwa Gospodarki oraz Polskiej Agencji Informacji i Inwestycji Zagranicznych dotycząca możliwości wejścia na rynek chiński przez polskich przedsiębiorców (http://www.gochina.gov.pl/ ekspertyzy_gochina), p. 33.

Bogusława Drelich-Skulska, Sebastian Bobowski, Anna H. Jankowiak, Przemysław Skulski, (2012), Nisze rynkowe dla polskich produktów w Chinach", Ekspertyza przygotowana na zlecenie Ministerstwa Gospodarki oraz Polskiej Agencji Informacji i Inwestycji Zagranicznych dotycząca możliwości wejścia na rynek chiński przez polskich przedsiębiorców (http://www.gochina. gov.pl/ekspertyzy_gochina).

Bogdan Góralczyk, "Miejsce Polski w strategii gospodarczej i polityce zagranicznej Chin po przekazaniu władzy na XVIII zjeździe KPCh", ekspertyza dla PAIZ Warszawa, 2012. (http://www.gochina.gov.pl/ekspertyzy_gochina).

Ewa Kaliszuk, "Chinese and South Korean Investment in Poland: A Comparative Study", *Transnational Corporations Review*, 8(1), pp. 60-78, 2016.

http://www.vanpur.com/?plus18=1.

http://www.gochina.gov.pl/.

https://www.money.pl/gospodarka/wiadomosci/artykul/jedwabny-szlak-chiny-polska-brama-do-ue,103,0,2318439.html.

Sino-European research and academic cooperation under BRI Framework: Social Sciences as a tool to improve Europe-China relations

Dr Łukasz Zamęcki

Abstract

The EU and China are already important economic and research partners, and the Belt and Road Initiative is creating a huge potential to boost this cooperation. The aim of this essay is to discuss the possible role of social sciences in the mutual understanding of Europe and China. The author's stance is to demonstrate the important areas and possibilities in which the cooperation on the field of social sciences can contribute to Sino-European understanding, despite different cultural backgrounds. Cooperation in the field of social sciences is not only coherent with BRI principles, but can also accelerate the still underestimated cooperation in other fields. The author proposes launching an institutional project (in the framework of an international board) under BRI, called the "Belt and Road Initiative Social Science Fund", which entails establishing research units and networks, joint publishing of books, organizing joint conferences, funding individual and team grants, establishing anopen-access scientific journal, supporting exchanges of professors and young researchers, and launching an Annual Sino-European Forum for Social Sciences Researchers.

Introduction

This paper does not present the research of grounded assumptions. The aim of the essay is to discuss the possible role of social sciences in the mutual understanding of Europe and China. The idea for this paper was born during the conference organized by the Sichuan University in 2017. The author aims to prove that the important possibilities stemming from the cooperation on the field of social sciences can contribute to Sino-European understanding. Furthermore, considering that the Belt and Road Initiative has already shown the potential to give a tremendous boost to the cooperation between both sides, I try to show the possibility to expand the BRI with research activities in social sciences. Cooperation in this field would not only be coherent with BRI principles but could accelerate the still underestimated cooperationin other fields.

1. Principles of the Belt and Road Initiative

The main goal of the Belt and Road Initiative, announced in 2013 by President Xi Jinping, is to "promote the economic prosperity of the countries along the Belt and Road Initiative and regional economic cooperation, strengthen exchanges and mutual learning between different civilizations, and promote world peace and development". According to this announcement, the general principles of BRI uphold mutual respect for each other's sovereignty and territorial integrity and advocate mutual nonaggression, mutual non-interference in each other's internal affairs, equality, mutual benefit, and peaceful coexistence. Furthermore, as the official presentation of the Belt and Road Initiative underlines, its goal is to achieve "...win-win cooperation that promotes common development and prosperity [...] by enhancing mutual understanding and trust, and strengthening all-round exchanges"[1].

---

[1]   *Vision and Actions on Jointly Building Silk Road Economic Belt and 21st-Century Maritime Silk Road,* retrieved from: http://en.ndrc.gov.cn/newsrelease/201503/t20150330_669367.html.

Since 2013 the Initiative has introduced comprehensive cooperation and investment in the fields of connectivity, international trade, tourism or financial integration. We are witnessing a variety of infrastructural proposals in Asia and Europe, co-financed in the frameworks of BRI. However, the BRIaims and principles can also be applied for the **research cooperation** among countries located on the B&R route. The quotation "Tolerance among civilizations respects the paths and modes of development chosen by different countries and supports dialogues among different civilizations" can be better understood when we considerthe efforts of the researchers who build the groundwork for cultures (what social scientists do); "wisdom and creativity" are obvious values of science;even the "common prosperity" can be better assisted by academic teamwork. Therefore, academic cooperation can be an important instrument of BRI.

The BRI acknowledges the need for "cooperation in science and technology"; it has already stressed the need to "establish joint labs (or research centres)". During the Belt and Road Initiative Forum for International Cooperation in 2017, President Xi Jinping underlined that "Innovation is an important force powering development". The main fields of cooperation were mentioned: artificial intelligence, nanotechnology, quantum computing, and smart cities[1].

2. Sino-European academic cooperation under BRI

The EU and China are responsible for almost 40% of the global GDP. Both actors are also important as world traders-they accounted for 33% of the global export and 27% of global import. European Community and the PRC cooperate quite strongly. The EU is, in fact, the largest trading partner for China

---

[1] D. Normile, *China's belt and road Initiative infrastructure plan also includes science*, retrieved from: http://www.sciencemag.org/news/2017/05/china-s-belt-and-road-infrastructure-plan-also-includes-science.

and China is EU's second-biggest trading partner.

The EU and China also collaborate in the field of scientific research, recognizing its rising importance. In 1998, the European Community and China signed the Agreement on Cooperation in Science and Technology. The Agreement was renewed on December 2004, then subsequently on November 2009, and, for the third time, on December 2014.Every year, among many other sectoral dialogues, a discussion on the field of S&T takes place. Nevertheless, the EU-China dialogue on Science and Technology was one of the first areas of cooperation between the EC and China.

Both actors have established mechanisms to finance joint cooperation. The Chinese Government and the EU have also established the Co-funding Mechanism to support joint research and innovation projects between European and Chinese universities and research institutions.The initiatives that are flagships for the cooperation are the following: Food and Agriculture; Environment and Sustainable Urbanisation; Transportand Biotechnologies.

The Belt and Road Initiative has opened new mechanisms of financing Euro-Chinese cooperation. One of the fields of this financing is academic collaboration. The academic cooperation under BRI already covers various forms of activity-scientific conferences, student[1] and academic exchanges. To give only a few examples of cooperation between the Sichuan University and University of Warsaw (Poland), both sides agreed on:

- a joint study program "2+1+2" (so-called "Polish +") and joint study program "3+1+1";
- a joint Center for Polish and Central European Studies;
- joint seminars twice a year;
- summer schools.

The American think-tank, Center for Strategic and International Studies, based on the data from the Chinese Ministry of Education, states that by the end

---

① Zhao Xinying, *President's initiatives spur plan for new scholarship*, retrieved from: http://english.gov.cn/news/top_news/2015/04/20/content_281475092513397.htm.

of April 2017, 45 educational agreements had been signed between China and B&R countries. According to the Ministry of Education of China, due to the newly established bilateral exchange programs over the next several years, 2,500 Chinese students will leave the country annually to study abroad. What is more, every year, China offers 10,000 places for students "whose home countries are identified as part of the Belt and Road Initiative". In 2016, 284,141 students from 64 of the 68 B&R countries studied in China[1]. The best world universities (e.g. University of Cambridge) have already launched B&R research centers[2] and the University Alliance of the Silk Road already connects more than 120 academic institutions. These activities constitute great investments in the mutual understanding of both sides and promoting their ownvisions of cultural values.

Bai Chunli, the president of the Chinese Academy of Sciences, in the context of the May 2017 Belt and Road Initiative Forum for International Cooperation, underlined that his institution alone has trained about 1,800 people from Belt and Road Initiative countries (focusing on issues such as climate change, water security, green energy, and disaster prevention and relief). The academy, furthermore, hasset up 9 overseas centers for science and technology cooperation and has launched more than 20 science projects. He also stressed that more than 30,000 foreign scholars visit the academy every year to take part in exchanges and cooperation[3].

China also plans to further strengthen the scientific cooperation under BRI. Bai Chunli, at a press conference on 9 May 2017, announced a plan to reinforce the research cooperation along the Belt and Road Initiative countries[4]. The project calls for training 5,000 foreign scientists and engineers over the next 5

---

[1] CSIS, *Is China both a source and hub for international students?*, retrieved from: https://chinapower.csis.org/china-international-students/.

[2] Xinhua, *Belt and Road Initiative Int'l center officially launched at University of Cambridge*, retrieved from: http://news.xinhuanet.com/english/2017-09/30/c_136649608.htm.

[3] Zhang Zhihao, *Science, innovation cooperation to benefit Belt and Road Initiative countries*, retrieved from: http://europe.chinadaily.com.cn/china/2017-05/09/content_29266235.htm.

[4] *China unveils "Belt and Road Initiative" science plans*, retrieved from: http://www.researchresearch.com/news/article/?articleId=1367868.

Students from B&R countries

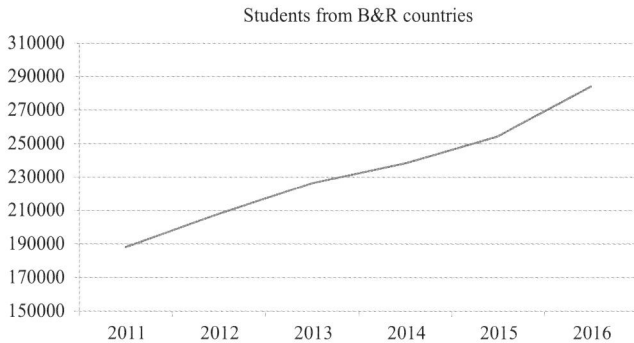

Figure 1. Students from B&R countries in China
Source: https://chinapower.csis.org/china-international-students/

years, as well as welcoming young scientists to China on short-term research visits. In addition, the initiative plans to set up 50 joint laboratories[1].

3. Challenges of the Sino-European social sciences researches

One of the concerning issues is the lack of existing instruments under BRI framework for research cooperation in the field of social science. Questions about the reasons for this situation must be raised, together with the appeal for the appreciation of social sciences and humanities.

A simple observation thus shows us that over the last few decades, applied sciences have hoisted everywhere in the world (as we can see above, China's most prolific research areas are also applied sciences). Without depreciating the world's pursuit of economic development, it is nowadays unquestionable that the world has alsonoticed the traps of ill-conceived technocratization, such as weakening communities and social ties, deprivation and dehumanization of man. Social sciences and humanities can be thus an interesting antidote to the

---

[1] D. Normile, *China's Belt and Road Initiative infrastructure plan also includes science*, retrieved from: http://www.sciencemag.org/news/2017/05/china-s-belt-and-road-infrastructure-plan-also-includes-science.

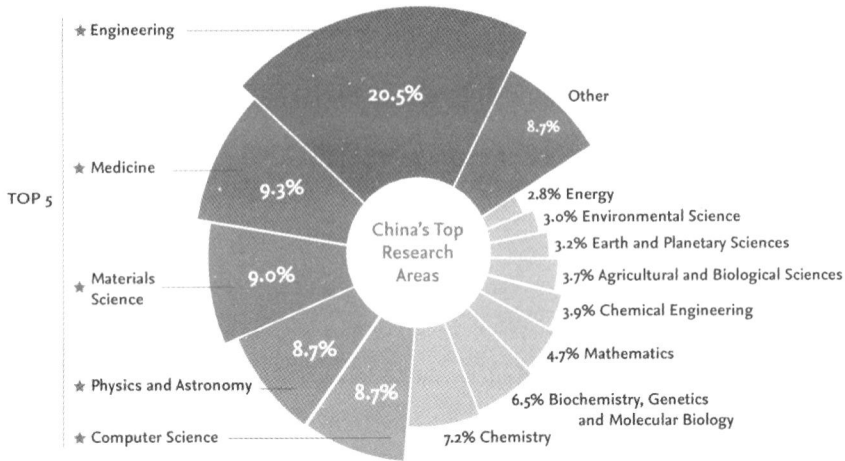

Figure 2. China's Most Prolific Research Areas (2011-2016)
Source: https://www.elsevier.com/research-intelligence/campaigns/onebeltoneroad

errors of rash modernization; they can contribute to the process of building the cultures of nations, mutual understanding and trust among people, and can aid in bringing peace, learning creativity and human rights. Social sciences are frequently underestimated by exact or applied sciences, often because of the accusation of being "not-measurable", "presenting a variety of paradigms" and "being susceptible to political involvement". However, the role of the social sciences among nations and cultures is to shape "collective consciousness". This does not mean homogenisation, but mutual understanding, which is exactly what stands as the core aim of BRI.

I believe that among the projects which support the activities with China, Sino-European research activities in the fields of humanities and social sciences need to be strengthened. It might be indeed somewhat more uncertain than the cooperation among applied sciences (due to different visions of political values), but it needs to be acknowledged that not only financial capital and knowledge but also social trust, human empowerment, reciprocity and social networks build prosperity (values which are studied and developed by social scientists), which are crucial important elements of economic development(especially to avoid themiddle-income trap).What is more, creativity, free discussions, and outside-of-the-box thinking are all essential to the progress in public policies and technology. These are just some from among countless reasons why social sciences and humanities should be strengthened.

Another problem is the lack of Sino-European social science grants or scientific journals. For instance, Poland participates in European grants such as HERA (Humanities in the European Research Area) and conducts research programmes with countries such as Germany, Lithuania or India (EU-India Platform for Social Sciences and Humanities) but it does not have any common programmes with China. Even in the field of engineering, Polish institutions cooperate with Chinese ones but only to a small extent. In the field of European Union grants, the situation does not look better; the cooperation with China inthe field of social sciences is very limited. One of the possibilities for social scientists is the Jean Monett Programme, however, its activities focus on the dissemination of knowledge about the European Union in other countries and are not directly aimed at cooperation.

4. Social sciences strengthening the Europe-China cooperation

The problems in building mutual trust in Sino-European relations stem from different cultural backgrounds of both civilizations and dissimilar political systems. That is why the mutual understanding and synergy of our activities require appreciating that the Chinese political identity is built around the image of being a developing country, emerging power, eastern civilization, and a socialist state. At the same time, Europe is proud to be a developed region, post-modern model, western civilization, a human rights defender and European welfare democracy (Wang, 2012).

The importance of the mutual understanding of organizational cultures can be seen on the examples of failed Chinese investments in Europe. One of them is the experience of China Overseas Engineering Group (COVEC) works in Poland. In 2009, COVEC, a subsidiary of China Railway Group Limited, won a contract to build a 50-km stretch of highway in Poland. It was the first large-scale Chinese infrastructure project won in an EU country. In 2011, because of financial problems rooted in the misunderstanding of investment processes in Europe, the ambitious plan of COVEC ended up as a failure, forcing them to withdraw.

Cooperation is not based on negating the differences but on better understanding and persuading. Social sciences can help us imagine the results of the development of technology and create predictions of alternative futures. A development without such reflection can be dangerous. Social scientists have developed policies which allow us to live longer and with better conditions; in the grand scheme of things, they can contribute to making the world safer.

Cooperation in the field of social sciences can also lead to the establishment of a platform for mutual recognition. If we consider that nowadays, 66% of internationally recognized papers on the field of social sciences are published by only 5 publishers (Larivière, Haustein, Mongeon, 2015), we are forced to ask the question: who uses the knowledge accumulated by the mainstream modern social sciences? Should the role of science be reinforcing the legitimacy of the existing order or searching for new solutions and serving cultures and nations? The platform for cooperation between social scientists can build wider pluralism in the field of social sciences.

Sino-European cooperation can change the current state of research and the publishing structure which supports and reproduces the hegemonic paradigms of the modern social science world. It can build an alternative for the current structure of "semi-peripheries-core regions".

5. The groundwork for further cooperation

This is the time for Chinese academic institutions to propose research activities under BRI, taking into consideration the pluralism of values, considering President Xi Jinping's call for BRI to be based on principles of peace and cooperation, openness and inclusiveness, mutual learning and mutual benefit. Xi also said that "Innovation is an important force powering development"[1]; and that "we should build the Belt and Road Initiative into a road connecting different civilizations. In pursuing the Belt and Road Initiative, we should ensure that when it comes to different civilizations, exchange will replace estrangement, mutual learning will replace clashes, and coexistence will replace the sense of superiority. This will boost mutual understanding, mutual respect and mutual trust among different countries"[2].

I therefore propose to establish the "Belt and Road Initiative Social Science Fund".

Aims

Joint research programmes should focus on social science issues such as social policies, regional policies, international relations, and political systems. The goals of cooperation should be the exchange of knowledge and better mutual understanding. Cooperation in other fields can also benefit from the social sciences collaboration.

Instruments

• Research units and networks;

• Books (publishing books series, e.g. books concerning China published in Poland and books concerning Poland published in China);

• Joint conferences;

• Establishing an open-access scientific journal, e.g. "Sino-European Journal of Social Science" or "Sino-European Belt and Road Initiative Journal" [3];

---

[1]   Xi Jinping, Belt and Road Initiative Forum, 14 May 2017, retrieved from: http://news. xinhuanet.com/english/2017-05/14/c_136282982.htm

[2]   Xi Jinping, Belt and Road Initiative Forum, 14 May 2017, retrieved from: http://news. xinhuanet.com/english/2017-05/14/c 136282982.htm

[3]   Journal needs to meet the basic requirements such as: standards of peer-review;diversity in geographic distribution of editors (editors should be also attractivefrom the point of view of the authors) and authors;ethical publishing practices (predatory publishing practices or editorial instructions leading to inauthentic journal self-citation are not acceptable), possessa good electronic format, well-designed website and clear abstracts;have interesting aims; havetimelines/regular publications (be published according to its stated frequency);be published in good-quality English; be cited world-widely (self-citation rates should be low).

- Individual and team grants for research projects;
- Professor and young researcher exchanges;
- Annual Sino-European Forum for Social ScienceResearchers.

Founders:

Founding institutions could be countries which take part in cooperation in the format 16+1. Host organization could be specially established for this purpose or be chosen among Chinese universities.

Funding opportunities

- Financial instruments of the Belt and Road Initiative;
- Governmental support;
- University funds;
- Private support;

Eligible partners

Universities from Europe, China, Central Asia, South Asia (universities on the road of BRI)

Structure

The Fund should have its international Board, which would decide about calls for projects and the strategic goals of BRI Social Fund. The Board can be composed of Chinese scholars and of the same number of scholars from the participating countries. The Board Members could be chosen either by the host Chinese university or by the cooperating countries. Furthermore, each country should have a national coordinator who will bridge the communication of universities from his country with other countries. National coordinators should also care about the dissemination of information in their countries. They can be chosen by the ministries of higher education of their respective countries.

Topics

Topics of possible cooperation can include:

- European and Chinese perspectives on BRI,
- European Integration,
- EU institutions and law,
- EU policies,

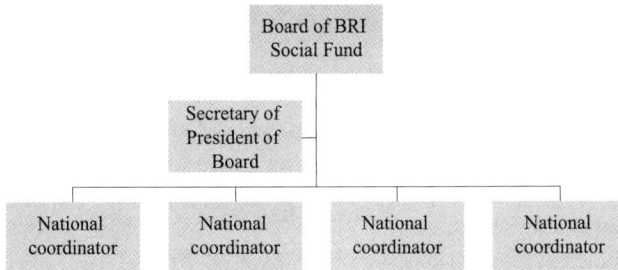

Figure 3. Simplified organizational chart of BRI Social Fund (proposal)
Source: own

- Public policies in Europe,
- 16+1 format,
- Models of public policies,
- Migration and migration policy.

Expected benefits:

Building international research teams basing on the above-mentioned instruments (researches, conferences, publications, etc.).

Summary

There are already various formats of collaboration under BRI and China-CEE cooperation, under 16+1 frameworks: in the field of tourism, among young political leaders, think-tanks or on education policy. There is, however, no forum on the cooperation in social science research. The BRI initiative simply cannot exist without a close cooperation between Europe and China. As already mentioned, the EU stands for 20% of the world's GDP and China, as of today, accounts already for about 14%. The mutual understanding between those two regions can foster stronger cooperation in different fields. This is the great role of social science; even despite the challenges stemming from different visions of political values, cooperation in social sciences is possible and beneficial. As the Chinese proverb says "the hardest stage is the beginning", thus, let us start with the beginning: the Social Science Belt and Road Initiative Cooperation, aiming at the creation of lasting mutual development and understanding.

References

China unveils 'Belt and Road Initiative' science plans, retrieved from: http://www.researchresearch.com/news/article/?articleId=1367868.

CSIS, *Is China both a source and hub for international students?*, retrieved from: https://chinapower.csis.org/china-international-students/.

Vincent Larivière, Stefanie Haustein, Philippe Mongeon, "The Oligopoly of Academic Publishers in the Digital Era", *PloS One*, Vol. 10 (6), 2015.

Dennis Normile, "China's Belt and Road Initiative infrastructure plan also includes science", *Science*, May 16, 2017. Retrieved from: http://www.sciencemag. org/news/2017/05/china-s-belt-and-road-infrastructure-plan-also-includes-science

Vision and Actions on Jointly Building Silk Road Economic Belt and 21st-Century Maritime Silk Road, retrieved from: http://en.ndrc.gov.cn/ newsrelease/201503/t20150330_669367.html.

Xi Jinping, Belt and Road Initiative Forum, 14 May 2017, retrieved from: http://news.xinhuanet.com/english/2017-05/14/c_136282982.htm.

Xinhua, *Belt and Road Initiative Int'l center officially launched at University of Cambridge*, retrievedfrom: http://news.xinhuanet.com/english/2017-09/30/ c_136649608.htm.

Yiwei Wang, (2012), China and the EU in Global Governance: Seeking Harmony in Identities, in J. Wouters, T. de Wilde, P. Defraigne (eds.)(2012), China, the EU and Global Governance, E. Elgar, Cheltenham, pp. 50-61.

Zhang Zhihao, *Science, innovation cooperation to benefit Belt and Road Initiative countries*, retrieved from: http://europe.chinadaily.com.cn/ china/2017-05/09/content_29266235.htm.

Zhao Xinying, *President's initiatives spur plan for new scholarship*, retrieved from: http://english.gov.cn/news/top_news/2015/04/20/content_281475092513397.htm.

EU-China Experimental Research-Cooperation between Sichuan University and Bonn University for nearly Two Decades[*]

Heike Hennig-Schmidt and Zhuyu LI

Abstract

This paper reports the results of the long-term Sino-German research cooperation between scholars from Bonn University and Sichuan University.

* **Acknowledgements:** Much of the work reported in this article could not have been done without the support of a great many people and institutions. We are especially grateful to Dr. Gari Walkowitz, Dr. Hong Geng and Dipl. Übersetzer Chaoliang YANG for their invaluable research assistance at the University of Bonn. They were involved in designing and running experiments in Germany and China and evaluating the verbal and the behavioral data. In particular, we thank Chaoliang YANG for translating the instructions and other material as well as the decision screens into Chinese. He also was involved in translating Chinese transcripts into German.

  Financial support is gratefully acknowledged by Heike Hennig-Schmidt from German Research Foundation (Deutsche Forschungsgemeinschaft DFG: Sonderforschungsbereich 303, HE 2790/2, 446 CHV-111/1/00, CHV 113/174/0-1), EU-TMR Research Network ENDEAR (FMRX-0238). She also appreciates a fellowship at Käte Hamburger Kolleg/Centre for Global Cooperation (Duisburg). Financial support is gratefully acknowledged by Zhuyu LI from EU-China Higher Education Cooperation Programme (No. 4040060/99, 2673123/00), the National Natural Science Foundation of China (NSFC, No. 79970099, No. 7010100005), the National Planning Office of Philosophy and Social Sciences of China (NPOPSS, No.01BTJ003, No.07BTJ003), European Studies Centre Programme (ESCP/G001-SCU-1) and EU Jean Monnet Programme (JMC 2008-2753, JMCE 2011-2869). Both authors are grateful to the Sino-German Center for Research Promotion, Beijing (GZ379, GZ414). Moreover, our research was supported by Sichuan University, Southwest Jiaotong University, Cologne University and Bonn University.

  We are also grateful to a great many Chinese and German student research assistents at Bonn University who transcribed the German and Chinese videos, did the back-translation of instructions and other material to check for consistency and provided valuable assistance in text analyzing the transcripts.

  This paper is a revised and updated version of Hennig-Schmidt and Li (2013). Parts of it are taken from Hennig-Schmidt et al. (2010) and Hennig-Schmidt (2016).

Since 1999, the authors and their research groups have been conducting cross-country and inter-country EU-China studies in experimental economics, which is unique in China. Our research has been guided by the idea that a two-way exchange of information between countries and cultures is important. When being ignorant about each other's goals, motivations and behavior, interacting partners might fail to reach a mutually satisfactory exchange and agreement. One has to accept the necessity to change one's modes of understanding in order to capture the philosophical and cultural backgrounds of another culture; and one has to show respect and empathy.

Our reseach comprises experimental studies on cross-cultural and inter-cultural team negotiations in China and Germany, on bargaining power and on fairness perceptions in distribution conflicts. Further, we report results from comparative experimental studies between Germany and China. These include the effect of task presentation (framing) on behavior, corruption, voting procedures and how performance and cooperation are affected when appraisal systems are transferred from Germany to China. Supporting young researchers during their research career and organizing summer schools and conferences is a further result of our long-lasting cooperation.

Introduction

The Sino-German cooperation of researchers from Bonn University and Sichuan University has been lasting for nearly two decades by now. Since 1999, Bonn EconLab-the Laboratory for Experimental Economics at the University of Bonn and the European Studies Center at Sichuan University have been conducting cross-country and inter-country EU-China studies in experimental economics. This is unique in that no other Sino-German research team has been doing such long-term cross-country studies in experimental economics. We not only did joint research, we also supported young Chinese and German scholars by giving them the opportunity to write their dissertations, Bachelor, Diploma and Master theses on topics related to China-EU experimental research. Further, we organized Sino-German Summer Schools and Workshops for young scholars and established scientiests.

Our research has been guided by the idea that a two-way exchange between countries and cultures is necessary and important. Not only should China get information about the EU; it is as important for inhabitants of EU member states to learn about China. The reason is that stylized facts taken for granted in one's own culture may have no or minor significance in the other. When members of the different cultures interact with each other, the similarities that are to be expected (c.f. Allison 1989) will be helpful for cooperation, yet, it will be the differences that might cause frictions. When being ignorant about each other's behavior, goals and motivations, interacting partners might fail to reach a mutually satisfactory exchange and agreement. Cross-cultural and inter-cultural studies, including economic experiments, can help to overcome the problems but involves quite a few challenges. The reason is that results derived in other cultures/countries may appear to be inconsistent and cannot be explained by methods and models which researchers are used to in their home culture/country. An easy but, of course, inadequate 'solution' would be to dismiss the seemingly inconsistent findings under the heading that people did understand the situation or that they act irrationally.

Another way of dealing with the challenge is more difficult but also more promising. It involves accepting that it may be necessary to change one's modes of understanding in order to capture the philosophical and cultural backgrounds of another culture. One has to realize that due to one's own education and experiences one may not be able to envision which specific rules apply in another culture and which kinds of behaviour are adequate and reasonable because those rules and behaviour are the consequences of culturally different education and experience. Thus, differences/peculiarities cannot be accepted as adequate for the respective culture and, therefore, not adequately dealt with. This dilemma most often results in a bias in perceiving, understanding and being willing and ready to account for existing dissimilarities. (see also Hennig-

Schmidt et al. 2010). This bias may lead to constructing decision models that neglect important explanatory variables from other parts of the world. An example is Hofstede's 5-dimension model developed to explain cultural differences (Hofstede 1980, 2010). The fifth dimension was only added after researchers concerned with the Confucian value system (the Chinese Culture Connection) found that these values were not adequately represented in the original 4-dimension model (Chinese Culture Connection 1987).

To overcome the 'culture' bias it is important and necessary to be open for potential peculiarities of people with different cultural and philosophical backgrounds, to show respect and empathy and to question whether one's own perspective is universally valid. Being willing to extend one's own appreciation and comprehension is not enough, however. Cultural diversity should be substantiated and, if possible, it should be quantified.

Different methodological approaches are used in EU-China research like surveys, field or questionnaire studies. We decided to use laboratory experiments and vido experiments in particular because this method allows the observation of behavior in controlled, simplified situations and has several advantages.① First, the experimental method allows to control the decision environment such that only ceteris-paribus changes are implemented, i.e. only one variable is changed at a time in order to check for causal relationships. Second, decisions are financially incentivized, i.e. experimental participants are paid depending on their own and on choices of other participants with whom they interact. Third, laboratory experiments are allowed to test institutional changes before they are implemented in the real world. Fourth, they enable robustness checks of the results because different scientists can rerun the experiments under exact the same conditions. Finally, using the same design in

---

① For the following arguments see, e.g., Davis and Holt (1993), Falk and Heckman (2009), Hennig-Schmidt et al. (2011).

different countries facilitates cross-country comparability[①].

In several experiments that we report below, the video method was used. Single players are represented by multi-person groups, who had to take a consensus decision. The discussions within the groups are video-taped and are transcribed word for word into text protocols by graduate students particularly trained and instructed for this task.[②] Video experiments are well-suited for cross-cultural and intercultural research (see e.g. Kerr et al. 2000) as running video experiments with exactly the same experimental design in different countries allows to directly comparing discussions and arguments across cultures. These discussions not only refer to the same well-defined experimental context but also the identical situations during a decision-making process.[③]

Our studies focused on China-German inter-country and cross-country research. Both countries differ in many respects. Germany-being a central part of Europe-is influenced by the Greek/Christian culture and philosophy, whereas China is shaped by Confucianism/Taoism (Jullien 2004). Both societies diverge strongly with regard to characterics like trust, rule of law, GDP, democracy, power distance, individualism and uncertainty avoidance (Herrmann et al. 2008b, Gächter et al. 2010). These differences are likely to influence behavior. Similar behavior and guidance with the same principles would, however, make strong cases for validity across cultures.

---

① When running experiments in different cultures one must pay attention to issues like language, currency effects, stakes, and experimenter interactions as all of them can affect cross-cultural comparability (cf. Roth et al. 1991, Henrich et al. 2001, 2004, Herrmann et al. 2008a, b). These effects were taken into account in our studies in the following way. We used the back-translation procedure (Brislin 1970), calculated participants' rewards to equal the hourly wage in a typical students' job in both countries and had all sessions run by native experimenters. All researchers involved in conducting the experiments were provided with an extensive procedural protocol in English to guarantee that the experiments in both countries were conducted as similarly as possible.

② All Chinese texts were translated into German allowing German and Chinese researchers to simultaneously work on the verbal material.

③ For advantages and disadvantages of video experiments, see Hennig-Schmidt and Li (2001) and Hennig-Schmidt et al. (2010).

Our Sino-German research group touches a great variety of topics of mutual interest and importance for a German and Chinese audience. In particular, we report results from video experiments on why people reject favorable offers, on cross-cultural and inter-cultural negotiations in China and Germany with regard to negotiation styles, bargaining processes, on how moral entitlements are derived and how they materialize, on bargaining power and on fairness perceptions in distribution conflicts. Further, we report on results from comparative experimental studies between Germany and China based on individual choices regarding the effect of task presentation (framing) on behavior, corruption, voting procedures and the effects on performance and cooperation in teams when appraisal systems are transferred from Germany to China.

The remainder of the paper is organized as follows. In Section 2, we report on research that resulted from our Sino-German cooperation while Section 3 describes the support we gave to young Chinese and German scholars. Section 4 is the conclusion.

1. Research

1.1 Why people reject advantageous offers

Hennig-Schmidt, Li and Yang (2008) contributed substantially to understanding a phenomenon that at first sight looked astonishing: The authors found that in an Ultimatum Game experiment run in China, more than half of the players rejected low *and* very high offers; and no such behavior was found in the same experiment conducted in Germany.

The Ultimatum Game is an important experimental tool to analyze social preferences in distributional conflicts. In the standard Ultimatum Game (Güth et al. 1982), a proposer can decide on how to split a given amount of money (the pie) between herself and a responder. After having seen the proposal, the responder can either accept or reject it. In case of acceptance, both receive the amounts as allocated; in case of rejection both receive nothing.

To learn about the motivations behind the players' behavior, Hennig-Schmidt et al. (2008) run a video experiment as described in the introduction. The UG design was changed in that responders were not informed about the proposal before deciding, but had to state for each possible offer whether to accept or reject (strategy method). Single proposers as well as responders were represented by three-person groups each. The discussions within the proposer and responder groups were video-taped and transcribed into text protocols.

The video transcripts allowed people to analyze the underlying motives for the non-monotonic strategies by content-analyzing the transcripts of 72 groups-half of them proposers and responders, respectively (comprising 208 participants in total). It has been argued that economic agents dislike being treated unfairly, i.e. they dislike inequality to their disadvantage, but also to their advantage (see the models, e.g., by Fehr and Schmdt 1999, and Bolton and Ockenfels 2000). When offers are low in an Ultimaum Game, the responders are likely to perceive disadvantageous allocations as unfair because they are left with (much) lower payoffs than the proposers. Rejecting a low offer becomes a likely action because the monetary and the motivational incentives are not at odds. When confronted with allocations that offer more than 50 percent of the pie, being treated unfairly corresponds to responders' payoffs being (much) higher than for proposers. This means that the monetary and the motivational incentive are in conflict. If, however, the motivational incentive prevails what are the reasons for such behavior?

The content analysis of Hennig-Schmidt et al (2008) revealed that the main motivation for refusing advantageous proposals is social concern capturing the basic idea of social preferences, but includes in addition to aversion against advantageous inequality-further aspects of subjects' caring about others. These aspects are mutually unacceptable allocations, injuring bilateral fairness, allocations to the disadvantage of either player are unlikely, rejecting all but middle (balanced) allocations and extensive responder's profit.

This finding is in agreement with models of inequity aversion, but reveals also other important motives that were not raised in the literature before. Moreover, these arguments are in line with requirements for social harmony and pro-social behavior-Chinese values that are still important in China today (e.g., Faure and Fang 2008, Chen 2010, Kuhlich and Zhang 2010).

Other motives are also mentioned but turned out less important: for instance, beliefs about proposer behavior, in particular non-expectancy of high offers, emotional, ethical, and moral reasons, and aversion against unpleasant numbers. Reciprocity avoidance that was advanced as a motive for high offer refutations by Henrich et al. (2001) and captures arguments in favor of status-seeking through gift-giving was not found during content analysis.

The robustness of the results in the group experiment was assessed by repeating the experiment with 179 individual participants who were not observed[1]. The individual responders show the same rejection behavior regarding high offers as groups do. Thus, motivations revealed during group discussions seem to pertain to individuals as well.

Similar findings as in Hennig-Schmidt et al. (2008) have been reported earlier by, for instance, Henrich et al. (2001), Bahry and Wilson (2006) orBellemare et al. (2008) who, however, did not provide consistent explanations for this phenomenon because most of the available data allow indirect inferences only, based on observed decisions, participants' social characteristics, questionnaires, debriefings and/or conversations.

The finding that social concern was the main motivation for non-monotonic strategies shows that models of social preference, in particular models of inequity aversion, capture an important behavioral aspect in ultimatum bargaining. On the other hand, advantageous offer rejections cannot be handled by these models because they restrict the parameter space: The ERC model by Bolton and Ockenfels (2000) does allow for declining advantageous

---

① 　We thus analyzed data of 387 Chinese participants in total in the individual and in the group experiments.

offers but assumes a rejection threshold not higher than the Equal Split. In the Fehr/Schmidt model (1999), the specification of the model parameters rules out rejections of advantageous offers. Thus, the empirical findings of Hennig-Schmidt et al. (2008) might contribute to re-examining the assumptions that underlie models of inequity aversion to capture behavior of participants in all parts of the world.

1.2 Video experiments on bargaining

Bargaining is one of the most frequent social interactions in business life, international trade, national and international politics. For negotiations to be successful in an intercultural context it is important to understand goals and motivations of the bargaining partner as well as socio-emotional factors influencing the decision process. A lack of understanding will make mutually satisfactory agreements extremely difficult.

Field data on bargainers' motives are difficult to obtain. Video experiments are one tool to gain the required empirical evidence under controlled conditions as the situation to be studied is well defined. Observing experimental negotiators when making their decisions can reveal their motives and goals.[1]

1.2.1 Negotiations: Cross-cultural comparison

The formation and adaptation of bargaining goals and potential differences between German and Chineses negotiation teams were studied by Hennig-Schmidt, LI and YAN (2009) and by Hennig-Schmidt and Walkowitz (2017). The latter authors extend the analysis of the former by investigating how asymmetric legal rights shape bargainers' aspiration levels (bargaining goals)

---

[1] One might be concerned about using student participants as negotiators. Yet, students do provide valid information. Not only will they play an important role after graduation, for instance, in business as future managers. It has also been shown that behavior in experiments is a predictor for behavior in later work environments (see the references in Hennig-Schmidt et al. 2018).

through moral entitlements derived from equity norms and number prominence. As aspiration formation is typically hard to observe in real-life a video experiment was run mimicking a real-life bargaining situation in the laboratory.

The experimental design is based on a non-cooperative model of characteristic function bargaining (Selten 1981), and was developed by Hennig-Schmidt (1999). Two teams bargain on the distribution of a given amount of money (the pie P) by alternating offers. Over the course of the negotiation, bargainers make alternating offers over the distribution of P until they consent or break off. If teams settle on an allocation they receive the amounts as agreed upon; if not, they receive an outside option, which is higher for the strong than for the weak team. Teams were assigned randomly to be strong or weak. Teams did not bargain directly with each other because the research interest focused on learning about the strategic arguments within a bargaining team. Therefore, the experimenter transmitted the decisions between the interacting teams. The unique experimental data set involves 15 negotiations from Germany and China. Within-team discussions were videotaped and coded. In total, verbal data from 30 teams (involving 89 participants), 1,100 pages of transcripts, and 65 hours of discussions were content-analyzed.

In many bargaining situations, bargainers bring justifiable entitlements to the negotiation table. Entitlements are subjectively perceived rights that go beyond abstract legal rights and go along with a motivational disposition to defend them (Schlicht 1998). They are often derived from the bargainers' outside options, the status quo, historical claims, or custom. Generally, entitlements impact business relations, arbitration, wage setting, corporate mergers, peace treaties, and many other situations (e.g., Kahnemann et al. 1986). More specifically, they influence associated bargaining processes and the bargaining outcomes (Gächter and Riedl (2005). Moreover, tensions in entitlements extend negotiations and is one reason for the often observed "deadline effect" of last-minute agreements (Roth et al. 1991).

Entitlements also shape the concessions necessary to reach an agreement and highly correlate with agreement outcomes. Previous evidence suggests that entitlements are so influential because they constitute so-called "moral property rights" in bargaining situations, which exist independently of legal (i.e., enforceable) property rights (Gächter and Riedl 2005). *Moral* entitlement in the present experiment are defined as an entitlement that bargainers subjectively derive from their outside option and that concerns their share of the pie at stake. This entitlement typically goes beyond their *legal* right (i.e., their outside option). Aspiration levels (i.e., the distributive goals the negotiators want to achieve in the negotiation, see Sauermann and Selten 1962, Selten 1998) together with their claims (expressed via proposals in the negotiation) can be seen as *manifestations of moral entitlements*. This is because they operationalize the negotiators' subjectively derived entitlements about the specific part of the pie they feel morally entitled to and are willing to defend.

Contrary to other studies, legal rights in the experiment are not previously earned and are not sunk. Therefore, if the accountability principle (Konow 2000) were applied[1], one should observe that outside options do not create moral entitlements, which differ between strong and weak parties, and both shold strive for equal shares. The main finding however, conveys that randomly assigned, not earned asymmetric outside options do have normative power and do shape the negotiation process. Strong negotiators (self-servingly) derive moral entitlements from their randomly assigned outside options. They strive for equitable[2] but unequal distributions, i.e., proportionality with regard to

---

[1] The accountability principle says that assigned legal rights do not constitute moral entitlements, which exceed an equal outcome (Konow 2000).

[2] The equity principle (Selten 1978, 1987) asserts that in distributive conflicts the amount to be distributed (for instance, money or costs) is to be allocated to the actors involved in such a way that they are treated equally according to a given distribution standard. The equity principle also takes into account that not only one but several distribution norms might exist, and that they can be relevant for the decision process. Prominent norms are Equal Split, Split the Difference and Proportional Split.

Equal Split: P is divided equally between the actors. Proportional Spit: P is divided in proportion to the outside options. Split the Difference: Each actor receives his/her outside option. In addition, each actor gets an equal share of the remainder of P after outside options have been deducted.

outside options and splitting the difference. Thus, moral entitlements materialize in the recorded aspiration levels and the final payoffs, which exceed the Equal Split. By contrast, weak negotiators do not express an obligation to comply with the strong party's demands and request equality. Over the course of the negotiation, equity tends to loose, while prominence of round numbers gains importance when adapting the bargaining goals to reach an agreement. These results hold for both the Chinese and the German subject pools. Notably, goal formation of the Chinese as well as the German negotiators at the beginning of the negotiation is strongly influenced by equity considerations, which make a strong case for this principle's cross-cultural validity.

Even though the bargaining outcomes of the Chinese and the German teams are not different, strong differences are found with regard to the negotiation process. Germans steadily reduce their goals and make concessions. In contrast, Chinese negotiations are characterized by long periods of stagnation, only minimal concessions, and the communication of false goals. Yet, the Chinese delay strategies do not result in active negotiation break offs as with German participants.[1]

1.2.2 Negotiations: Inter- and intra-cultural comparison

The importance of aspiration formation in combination with equity concerns has also been found by Hennig-Schmidt and Walkowitz (2015) who analyzed an experiment on *inter-cultural* in addition to intra-cultural negotiations. The paper, thus, contributes to better understand negotiation behaviour *between* Germans and Chinese. The authors study a negotiation experiment based on alternating offers but *with earned assignment of outside options and face-to-face bargaining*. Two teams of five persons each bargain on the distribution of a pie P. Teams earned their position as a high or low outside option player in a quiz preceding the experiment. Between-team bargaining was face-to-face. Before and after the negotiation phases, teams had internal

---

[1] See also Hennig-Schmidt, LI, LU, and YANG (2001), LI, LU and Hennig-Schmidt (2002).

within-group discussions to elaborate on their strategies. Negotiations lasted for three hours each and consisted of 12 teams bargaining in two German-German, two Chinese-Chinese and two Chinese-German negotiations. The analysis was based on team decisions and on the verbal transcripts of the video-recorded within- and between-team discussions. Involved were 59 PhD students graduating in Economics or Management Science as well as young staff of economics and management faculties of various universities from all over China and Germany. They participated in the first or second Sino-German Summer School on Experimental Economics organized by Hennig-Schmidt and Li 2006 at Sichuan University, Chengdu, China, and 2007 at the University of Bonn, Germany.

Hennig-Schmidt and Walkowitz (2015) find that all teams-the Chinese as well as the Germans-formulate bargaining goals before the negotiation starts. These aspirations apparently help to structure the bargaining process, as many features of the subsequent negotiation like offers, demands, final outcomes, or concessions can be traced back to these previously formulated goals. Carefully preparing the negotiation, reasoning about the counterpart's aspirations, gathering as much information on the counterpart as possible, anticipating their behaviour by "imaginary bargaining", and using "role play" appear to be good strategies for reaching at least an acceptable negotiation outcome. The Chinese teams, in particular, make use of these techniques, which may be the reason why there are, on average, more successful negotiators in our experiment than the German participants.

The data also show that fairness concerns play an important role in the negotiation processes. Particularly German teams repeatedly request specific explanations and justifications from their counterparts on why a proposed offer or demand can be considered fair. Chinese teams also talk about fairness issues but to a much lesser extent. Both Chinese and German bargainers often agree upon an allocation based on the equity norm of Split the Difference. Relying on this norm seems to represent a feasible and justifiable compromise for both parties, which takes both negotiators' outside options into account. Equally splitting the surplus combines the strong teams' aspirations for more than half of the joint profit (their moral entitlement due to their earned strong position) with an element of equality. Split the Difference, thus, satisfies the German teams' specific request that an allocation has to be fair.

The verbal transcripts show that bargaining parties have the chance to reach mutually acceptable agreements if they carefully analyse the bargaining situation, the amount initially at stake for negotiation, and, more importantly, their counterpart's legal entitlement represented by his/her outside option as well as the potential impact of their own. Based on these variables, negotiators can effectively try to anticipate the bargaining process by defining the different equitable allocations the bargaining situation allows for, by formulating own aspirations, by reflecting about their counterpart's aspirations, by calculating fair/equitable allocations-especially compromises like Split the Difference-and by making them salient during the negotiation process.

Hennig-Schmidt and Walkowitz (2015) find support for the idea that successful negotiators need specific traits, which Thompson (2009) lists as predictors of success in inter-cultural interactions. Those are, for instance, empathy, openness to different points of view, interest in the counterpart's culture, cultural flexibility, patience, inter-cultural sensitivity, and skills in collaborative conflict resolution.

1.2.3 On power in bargaining

The impact of power in bargaining was analyzed by Hennig-Schmidt and Li (2006). They experimentally study the influence of bargaining power, defined options outside the bargaining deal, on negotiation outcomes. The experimental bargaining literature mainly focuses on symmetric power situations (see, for instance, the studies on ultimatum bargaining following Güth et al., 1982, and Rubinstein, 1982). Power asymmetries typically are neglected even though in reality power differences exist in many bargaining situations. Only a few studies incorporate power disparity (see for a recent study Hennig-Schmidt, Irlenbusch, Rinke and Walkowitz 2018). Predictions on the impact of bargaining power on outcomes are not clear cut. According to the Nash bargaining solution (Nash 1950), bargainers' final payoffs should reflect power differences, while Binmore, Morgan, Sutton and Shaked (1991) argue that outside options matter only when offers are lower than guaranteed payoffs (see also Konow 2000).

To investigate the impact of power differences on bargaining outcomes, Hennig-Schmidt and Li (2006) investigate the full set of decision and verbal data of the two-player bargaining video experiment in Germany (Hennig-Schmidt 1999) and the Chinese data analyzed by Hennig-Schmidt et al. (2011) and by Hennig-Schmidt and Walkowitz (2017).

Two treatments characterized by high and low power asymmetry were run at Bonn University and did not reveal evidence that power differences are reflected in bargaining outcomes for players with high and low outside options. However, running the high asymmetry treatment in the People's Republic of China shows that more powerful players are able to enforce significantly higher payoffs in China than was the case in Germany. The video tapes reveal that the behavioral disparity can be attributed to different lines of reasoning in the two subject pools. Most German participants did not draw on the given power relation. They took the Equal Split as their reference point whereas Chinese subjects did take the given power asymmetry into account. Their bargaining behavior was based on a Split-the-Difference argument. Thus, the significance of outside options differed in both subject pools. While the disparity in outside options did not constitute a corresponding perception of power disparity for German subjects, the Chinese participants took the power asymmetry as given. This result is in line with predictions based on Hofstede's power distance measure (see Hofstede 1980, 2010) and seems to reflect the cultural background of the experimental subjects.

Apparently, environmental conditions influence perceptions and behavior. Culture certainly is a crucial factor, promoting an egalitarian perspective as in most German groups or a hierarchical viewpoint as in the Chinese sessions. Culture also seems to have some bearing on how theory is modeled. While

Western researchers stress the egalitarian viewpoint (e.g. Fehr and Schmdt 1999, Bolton and Ockenfels 2000), business studies (e.g. Fang 1999) as well as investigations of moral behavior and social interactions in Chinese society (e.g. Gabrenya and Hwang 1996) stress the respect for hierarchy and harmony in all dimensions of life to be an important influencing factor on Chinese behavior.

1.2.4 Fairness concerns in distribution conflicts

Justice and fairness in the sense of impartiality and lack of bias towards everybody are of central concern in Western thinking rooted in the Greek philosophy. Given the differences in fairness conceptions in the East and the West, one might conjecture that fairness and related arguments are likely to play an important role in Germany. Similarities across countries would make a strong case for its cross-cultural validity.

Walkowitz and Hennig-Schmidt (2017) analysed the transcripts of the above mentioned bargaining and Ultimatum Game video experiments[1] for the prevalence of fairness discussions, i.e. whether fairness was made an issue during the argumentation or not. Given that fairness is so important in Western countries, one might have expected that nearly all German groups talk about fairness. Notably, however, in only 76% of all 127 German groups analyzed above, fairness was made as an issue. This is about 7 percentage points more often compared to the frequency of fairness discussions in the 96 Chinese groups (69%) included in the analysis. The difference is not significant, however.

A separate analysis of the Ultimatum Game, where also German data were analyzed (see Fn 10) show some interesting features Also in this experiment, participants in German groups tended to talk about fairness more often than Chinese do (72.46% vs. 61.11%), and also this difference is not significant. However, a deeper analysis of the transcripts revealed some differences with

---

① Note that for the Ultimatum Game, in addition to the Chinese data of Hennig-Schmidt et al (2008) German data of 69 groups comprising 200 participants were included.

regard to fairness perceptions suggesting that even though fairness does not appear irrelevant for the Chinese, it seems more important for the German participants as Chinese player groups start discussing fairness much later during the negotiation process. Although the Equal Split is the pertinent fairness norm in both countries, less Chinese groups do discuss this fairness norm. Finally, fewer Chinese teams are concerned with their counterparts when discussing fairness. These findings suggest that culture might matter when fairness is concerned.

To get a more comprehensive picture of the prevalence of fairness discussions, Walkowitz and Hennig-Schmidt (2017) combine the data of the previously analyzed experiments with additional individual and group studies that one or both of the authors conducted in Germany and/or China.[1] The survey is based on 1,412 independent observations (833 in Germany and 579 in China) and includes 259 videotaped team discussions, 1,153 individuals' answers to open questions-i.e., data of 1,882 participants in total (1,115 in Germany and 767 in China). In the individual studies, participants decide individually and answer open questions on the influencing factors of their decisions. Their written statements were coded for fairness as in the group studies.

The finding that fairness is not an issue for all participants is corroborated, yet for teams much less so than for individuals. Numbers for the latter are 26.62% overall, 35.22% in the German and 14.69% in the Chinese subject pools. In the individual experiments, fairness seems to be more important for our German than for our Chinese participants as it is significantly more often mentioned by the former than by the latter. This seems to reflect the view of Bicchieri (1999) that fairness is context dependent, and also lend support to

---

[1]   The additional data include: Video experiments: Sadrieh and Hennig-Schmidt, (1999, unpublished German data), Bosman, Hennig-Schmidt, v. Winden (2006).
    Individual decision experiments: Kohnz, Hennig-Schmidt (2005, unpublished German data), Hennig-Schmidt and Schlüter (2009, unpublished German data), Bosman, Hennig-Schmidt and v. Winden (2017, unpublished Chinese data), Hennig-Schmidt et al. (2018, unpublished Chinese data).

Morris and Gelfand (2004) that the reason or rationale one has to give for one's own decision appears to be heavily influenced by one's own culture.

1.3 The effect of task presentation (framing) on behavior in different countries

Can it be taken for granted that the way how a task is described or how a product is presented or named has no influence on the behavior of those to whom the message is directed? This is an important question as-if this were not the case-global players in business, for instance, will have to take great care on how to instruct foreign employees differently from workers in their home country or how to name a product differently in order to achieve the expected results in foreign countries. To contribute to understanding the underlying processes, Goerg and Walkowitz (2010) studied whether it mattered how a task is presented (framed). In particular, they wanted to know whether Chinese and Europeans-here participants from Finland-respond similarly to identical decision problems presented in different ways. They also investigates how members of Middle East countries, i.e., Israelis and Palestinians behaved in the same task. Goerg and Walkowitz (2010) applied a two-person continuous prisoner's dilemma game, presented either in a 'give frame' where a transfer is positive for the counterplayer, or in a 'take frame' where money is taken from him/her. The experimental study involved 142 subjects, about 20 each from Abu-Dis (West Bank), Chengdu (PR China), Helsinki (Finland), and Jerusalem (Israel).

The authors found strong subject pool effects. Participants in Abu-Dis and Chengdu showed a substantially higher cooperation level in the give treatment than under the take frame. In Helsinki and Jerusalem, no framing effect was observed. These findings were also reflected in first-order beliefs, i.e. in how each player expected the counterpart to behave. The findings in Abu-Dis and Chengdu were in line with prior work on presentation effects in public goods games and with studies on goal framing. The authors suggested to explain the observed behavior by the concept of loss aversion and the so-called endowment effect. The Palestinian and Chinese subjects might be more sensitive to a loss induced by a second person (take frame), compared to a loss induced by themselves (give frame). To avoid an expected loss, players take more from the matched player and, thus, cooperation is lower in the give than in the take treatment.

An alternative explanation refers to the action itself. In the give presentation, action leads to cooperation, whereas under the take condition, the opposite holds, i.e., not taking money away from the counterpart. The difference in the sensitivity toward the given presentation might stem from a different attitude toward actions depending on power to control, i.e., to decide how much to transfer. The different perception of own power may deliver an approach to explain behavioral differences across subject-pools and potentially even cultures. Behavior in Jerusalem and Helsinki might be rooted in the fact that the subjects live in Western, more individualistic, and low-context societies who often behave more competitively and outcome-oriented in cooperation settings, compared to people from collectivistic and high-context societies. It is not clear whether Israelis and Finns actually *perceive* the two games as different presentation forms of the *same* decision problem, or whether they *apply different approaches* that lead to *similar* behavioral consequences and outcomes. The above discussion suggests the possibility that a frame may serve as a cue on comparable social situations and these cues may be subject-pool (culture) dependent.

1.4 Corruption

Understanding the factors that promote and reduce corruption-defined as "the misuse of entrusted power for private gain" (Transparency International) - are necessary as corruption is a major economic problem around the world. In particular, it has huge negative welfare effects. Corruption and anti-corruption activities are important political issues for every country. In an environment where power is extremely a symmetrically distributed among different social classes (like in China) and officers have enormous such kind of authority, corruption is likely to grow easier. Corruption is significantly correlated to power distance (Husted 1999).

It has been argued that a certain degree of corruption may even speed up economic growth. But not only economic growth matters (Rose-Ackerman 2006). If corruption is indulged, social fairness and social harmony is likely to reach a critical unbalance and lead to a series of social problems like unraveling of trust. Corruption can also lower economic growth (Mauro 1997, Mo 2001). Anti-corruption policy is of special importance for countries developing at a high rate.

Basic for fighting corruption is to increase people's sensitivity to corruption. Perceptions of corruption are positively correlated with the intensity of anti-corruption programs(Rousso and Steves 2003).Educating the young generation is a key element in reducing corruption successfully since it changes young people's values and thus lowers their perception of corruption (Hauk and Saez-Marti 2002).

Geng and Hennig-Schmidt (2014) study in a bribery experiment whether Chinese subjects' sensitivity to corruption can be affected by directing their attention to the bribery context. The sensitivity to bribery was increase by having them make bribery decisions where they are informed about the negative consequences of a bribery scenario either with salient information (framed treatment) or with implicit information (neutral treatment).[1] In the loaded treatment, the decision-making task is presented as an interaction between a firm and a public official. The firm can make private payments to get the public official's permission for running a plant. The permission causes negative consequences to the public. Both the firm and the public official are better off when the private transfer is accepted and the permission is granted. The interaction with the same partner lasts for 30 periods. In the neutral treatment, no real-life context is used. The words firm (officer) are replaced by player A (B), private payment is replaced by transfer, and the decision on permission is

---

[1]　The experimental design is based on Abbink and Hennig-Schmidt (2006).

replaced by choose X or Y. 144 subjects participated in the experiment, 72 each in the framed and the neutrally connotated treatment.

Why does it make sense to run such a study in China? The Chinese culture is characterized by *guanxi* networks which are traditional institutions to stabilize social relations and secure the market exchange of goods. *Guanxi* is an integral part of the Chinese social system; relationships and social connections are based on mutual interest and benefits (Taube 2013). The experiment mirrors several features of *guanxi* relationships. The strong trust-reciprocity design of the experiment features that favors received must be returned. Interaction for a large number of periods reproduces that transactions in *guanxi* networks are like an infinitely repeated game with a known set of people.

Geng and Hennig-Schmidt (2014) found that in contrast to the results Abbink and Hennig-Schmidt (2006) report about Germany, Chinese subjects' behavior is not stable across both conditions. While the Chinese firms do not behave differently, the Chinese public officers both accept significantly less bribe offers and grant significantly less permissions in the framed than in the neutral treatment. Participants in the role of officials show greater sensitivity to corruption than firms in the bribery context. They might perceive the neutral context as a *guanxi* environment whereas the loaded treatments is understood as a corruption scenario.

Together with the results of Abbink and Hennig-Schmidt (2006), the above findings suggest that subjects with different cultural backgrounds are differently sensitive to bribery. For one thing, the importance of social networks much more important in China than in germany where no explicit *guanxi* culture exists. On the other hand, the different treatment effects in the German and Chinese sessions may be due to the different current corruption situation and anti-corruption publicities in the two countries. The Chinese subjects may be more sensitive to the framed context of the experiment due to the strong anti-corruption campaigns in China.

The findings of Geng and Hennig-Schmidt (2014) are in line with recent anti-corruption compaigns in China. As firms are always motivated to offering bribes for higher corporate gain, public officials' intention to corruption may be reduced sharply by being sensitized of the corruption scenario and the anti-legal character of their reciprocal behavior. Subjects' tendency to engage in corruption seems to be reduced by repeated exposure.

1.5 Voting: The limited power of voting to limit power

Geng et al. (2011) run a voting experiment in Germany and China and experimentally approach the question which aspects of a voting procedure are able to restrict elected candidates' willingness to use their power in an opportunistic way. To this end, the authors analyse whether the presence of a voting procedure by itself matters for the exercise of power. By running a one-shot game, reelection concerns are ruled out. Two kinds of electoral campaigns are compared: self-descriptions of personality and promises regarding prospective in-office behaviour.

Geng et al. (2011) find that social approval as conveyed by a vote is not enough to induce pro-social choices by elected candidates. A voting mechanism leads to higher transfers if and only if it is coupled with electoral promises concerning the future allocation choices of candidates. Contrary to the implicit-reciprocity hypothesis, the social appraisal of a candidate's personality implied in the candidate's election does not induce, by itself, more generous behavior on the part of successful candidates. Rather, there seems to be a tendency for a personality-based vote to decrease elected candidates' generosity, even though this tendency is far from being statistically significant. Yet, the fact that this tendency is observed in the Chinese and the German subject pools and that in the German sessions, recipients expect this shift in generosity to happen suggests there may be more to it than mere chance. When campaigns are promise-based, elected candidates transfer more to their recipients than candidates selected by a random draw even though promises do not differ.

Overall, the results suggest that the power of voting to limit the self-oriented exertion of power is limited and context-specific. A voting mechanism as such apparently does not limit the opportunistic use of power by elected candidates. Rather, being elected on the basis of one's personality seems to induce a stronger sense of entitlement, leading to less welfare-oriented behavior. Once the voting mechanism is coupled with promises about prospective in-office behavior, a beneficial effect of elections is observed. This effect is not as strong as expected, though. Taken together, these findings seem to suggest that for elections to unfold their full potential as a power-limiting device, re-election concerns are indispensable.

1.6 Effects on performance and cooperation in teams when transferring appraisal systems from Germany to China

Organizational incentive strategies are frequently used to increase work performance and are applied in many industries and companies. Usually, managers decide on distributing bonuses from a bonus pool. They select the recipients and the level of bonus payments. Mostly, bonus payments are tied to employees' performance and subjective performance appraisals are used to evaluate an employee's performance. A typical problem in the field arises in that ratings are biased. Two biases are found: first the "Centrality Bias", which means that ratings are compressed and not all available ratings are used, and second the "Leniency Bias" meaning that supervisors are lenient in that ratings are too good. Possible consequences are negative effects on work motivation because high performance is not (adequately) rewarded and poor performance is not (adequately) sanctioned. Thus, marginal returns to effort decrease, resulting in weaker, more expensive incentives. There is evidence in the field of negative effects on productivity of compressed ratings (e.g. Bol 2011, Engellandt and Riphahn 2011).

Potential solutions are to introduce "forced ranking" systems, which imply that supervisors have to differentiate in their rankings and have to use (all of) given rankings. Also this incentive system is controversially discussed because it might cause a bad work environment; incentives may decrease incentives due to missing differentiation within an appraisal class. This may in turn cause employees' resistance against the system and lack of cooperation. The problems may even increase when (Western) performance appraisal systems are transferred to other countries with completely different value systems on the work place like, for instance, in Germany and China (see e.g. Gabrenya and Tang 1996; Singh, R. 1997; Björkmann and Lu, 2001a, b; Schulz, 2008; Jiang and Yang 2011). If companies are not aware of these problems, unintended negative effects on performance and team cooperation may result.

As there is lack of empirical evidence on the effects of transferring Western appraisal systems to China and controlled studies are missing, Harbring, Hennig-Schmidt and Walkowitz (2017) run an experimental study in Germany and China to analyze a comparable situation in the laboratory. Teams of four participants played together with three employees performing a repeated real-effort task and the supervisor appraising the performance of the employees. 216 students in 54 teams (24 teams in Germany and 30 in China) took part in the study.

Harbring et al. (2017) found a leniency and a centrality bias in both countries, yet the effects are stronger in the Chinese subject pool. Introducing a forced ranking system can pay off as output per Euro increases by 6%. If supervisors differentiate it is effective in the German subject pool: undeserved high rankings *demotivate* whereas low rankings *motivate* employees. In contrast, in China high ratings *motivate* high performers *and* low performers alike and Chinese employees want to avoid the worst ranking. Finally, forced ranking affects team cooperation-measured by a different cooperation game-in that employees tend to contribute less, yet supervisors contribute more.

The results of Harbring et al. (2017) suggest that in real-work settings companies have to make sure that the application of Western human resources practices applied in Non-Western work environments like China do not induce problems and that the systems are adapted to fit the work values of Chinese employees.

2. Support of young researchers and other intercultural activities

The cooperation between BonnEconLab and Sichuan University supported young researchers in many ways. In addition to participating in summer schools, workshops and seminars, young scholars were provided with many opportunities for joint research projects on the Ph.D.- as well as on the Diploma-, Master- and Bachelor level. Much of the basic research described above in Section 2 is based on young scientists' theses. Several of them contributed to the publications referred to in Section 2 and in the References.

At Bonn University, the following dissertations, Bachelor, Diploma and Master theses were accomplished.

Dissertations: Dr. Hong Geng "Experimental Studies on Cross-cultural Behaviour between Germans and Chinese" (2010); Dr. Sebastian Goerg "Four Contributions to Experimental Economics" (2010); Dr. Gari Walkowitz "On Cooperation and Trust in Strategic Games-Behavioral Evidence from the Middle East and Europe" (2010). Dr. Goerg and Dr. Walkowitz are currently Assistant Professors at the University of Florida, U.S.A., and the Technical University Munich, respectively. Dr. Geng has a leading position in one of the world-wide most important companies focusing on the individual needs for people with disabilities, which is located in Germany.

Diploma, Master and Bachelor theses:

Chinese students worked on "Behavioral differences of voting in China"; "Culture and negotiations"; "Decisions, expectations and fairness in symmetric and asymmetric ultimatum bargaining in Germany and China"; "Bargaining behaviour and aspirations"; "Decision processes in ultimatum bargaining".

German students' topics were "Efficiency of strategies in inter-cultural bargaining situations"; "Asymmetry and personality in ultimatum bargaining in Germany and China"; "Performance appraisal in China und Germany-Challenges when implementing Western Human Resource Management systems".

The studies of our research group were published in domestic and international journals: *Forecasting* 2001 (Chinese), *Chinese Journal of Management Science,* 2001 (Chinese with English Abstract), *Business Economics and Administration* 2002 (Chinese); *Nankai Business Review* 2006 (Chinese with English abstract); *Experimental Economics* (2006); *Journal of Economics, Behaviour and Organization* 2008; *Journal of Economics and Psychology* 2010; *Journal of Public Economic Theory* 2011, *Homo Oeconomicus* 2015; *Games* 2017 (2); *International Journal of Game Theory* (2018). Several analyses are not finished yet, see also the references. In 2008 we were awarded the "First prize for outstanding achievements in scientific research" by the Sichuan Institute of Quantitative Economics. Moreover, our research was presented at a large number of national and international conferences.

Members of our reseach group organized Summer Schools for young scientists and Workshops.

Sino-German Summer Schools

• Nine-day Sino-German Summer School 2006: "Culture and Negotiation in Management-Experimental Methods in Intercultural Relationships", Sichuan University, Chengdu, PR China, Organizers: Heike Hennig-Schmidt (Bonn University), Zhuyu LI (Sichuan University), Reinhard Selten (Bonn University)

• Nine-day Sino-German Summer School 2007: "Culture and and Behavioral Methods in Management-Theory, Experiments, Practice", Bonn University, Bonn, Germany, Organizers: Heike Hennig-Schmidt (Bonn University), Jianmin JIA (Southwest Jiaotong University), Reinhard Selten (Bonn University)

• Nine-day Advanced Sino-German Summer School 2008: "Research Frontiers in Management Science and Culture-Experimental Methods and Advanced Applications", Southwest Jiaotong University, Chengdu, PR China, Organizers: Heike Hennig-Schmidt (Bonn University), Jianmin JIA (SouthwestJiaotong University), Reinhard Selten (Bonn University)

64 Chinese and 54 German Ph.D. students and young staff participated

in these three events which were funded by the Sino-German Center for Research Promotion, Beijing. Students participated in lectures by reknown experimental experts, in experiments, working groups, sightseeing. At the end of the summer schools they presented their projects and the results of their joint work in the working groups. Some joint projects were published in international journals.

Workshops

• Four-day Sino-German Workshop 2010: "Advanced Topics in Experimental and Behavioral Economics-Intra-cultural and Cross-cultural Perspectives in Management Science", Sichuan University, Chengdu, PR China, Organizers: Heike Hennig-Schmidt (Bonn University), Zhuyu LI, Qiuping XU (Sichuan University).

• One-day International Workshop 2004: "Experimental Economics and its Application to Inter-cultural Research", Sichuan University, Chengdu, PR China, Organizers: Heike Hennig-Schmidt (Bonn University), Zhuyu LI (Sichuan University).

Further, Hennig-Schmidt and Walkowitz were founding members of ACCER, the Association for Cross-Cultural Experimental Economic Research (www.accer.org). By establishing a network of scholars working in this field, ACCER aims at encouraging and supporting a lively academic exchange to enhance intercultural understanding and to deal with intercultural differences. ACCER was co-organizer of six international Workshops between 2010 and 2017 where young scientists and established scholars presented their cross-cultural and intercultural experimental research.

Our research was funded by the European Union, the German Research Foundation (DFG), the National Planning Office of Philosophy and Social Sciences of China (NPOPSS), the National Natural Science Foundation of China (NSFC), the Sino-German Center for Research Promotion Beijing and other institutions like Sichuan University, Southwest Jioaotong University and the universities of Bonn and Cologne. See the acknowledgements for the specific grants.

3. Concluding remarks

We reported on a variety of research fields that were in the focus of our Sino-German cooperative research. Several of them are of political relevance like corruption and voting; some are important in the context of business and international negotiations. And some analyze moral and philosophical issues like moral entitlements and concerns for fairness and justice.

On the personal and instututional level, we created, maintained and extended a network of scholars working on research topics of mutual interest. We initiated and intensified lasting joint projects through personal contacts and provided young researchers and PhD students with a platform for experiencing intercultural exchange. We established a long-term sustainable collaboration by exchanging knowledge and creating understanding for the partners of the other culture. Mutual interest in EU-China cross-cultural and inter-cultural research, regular meetings and face-to-face interactions, doing research together and opening our minds for cultural differences have proved to be the warranty for our long-lasting cooperation and inter-cultural success.

References

* Authors' publications and research of authors' Sino-German collaborative research group.

* Klaus Abbink and Heike Hennig-Schmidt, "Neutral versus Loaded Instructions in a Bribery Experiment", *Experimental Economics*, 9, 103-121, 2006.

Robert E.T. Allison, "An Overview of the Chinese Mind". In: Robert E.T. Allison, (ed.), *Understanding the Chinese Mind. The Philosophical Roots*, Oxford University Press, Hong Kong, Oxford, New York, 1-25, 1998.

Donna L. Bahry and Rick K. Wilson, "Confusion or fairness in the field? Rejections in the ultimatum game under the strategy method", *Journal of*

Economic Behavior and Organization, 60, 37-54, 2006.

Charles Bellemare, Sabine Kröger and Artur van Soest, "Measuring Inequity Aversion in a Heterogeneous Population using Experimental Decisions and Subjective Probabilities", *Econometrica*, 76, 815-839, 2008.

Christina Bicchieri, "Local fairness", *Philosophy and Phenomenological Research*, 59, 229-236, 1999.

Ken Binmore, Peter Morgan, Avner Shaked and John Sutton, "Do People Exploit Their Bargaining Power? An Experimental Study", *Games and Economic Behavior*, 3, 295-322, 1991.

Ingmar Björkmann and Yuan Lu, "A corporate perspective on the management of human resources in China", in: Li, J.T. (Ed.): *Managing International Business Ventures in China*, Elsevier Science, Oxford, 153-163, 2001a.

Ingmar Björkmann and Yuan Lu, "The management of human resources in Chinese-Western joint ventures", in: Li, J.T. (Ed.): *Managing International Business Ventures in China*, Elsevier Science, Oxford, 181-201, 2001b.

Jasmijn C. Bol, "The determinants and performance effects of managers' performance evaluation biases". *Accounting Review* 86(5):1549-1575, 2011.

Gary Bolton and Axel Ockenfels, "A Theory of Equity, Reciprocity and Competition", *American Economic Review*, 90, 166-193, 2000.

* Ronald Bosman, Heike Hennig-Schmidt and Frans van Winden, "Emotion at Stake-The Role of Stake Size and Emotions in a Power-to-take Game Experiment in China with a Comparison to Europe", *Games*, 8 (1), 17, 2017.

* Ronald Bosman, Heike Hennig-Schmidt and Frans van Winden, "Exploring Group Decision Making in a Power-to-Take Experiment", *Experimental Economics*, 9 (1), 35-51, 2006.

Ritchard W.Brislin, "Back-translation for Cross-cultural Research". *Journal of Cross-cultural Psychology*, 1, 185-216, 1970.

Xinyin Chen, "Socio-emotional development in Chinese children", in: Bond, M. H., *Oxford Handbook of Chinese Psychology*, Oxford University Press, Oxford, New York, 37-52, 2010.

Chinese Culture Connection, "Chinese Values and the Search for Culture-free Dimensions of Culture". *Journal of Cross-Cultural Psychology*, 18, 143-164, 1987.

Chi-Yue Chiu and Ying-Yi HONG, "Justice in Chinese Societies, A Chinese Perspective", in: Henry S. R .Kao, and Durganand Sinha (eds), *Asian perspectives on psychology*. Thousand Oaks, CA, US: Sage Publications, 164-184, 1997.

Douglas D. Davis, and Charles A. Holt, *Experimental Economics*. Princeton University Press, Princeton, NJ, 1993.

Axel Engellandt, and Regina T. Riphahn , "Evidence on incentive effects of subjective performance evaluations". *Industrial Labor Relations Review* 64(2), 241-257, 2011.

Armin Falk and James J. Heckman, "Lab experiments are a major source of knowledge in social sciences", *Science,* 326, 535-538, 2009.

Tong FANG, *Chinese business negotiation style,* Sage, Thousand Oaks, CA, 1999.

Faure Guy O. and Tony Fang, "Changing Chinese Values: Keeping up with Paradoxes", *International Business Review* 17: 194-207, 2008.

Ernst Fehr and Klaus M. Schmidt, "A Theory of Fairness, Competition and Cooperation". *Quarterly Journal of Economics*, 14, 815-868, 1999.

William K. Gabrenya and Kwang-Kuo HWANG, "Chinese Social Interaction: Harmony and Hierarchy on Good Earth", in: Michael Harris Bond (ed.) *Handbook of Chinese Psychology*. Oxford University Press. Oxford. New York. 309-321, 1996.

Simon Gächter and Riedl Arno, "Moral property rights in bargaining". *Management Science*, 51, 249-263, 2005.

Simon Gächter, Benedikt Herrmann and Christian Thöni, "Culture and cooperation", *Philosophical Transactions of the Royal Society B*,365, 2651-2661, 2010.

* Hong Geng, Heike Hennig-Schmidt, "Sensitivity to Corruption[1]- An Experimental Investigation in China", University of Bonn, *Discussion paper*, 2014.

　　* Hong Geng, Arne Weiss and Irenaeus Wolff, "The limited power of voting to limit power", *Journal of Public Economic Theory*,13,695-719, 2011.

　　* Sebastian Goerg and Gari Walkowitz, "On the Prevalence of Framing Effects Across Subject- Pools in a Two-Person Cooperaton Game", *Journal of Economic Psychology*, 31, 849-859, 2010.

　　Werner Güth, Rolf Schmittberger and Bernd Schwarze, "An Experimental Analysis of Ultimatum Bargaining", *Journal of Economic Behavior and Organization*, 3, 367-388, 1982.

　　* Christine Harbring, Heike Hennig-Schmidt and Gari Walkowitz, "Performance Appraisal Systems and Cooperation in Teams-Evidence from a Lab Experiment in Germany and China", mimeo, 2017.

　　Esther Hauk and Maria Saez-Marti, "On the Cultural Transmission of Corruption." *Journal of Economic Theory*, 107(2): 311-335, 2002.

　　* Heike Hennig-Schmidt, *Bargaining in a Video Experiment-Determinants of Boundedly Rational Behavior*. Lecture Notes in Economics and Mathematical Systems, Vol. 467, Springer, Berlin, Heidelberg, New York, 1999.

　　* Heike Hennig-Schmidt, "When Research Migrates-On Understanding Behavioural Differences across Countries", in: Böckenförde, M., N. Krupke, and P. Michaelis (eds.): *A Multi-disciplinary Mosaic: Reflections on Global Cooperation and Migration*. Global Dialogues 13, Duisburg: Käte Hamburger Kolleg/ Centre for Global Cooperation Research (KHK/GCR21), 30-32, 2016. Doi: 10.14282 / 2198-0403-GD-13.

　　* Heike Hennig-Schmidt and Zhuyu LI, "Video Experiments-A New Method in Experimental Economics". *Forecasting*, 20(7), 116-118 (Chinese), 2001.

　　* Heike Hennig-Schmidt and Zhuyu LI, "On Power in Bargaining: An Experimental Study in Germany and The People's Republic of China". *Nankai Business Review*, 2, 31-38 (Chinese with English abstract), 2006.

　　* Heike Hennig-Schmidt and Zhuyu LI, "EU-China Experimental Research Results and Its Impact of Cooperation between Sichuan University

and Bonn University for More than a Decade", European Studies Forum, Sichuan University, 2013.

* Heike Hennig-Schmidt and Bastian Schlüter, "Choices, Beliefs and Fairness in Symmetric and Asymmetric Ultimatum Game Experiments", mimeo, 2009.

* Heike Hennig-Schmidt and Gari Walkowitz "Negotiations among Chinese and Germans-An Experimental Case Study", *Homo Oeconomicus*, 32 (3/4), 451-488, 2015. http://www.accedoverlag.de/index.php/en/homo-oeconomicus/inhalt/homo-oeconomicus-32-3.

* Heike Hennig-Schmidt and Gari Walkowitz,"Moral Entitlements and Aspiration Formation in Asymmetric Bargaining: Experimental Evidence from Germany and China". *Games*, 8(4), 44, 2017; doi:10.3390/g8040044.

* Heike Hennig-Schmidt, Hendrik Jürges and Daniel Wiesen, "Dishonesty in healthcare practice: A behavioral experiment on upcoding in neonatology, *Health Economics Research Network at the University of Oslo, Working paper* 2018: 3.

* Heike Hennig-Schmidt, Zhuyu LI and Ziyin YAN, "Equity and Prominence in Asymmetric Bargaining-An Experimental Study on Aspiration Formation and Adaptation in Germany and P. R. China", Discussion paper, University of Bonn, Germany, 2011.

* Heike Hennig-Schmidt, Zhuyu LI and Chaoliang YANG, "Why People Reject Advantageous Offers-Non-monotone Strategies in Ultimatum Bargaining", *Journal of Economic Behavior and Organization*, 65, 373-384, 2008.

* Heike Hennig-Schmidt, Reinhard Selten, and Daniel Wiesen, "How Payment Systems Affect Physicians' Provision Behavior-An Experimental Investigation", *Journal of Health Economics*, 30, 637-646, 2011.

* Heike Hennig-Schmidt, Bernd Irlenbusch, Rainer M. Rilke and Gari Walkowitz, "Asymmetric Outside Options in Ultimatum Bargaining: A Systematic Analysis", *International Journal of Game Theory*, 47, 301-329, 2018.

* Heike Hennig-Schmidt, Ulrike Leopold-Wildburger, Axel Ostmann and Frans van Winden, "Understanding Negotiations: A Video Approach in Experimental Gaming", in: Ockenfels, A. and A. Sadrieh Eds. *The Selten School of Behavioral Economics-A Collection of Essays in Honor of Reinhard Selten*, Berlin, Heidelberg: Springer-Verlag, 127-166, 2010.

* Heike Hennig-Schmidt, Zhuyu LI, Wanbo LU and Chaoliang YANG, "Concession Behavior in Negotatons: A Bargaining Experiment", *Chinese Journal of Management Science*, 9, 351-355 (Chinese with English Abstract), 2001.

Joseph Henrich, Steven J. Heine and Ara Norenzayan, "The weirdest people in the world". *Behavioral and Brain Sciences*, 33(2-3), 61-83, 2010.

Joseph Henrich, Robert Boyd, Samuel Bowles, Colin Camerer, Ernst Fehr and Herbert Gintis (eds.) (2004): *Foundations of Human Sociality: Economic Experiments and Ethnographic Evidence from Fifteen Small-Scale Societies*, Oxford University Press, 2004.

Joseph Henrich, Robert Boyd, Samuel Bowles, Colin Camerer, Ernst Fehr and Richard McElreath, "In Search of Homo Economicus: Behavioral Experiments in 15 Small-Scale Societies". *American Economic Review, Papers and Proceedings*, 91, 73-78, 2001.

Benedikt Herrmann, Chrictian Thöni, Simon Gächter, "Anti-social punishment across societies", *Science* 319, 1362-1367, 2008a.

Benedikt Herrmann, Chrictian Thöni, Simon Gächter, "Supporting Material for Anti-social punishment across societies", *Science* 319, 1362-1367, 2008b.

Gert Hofstede, *Culture's Consequences: International Differences in Work-Related Values*. Sage, Newbury Park, CA, 1980.

Gert Hofstede, Gert J. Hofstede and Michael Minkov, *Cultures and Organizations: Software of the Mind,* Third Edition. New York: McGraw-Hill, 2010.

Brain W. Husted, "Wealth, Culture, and Corruption". *Journal of International Business Studies* 30(2): 339-359, 1999.

Xiaochuan JIANG and Jianfeng YANG (2011): Understanding the Work Values of Chinese Employees, *Psychology* 2 (6), 579-583, 2011.

Francois Jullien, *Über die »Zeit«. Elemente einer Philosophie des Lebens, 2004*. Aus dem Französischen von Heinz Jatho, Diaphanes, Zürich, Berlin; Original: Du »temps«. Élements d'une philosophie du vivre, Grassiet and Fasquelle, Paris, 2001

Dainel Kahneman, Jack L. Knetsch and Richard Thaler, "Fairness as a constraint on profit seeking: Entitlements in the market". *American Economic Review*, 76, 728-741, 1986.

Norbert L. Kerr L., Joel Aronoff and Lawrence A. Messé, Methods of Small Group Research, in H.T. Reis and Charles M Judd (eds.), *Handbook of Research Methods in Social and Personality Psychology*, Cambridge University Press, Cambridge, UK, 160-189, 2000.

James Konow, "Fair Shares: Accountability and Cognitive Dissonance in Allocation Decisions". *American Economic Review*, 90, 1072-1091, 2000.

* Simone Kohnz and Heike Hennig-Schmidt, "Asymmetric outside options in ultimatum games-An experimental study", *Discussion Paper*, University of Bonn, 2005.

Steve J. Kulich and Rui ZHANG, "The multiple frames of 'Chinese' values: from tradition to modernity and beyond", in: Micheal H. Bond, M. H., *Oxford Handbook of Chinese Psychology*, Oxford University Press, Oxford, New York, 241-278, 2010.

* Zhuyu LI, Wanbo LU and Heike. Hennig-Schmidt, "The Impact of Concessions in Negotatons: An Experiment on the Bargaining Model", *Business Economics and Administration*, Vol.126 (4), 23-27. (Chinese), 2002.

* Wanbo LU, Zhuyu LI and Heike Hennig-Schmidt, "An Experiment on Ultimatum Bargaining and Testing on the Differences". *Proceedings of the Second International Conference on Game Theory and Applications(CMGTA'2007)*, World Academic Press, ISBN: 1-84626-166-X, pp. 130-134. (ISTP), 2007.

Paolo Mauro, *Why Worry about Corruption?*, International Monetary Fund, 1997.

John Nash, "The Bargaining Problem", *Econometrica*, 18, 155-162, 1959.

Pak Hung Mo, "Corruption and Economic Growth". *Journal of Comparative Economics*29(1): 66-79, 2001.

Michael W. Morris and Michele. J. Gelfand, "Cultural Differences and Cognitive Dynamics: Expanding the Cognitive Perspective on Negotiation". In: Ed. M. J. Gelfand and J. M. Brett, *The Handbook of Negotiation and Culture,* Stanford University Press Stanford, 45-70, 2004.

Rose-Ackerman, S. (2006). Introduction and Overview. *International Handbook on the Economics of Corruption.* Ed. S. Rose-Ackerman, Edward Elgar Publishing.

Alvin. E. Roth, Vesna Prasnikar, Masahiro Okuno-Fujiwara and Shmual Zamir, "Bargaining and Market Behavior in Jerusalem, Ljubljana, Pittsburgh, and Tokyo: An Experimental Study". *American Economic Review*, 81, 1068-1095, 1991.

Alan Rousso and Franklin Steves, "The Effectiveness of Anti-corruption Programs: Preliminary Evidence from the Post-communist Transition Countries". *International Handbook on the Economics of Corruption.* Ed. S. Rose-Ackerman, Edward Elgar Publishing, 2006.

Ariel Rubinstein, "Perfect Equilibrium in a Bargaining Model". *Econometrica*, 50, 97-109, 1982.

* Sadrieh Abdolkarim and Heike Hennig-Schmidt, "The Tripled Take Game-Text protocols of a video experiment". Sonderforschungsbereich 303, University of Bonn, *Experimental Data Documentation Series* No. 6.99, 1999.

Sauermann Heinz and Reinhard Selten, "Anspruchsanpassungstheorie der Unternehmung", *Zeitschrift für die gesamte Staatswissenschaft*, 118, 577-597, 1962.

Ekkehart Schlicht, *On Custom in the Economy*; Clarendon Press: Oxford, UK, 1998.

Schramm Matthias and Markus Taube, "Evolution and institutional foundation of the hawala financial system", *International Review of Financial Analysis*, 12, 405-420, 2003.

Siegmar Schulz, "Deutsch-chinesische Kooperationen: Das Beispiel

Volkswagen", in: Achim Hecker, Klaus Kammerer, Bernd Schauenberg, Harro von Senger (Eds.) *Regel und Abweichung: Strategie und Strategeme- Chinesische Listenlehre im interdisziplinären Dialog*, LIT Verlag, Berlin, 69-86, 2008.

Reinhard Selten, "The Equity Principle in Economic Behavior", in: *Decision Theory*, Social Ethics, Issues in Social Choice, Gottinger, H.W. and Leinfellner, W. (eds.), Dordrecht, D. Reidel Publishing Company, 289-301, 1978.

Reinhard Selten, "A Non-cooperative Model of Characteristic-Function Bargaining", in: *Essays in Game Theory and Mathematical Economics*, Aumann, R. J. et al. (eds.), Bibliographisches Institut AG, Mannheim, Wien, Zürich, 131-151, 1981.

Reinhard Selten, "Equity and Coalition Bargaining in Experimental Three-Person Games", in: A.E. Roth (ed.), *Laboratory Experimentation in Economics*, New York et. al., Cambridge University Press, 42-98, 1978.

Reinhard Selten, "Aspiration Adaptation Theory", *Journal of Mathematical Psychology*, 42, 191-214, 1998.

Ramadhar Singh, "Group Harmony and Interpersonal Fairness in Reward Allocation; On the Loci of the Moderation Effect", *Organizational Behavior and Human Decision Processes*, 72, 158-183, 1997.

Markus Taube, "Relational corruption in the PR China. Institutional foundations and its (Dys)-functionality for economic development and growth", *Zeitschrift für Vergleichende Polititische Wissenschaft (Suppl)* 7, 89-116, 2013.

Leigh L. Thompson, "Negotiation Behavior and Outcomes: Empirical Evidence and Theoretical Issues", *Psychological Bulletin* 108: 515-532, 1990.

Transparency International: http://www.transparency.org/whatwedo/ (downloaded February 17, 2013)

* Gari Walkowitz and Heike Hennig-Schmidt, "On the Fabrics of Fairness in Bargaining-Experimental Evidence from Germany and PR China", *Discussion paper*, University of Bonn, Germany, 2017.

Zhixue ZHANG and Chung-Fung YANG, "Beyond Distributive Justice: The Reasonableness Norm in Chinese Reward Allocation", *Asian Journal of Social Psychology*, 1, 253-269, 1998.

A Brief Academic CV of the Contributing Authors of this collection (following the alphabet of the last name)

- **Bogusława Drelich-Skulska**

Bogusława Drelich-Skulska is a Professor in Economic Sciences: International Business Relations. She is a Head of the Department of International Economic Relations and Vice-Rector for International Co-operation at **Wroclaw University of Economics**, Poland (2016-2020). Prof. Skulska is the founder of the Asia-Pacific Research Centre at the same university (since 2010). Her research focuses on international integration processes and foreign economic policy, particularly in East Asia. Prof. Skulska publishes extensively in Polish and in English on various aspects of this field of research, as well as on aspects of foreign trade in Poland and other East European countries. She managed research projects: New Regionalism in Eastern Asia. Evolution-Institutionalization-Actors (2011-2013) and Clusters as an innovation carrier of enterprises and regions. Verification and implementation of Asian models in terms of the Polish economy (2011-2014). Participated in over 80 national and international conferences and published as author & co-author 6 books and more than 60 scientific articles. She was a visiting professor at the University of Neuchatel (Switzerland) and in the Center for Asian and Pacific Studies (CAPS), Seikei Univeristy in Tokyo (Japan).

- **Gustaaf Geeraerts**

Gustaaf Geeraerts obtained his PhD from **Vrije Universiteit Brussel** (VUB). Currently he is Distinguished Professor at the School of International

Relations and Public Affairs and Co-director of the Center for China-EU Relations, **Fudan University**, Shanghai. He is also Professor Emeritus and founding director of the Brussels Institute of Contemporary China Studies (BICCS), Vrije Universiteit Brussel (VUB). His research interests centre on international relations theory, China's foreign policy, global governance and EU-China relations. He is currently working on China's rise and the new multi-polarity, with special attention for the Belt and Road Initiative. Besides that, he is involved with basic research on the concept of strategic hedging, especially regarding second-tier states. Recent publications include "The Changing Global Context of China-EU Relations", *China International Studies* (2013), (with M. Salman) "Measuring Strategic Hedging Capability of Second-Tier States under Unipolarity," in *Chinese Political Science Review* (2016), "China, the EU, and Global Governance in Human Rights," in J. Wang and W. Song (eds.), *China, the European Union, and the International Politics of Global Governance*, (Palgrave, 2016); (with Huang Weiping), "The Economic Security Dimension of the EU-China Relationship: Puzzles and Prospects" in E. Kirchner et. al. (eds.) *Security Relations between China and the European Union from Convergence to Cooperation*? Cambridge: Cambridge University Press.

- **Guenter Heiduk**

Guenter S. Heiduk studied Economics at Friedrich-Alexander-University Erlangen-Nuernberg and Albertus-Magnus University Cologne, Germany, where he got his Diploma in 1968. After finishing his PhD dissertation as well as his habilitation at RWTH Aachen University he had been appointed Assistant Professor. In 1981 he accepted an appointment as Professor of International Economics at Duisburg-Essen University (former Duisburg University) from where he retired in 2007. During his tenure he served as Dean of the Faculty of Business and Economics as well as Vice-Rector for International Academic Affairs. In 1983 he co-founded the East Asian Studies Programme. He had been invited as Visiting Professor/Researcher at Fudan University, Kyoto University,

Tokyo Keizai University, Wuhan University. He also worked as long- and short-term expert in several higher education projects of the European Commission (including for example as Academic Advisor to the EU-China European Studies Centre Programme, 2004-2008). Since December 2007 he had been appointed Professor at the World Economy Research Institute/East Asian Research Unit at **Warsaw School of Economics**, Poland. Furthermore, he has frequently been invited to serve as guest lecturer at International Summer Schools at Renmin University as well as University of International Business and Economics, Beijing. He organized a number of international conferences at Duisburg-Essen University and Warsaw School of Economics. With regard to research, he published 25 books and more than 75 articles. The topics are ranging from theory of international trade, Asian economic integration, production networks in Europe, China's investment in Central and Eastern Europe, to WTO and global trade. His most recent research interests involve China's Belt & Road Initiative.

- **Heike Henning-Schmidt**

Dr. Heike Hennig-Schmidt is senior researcher at BonnEconLab, the Laboratory for Experimental Economics at **Bonn University**, Germany. She also holds a position as senior researcher at the Department of Health Management and Health Economics at the University of Oslo, Norway. She received her PhD in Economics from Bonn University under the supervision of Prof. Dr. Dres. h.c. Reinhard Selten, Nobel Laureate in Economics. Her research and publications are in the fields of experimental economics and experimental methods, in particular cross-cultural and intercultural experimental studies on bargaining, fairness, justice and equity, the impact of emotions on decision making, group decision making, framing and presentation effects. She initiated the field of experimental health economics and introduced video experiments into economics.

Heike Hennig-Schmidt is a renowned expert on inter-cultural and long-distance economic experiments and is one of the very few researchers that authored, co-authored and published papers on such topics. She has conducted studies in China, Israel, Westbank (Palestine), Norway and the Russian Federation. Heike Hennig-Schmidt is founding member of ACCER (Association for Cross-Cultural Experimental Economic Research), a research network bringing together international scholars who work in the field of cross-cultural and intercultural experimental economics. She publishes in top-ranked international peer-reviewed journals related to economic decision, organization and behavior, economic experimental research, strategic interaction, game theory and its applications, economics of health and medical care, law and psychology. Besides presenting her research at national and international conferences she is organizer of several international workshops, conferences and Sino-German Summer Schools. Heike Hennig-Schmidt got several research grants from the German Science Foundation (DFG) and has been reviewer for various international peer-reviewed journals. She also has long-lasting administrative experience while being appointed Head of BonnEconLab, which-founded in 1984 by Reinhard Selten-is the oldest institution of its kind in Europe.

- **Anna H. Jankowiak**

Anna H. Jankowiak, Ph. D., Assistant Professor in the Department of International Economic Relations and Head of the International Cooperation Center at the Wroclaw University of Economics; co-founder of the Asia-Pacific Research Centre and the main coordinator of Asian Conference at **Wroclaw University of Economics**; author and co-author of 45 articles and 8 books in Polish and English concerning the issues of the Asian regionalism, Asian economies, transnational corporation, international business, global production networks and clusters in global economy; co-creator of the research project "Clusters as an innovation carrier of enterprises and regions. Verification and implementation of Asian models in terms of the Polish economy", funded by National Science Centre, Poland; co-author of the expertise Niche markets for Polish products in China, prepared at the request of Polish Information and Foreign Investment Agency; visiting professor in the Center for Asian and Pacific Studies (CAPS) at Seikei University in Tokyo (Japan), in the School of Business at the University of Iceland (Reykjavik, Iceland), in the Beijing Foreign Study University (China), Tallinn University of Technology (Estonia) and School of Interdisciplinary Area Studies, University of Oxford (Oxford, Great Britain). She was a member of experts group for the Polish export to China, formed in the Ministry of Economy of Poland. She was a visiting scholar at Seikei University in Tokio, Japan and St. Mary's University in Halifax, Canada. She is a member of European Association for Southeast Asian Studies and International OVOP Policy Association.

- **Elżbieta Kawecka-Wyrzykowska**

Elżbieta Kawecka-Wyrzykowska, Ph.D., full professor since 1992. Head of the Jean Monnet Chair of European Integration at the **Warsaw School of Economics** since 1997, Jean Monnet Professor ad Personam since 2007. In 2008-2013 she was Vice Rector of the Warsaw School of Economics in charge of Foreign Cooperation; in 2002-2005-a member of the team of advisors to the President of the Republic of Poland, and in 2012-2015 a member of the Senate of the University of Management and Economics (ISM) in Vilnius (Lithuania). Visiting Fellow at universities in the USA (1983 and 1997), Italy (1998) and Japan (1990), a consultant of the Economic Commission for Europe (1994) and of the OECD (1995). Co-ordinator of and participant in several national and international research projects. She is the author of over 120 research papers and co-author of over 100 books on Poland's integration into the European Union, on the EU and on GATT and the World Trade Organisation. Her research interests include: economic areas and policies of European integration, Poland's position in the EU, preferential trade agreements, international trade and trade policy. She has extensive teaching experience at universities in Poland and abroad (for more information visit: kawecka.eu).

- **Zhuyu LI**

Zhuyu LI studied mathematics at **Sichuan University**, China and had her Master and Doctor degrees in applied mathematics and statistics, Hiroshima University, Japan. She finished her two year post-doctoral research at Statistical Consulting Centre in Multivariate Analysis and Data Analysis, Pennsylvania State University, USA in 1994-1996. She had been employed as the full-time researcher at Department of Economics II, University of Bonn, Germany in 1996. Ms. Li came back to Sichuan University in 1998, and then has been employed as a professor since 2002. From 2008, due to her rich experiences in international research cooperation and in projects'management, she has been employed as the executive vice director & academic coordinator at the Centre for European Studies / Jean Monnet Centre of Excellence. She has visited more than 20 universities in Asia, Europe and The United States. She has hosted over 25 academic projects both in and outside China, including the projects from NSFC, DFG, EU Erasmus Mundus, Erasmus + and Jean Monnet Project, etc. She has published over 60 academic papers both in and outside China, and published one book, which won the 2nd prize of the Ninth National Statistical award outstanding achievements in scientific research, Chinese National Bureau of Statistics.

- **Agnieszka McCaleb**

Agnieszka McCaleb, PhD, is an Assistant Professor at the East Asian Research Unit, World Economy Research Institute of the **Warsaw School of Economics**. She holds a PhD in Economics from the Warsaw School of Economics and a MA in Sinology (Chinese Studies) from Warsaw University. Agnieszka wrote her doctoral dissertation on the role of central and local governments in internationalization of Chinese firms. In 2016, she was awarded the Dekaban-Liddle Scholarship at Adam Smith Business School at University of Glasgow. Agnieszka's research interests focus on Chinese multinational corporations and foreign direct investment, Asian national innovation systems and competitiveness.

- **Arkadiusz Michał Kowalski**

Arkadiusz Michał Kowalski is an Associate Professor and Head of East Asian Research Unit in the World Economy Research Institute in the **Warsaw School of Economics**. He received his habilitation degree in Economics in the Collegium of World Economy in 2013 and Ph.D. in the Collegium of Economic Analysis in 2006. His research and academic teaching focus on innovation systems, clusters, international competitiveness, internationalization of firms, and economies in East Asia. He has been involved as a manager or researcher in different European or domestic research projects in these areas, which resulted in more than 60 publications, including books, chapters, articles in scientific journals and expert's reports. In particular, he is a Manager of project financed by National Science Center (OPUS11) "The Dynamics and factors of innovation gap between Poland and China-international and regional dimensions". He has been engaged into consultancy work with international organizations, governmental bodies, national parliament, enterprises, and clusters. He is also a member of the Microeconomics of Competitiveness (MOC) Network, coordinated by the Institute for Strategy and Competitiveness, Harvard Business School, Boston, USA.

- **Jian SHI**

Jian SHI is Jean Monnet Chair Professor in European Culture Studies and EU studies (2008-), pre-vice president of **Sichuan University** for the international affairs (2004-2014), Chair of Academic Board of Brussels Academy for China and European Studies (BACES) since 2014, and the director of the Centre for European Studies /Jean Monnet Contre of Excellence. Prof. Dr. Shi has his PhD from Lehigh University, U.S.A, and his research focus on EU Studies, European Culture, European Integration and European society studies, and he is active in promoting China-EU people to people dialogue. He has been leading EU Jean Monnet and

Erasmus funded projects, and has published 10 books and over 70 papers in academic journals. Prof. Dr. Shi has also offered courses in European / EU studies both at the undergraduate and post graduate levels at Sichuan University.

- **Ágnes Szunomár**

Ágnes Szunomár is a research fellow at the Institute of World Economics, Centre for Economic and Regional Studies of the **Hungarian Academy of Sciences**, where she is the head of Research Group on Development Economics. She holds a PhD in Economics from the Corvinus University of Budapest. Her research focuses on China's foreign economic relations including the relation between China and Central and Eastern Europe. She also made research on emerging markets as well as on foreign direct investment issues and related policies. She participated in several international as well as Hungarian research projects, and currently leads a research focusing on emerging market MNCs activities in East Central Europe. She published articles and studies in Hungarian, English and Chinese and edited several scientific volumes.

- **Tianqin YAN**

Tianqin YAN has his PhD in European Studies, and he is now associate professor at the School of Foreign Languages and Cultures and the Centre for European Studies/Jean Monnet Centre of Excellence, **Sichuan University**. He is visiting scholar of Sabanci University in Turkey and Pavia University in Italy. He has published a series of academic papers in the fields of Turkish studies and European studies. At present, he is undertaking two research projects founded by China's Ministry of Education, one of which is entitled "Approaching the Changing Foreign Policy of Turkey under the Background of Building the Belt and Road Initiative". In 2017, he had a monograph published, which is entitled as *The Other Wandering at the Gate to Europe--A Study of Turkey's Identification Dilemma*.

- **Dan YI**

Dan YI is a professor of Literature at the College of Literature and Journalism at Sichuan University, China. He has been teaching foreign literature and critical theories since 1985. From 1996, he has been a visiting scholar at various American and European institutions including Harvard, KU Leuven, to carry out research projects sponsored by China CSC, EU Jean Monnet and Erasmus funds. He has published monographs and academic papers in Western literature and critical theories, arts, and European identification. He is also the director of academic committee of the CES of SCU.

- **Łukasz Zamęcki**

Łukasz Zamęcki, PhD in political science, assistant professor at the Faculty of Political Science and International Studies (**University of Warsaw**). Deputy Dean of Faculty of Political Science and International Studies (2016-onwards); Deputy Director of Institute of European Studies (2012-2016). Conducting lectures in following areas: Poland in the process of European integration; Integration of Poland with the EU; Finances of the EU; Business starting-up in the EU; European Workshops; Poland and Europe: history and present days; Theory of European Democracy; Methods of didactics; Methods of research activities; EU trade policy, EU strategies; EU-China relations. Successful social science teacher in top-ranking high school. Associate with Central Examination Board (2011-onwards), Regional Examination Board in Warsaw (2011-onwards), "Universitatis Varsoviensis" foundation (2007-2016). Member of scientific quarterly "Society and Politics. Educational Journal" (2008-2016) and scientific journal "Przeglad Europejski" (2012-onwards). Supervisor of 46 BA thesis, adviser of 27 MA thesis, tutor for Chinese students   Faculty of Journalism and Political Science. Author and editor of eight publications and dozens of scientific articles and chapters in collective works. Guest lecturer at foreign universities. Head of three research projects. Involved as the coordinator in the research project Jean Monnet Network More EU More Europe to overcome the Crisis realised at University of Warsaw within the consortium of Scuola Superiore Sant'Anna (leader), Notre Europe-Institute Jacques Delors, Paris (France), CEU San Pablo University, Madrid (Spain) and Nova Law School, Lisbon (Portugal).